ORGANISATIONS OF SCHEDULED CASTES AND SOCIAL CHANGE

ORGANISATIONS OF SCHEDULED CASTES AND SOCIAL CHANGE

Dr. SINDHE JAGANATH R.

Publications

KALPAZ PUBLICATIONS

DELHI-110052

Organisations of Scheduled Castes and Social Change

Rs. 690

ISBN: 81-7835-408-X

Published in 2005 in India by
Kalpaz Publications
C-30, Satyawati Nagar, Delhi-110052
E-mail : Kalpaz@hotmail.com

Laser Typesetting at : Master Computers, Delhi
Printed at :
Raidhani Printers Ph : 011-23215190

Dedicated to
My
Late Father

Dedicated to

Contents

List of Tables

Foreword

Having proclaimed to constitute ourselves into a Secular and Democratic Republic and having been wedded to the policy of Welfare State since independence, the Union of India has been envisaging, devising and experimenting various measures and strategies to realize this ideal, with varying results. As acknowledged, world over, none can match the vision, wisdom and idealism with which the policies are formulated in India, but, the implementation lags far behind in realizing the goals and ends sought to be achieved by these lofty policies. The policy of Protective, Discrimination has been looked upon as strategy and approach to bring about the much deserved distributive social justice and equity through emancipation, liberty through enlightenment and fraternity through elimination of unfounded, unjustified and unqualified inequities and social barriers. Inspite of such insightful policies and programmes, the government agencies vested with the responsibility of enforcement of these policies and legislations have not been able to achieve the desired results, with much of inequity and injustice of the past continuing to haunt the social fabric.

This situation has warranted the emergence of Dalits, backward classes and minorities movements to act as pressure groups and instruments for the advocacy not only of implementation of the existing ameliorative policies but also enactment of several additional legislations, in tune with the Welfare State goal and changing socio-economic scenario world over. In doing so, these movements have functioned as harbingers of positive social transformation and instruments or vehicles of social change in the traditional social order. Associations and institutions and the success of any movement, to a considerable extent, depends upon the structure, strategies, functioning and leadership of these organisations, which need to be studied systematically, scientifically and empirically. The impact of these movements on the fabric of Indian society can be ascertained objectively only through empirical studies of the organisations representing these movements.

It is precisely owing to this logic, rationale and reasons, the book entitled "Organisations of Schedule Castes and Social Change" authored by Dr. Sindhe Jaganath gains prominence and occupies a place of pride in the literature on Dalit movements in the context of contemporary Indian society. It is a fascinating study on the structure and functioning of Scheduled Caste Organisations and their implications for material and social conditions of existence of people belonging to these sections of Indian society on the one hand and thereby for the structure of Indian society at large on the other.

Dr. Sindhe Jaganath has focused empirically upon the structural and functional dimensions of the Scheduled Caste Organisations, particularly as institutions spearheading the Dalit Movement in this part of the Country in their pursuit of social equity and social justice, resulting in positive as well as creative and constructive social change. Much of the literature on Scheduled Castes is about the antecedents, anecdotes and rise of reformative and revolutionary movement and their assumed impact on these sections of society on the one hand and the social and power structure of the society at large, but there are few studies focusing on the organisations of scheduled castes that provide fillip and impetus and concrete or tangible existence to the movement. Every movement to be of some implications has to have a structure represented by an organisation with its own hierarchy of statuses and roles, division of labour and delegation of authority, its own letter of establishment specifying the norms, rules and regulations governing the functioning of the organisation. But seldom this dimension of the phenomenon has come under the sociological scrutiny, warranting a study as the one undertaken by Dr. Sindhe

Jaganath. It is precisely owing to its being a pioneering study an area of applied sociological specialization and focusing on the crucial issues that concern a vast section of Indian society that this work deserves unreserved praise. The book has captured these organisations in all their dimensions, in all their manifestations and in all their ramifications to provide one with rare intellectual, theoretical and empirical insights into the intricacies of these organizations, without which a vast majority of the scholars, researchers, activists and even the intellectuals would have been myopic to the social realities pertaining to the structural and functional dimensions of one of the most prominent social movements in contemporary India. I am sure; the book will be well received in academic, research and non-academic circles and at the same time it would prove an invaluable reference material for providing significant and meaningful leads for future research in this area. Dr. Sindhe Jaganath has exhibited rare skill and aptitude required in dealing with a very pertinent as well as complex phenomenon. The deep theoretical moorings and methodological finesse he has, have stood him in good stead in an academic endeavour as the present one and I wish many more such works of academic excellence and empirical significance from him of which he is more than capable.

Prof. S.L. Hiremath
Department of Sociology
Gulbarga University
Gulbarga

Preface

The present book is an outcome of my long-standing interest in issues concerning the weaker and downtrodden sections of society and my association and acquaintance with theoretical and empirical literature dealing with these issues. All through my post-graduation, I was fascinated by the sociological perspectives evolved in approaching the phenomenon of caste and caste dynamics and was equally perturbed owing to the physical and social conditions of existence of masses of people belonging to these sections, inspite of several statutory and voluntary efforts towards their emancipation. It is precisely at this point of time in my academic career and owing precisely to these intellectual questions, I decided to take up an empirical investigation focusing on the problems and prospects of scheduled castes in the context of the contemporary Indian society. Further, exploration revealed to me that it is the organizations of scheduled castes that are spearheading both the concerted movements as well efforts towards bringing about positive social transformation aimed as social equity and justice. It is needless to say that I was immensely influenced by the education I received during my post-graduation, the training in research I had during my MA and M.Phil., Courses and the discussions I had with enlightened teachers, intellectuals, social workers and activists, that ultimately prompted and motivated me to take up the research of which present book is the product.

Consequently, I undertook research work at the Department of Sociology, Gulbarga University, Gulbarga, Karnataka under the supervision and guidance of Dr. Meti Sheshan, Reader in Sociology, to whom I am indebted for invaluable suggestions, academic inspiration and constant encouragement in completing this work.

It gives great pleasure to extend my sincere thanks to Prof S.L. Hiremath, Department of Sociology, Gulbarga University, Gulbarga for his valuable suggestions and encouragement. My thanks are also due to Dr. (Smt.) Nusrath Fatima, Lecturer in Sociology for cooperation and suggestions.

I acknowledge my sincere gratitude to Prof. L.S. Ainapur (Retd.) and Prof. M.S. Dhadave (Retd.) for their wholehearted support and cooperation throughout my work.

I particularly, acknowledge my everlasting debts of gratitude to my Uncle, Sri Sindhe Bhimsain Rao, Under Secretary to Chief Minister, Government of Karnataka, Aunt, Prof. Chandramma S.B. Rao, Director, Devaraja Urs Research Institute, Bangalore, who have always been tower of strength and source of inspiration in all my academic endeavours.

I owe my heartfelt gratitude to my father-in-law, Ambanna, mother-in-law, Shantabai, Uncle Sharanappa, Aunt Laxmibai, Brother, Basavaraj Sindhe, Range Forest Officer, for their parental care which made me to come up in my life.

I express my gratitude to my brother-in-law, Ravi Dange, M/s Sona Gas Agency, Bhalki for his encouragement and cooperation all through my work.

My thanks are also due to my well-wishers and friends Prof. S.P. Melkeri, Prof. C.M. Yatnoor, Dr. Sreeramulu, Dr. C. Somashekar, Dr. T.M. Bhaskar, Dr. H.T. Pote, Dr. Shantinath Dibbad, Dr. Basavaraj Sannakki, Dr. Babanna, B.L., Sri Shivaputra Potalkar, Sri Tuppad Veeranna, Sri Ramankumar A.G., Sri Chandrashekhar Sangavi, Smt. Nirmala Sangavi and my brothers Sri Sadanand, Dr. Vishwanath and Late Sri Nityanand for their kind help and cheerful encouragement during the course of my study.

My sincere thanks are due to Prof. V. Ramaswamy, ISEC, Bangalore for data analysis and for his valuable suggestions.

I will be failing in my duty if I do not record my gratitude to all respondents/office bearers of Scheduled Castes

Organisations, Elites, Senior Caste men of Gulbarga whose spontaneous cooperation went a long way in shaping this work.

My deepest gratitudes are due to my wife Smt. Indubai, who put up with all inconveniences caused by a study of this nature with immense patience. Without her constant encouragement and support. I am afraid, this study would not have been possible. My daughter Pallavi deserves a mention, as she did not receive due attention at a tender age owing to my pre-occupations with this study.

Once again I thank one and-all who have helped me either directly or indirectly in bearing fruits to my long cherished work.

Dr. Sindhe Jaganath R.

1

Introduction

Study of organisations is not a new phenomenon. There are scholarly several studies focusing on various dimensions of organisations.[1] Organisations emerge due to various factors. Organisations can be classified based on the purpose for which they are emerged or established like social organisation, cultural organisation, literary organisations, voluntary organisations, political organisations, protest organisations, religious and reformation organisations, caste organisations, trade union organisations, etc. It is very difficult to trace the very origin of 'organisation' because it emerged with the history of the primitive man. The process of its development is seen along with the development of human civilization itself. Today we find an organisation at the bottom of a small community to that of an international level. Every organisation has a specific purpose or objective for the improvement or protection of the interests of its members.

International Organisations

The process of formation of an international organisation had started during the nineteenth century, largely in Europe. Industrial development, improvement in transportation and communication, urbanization, trade and commerce, education and advancement of science and technology etc laid foundation for several types of organisations. The first to emerge were the International Telegraphic Union (1865), Universal Postal Union (1874) etc.[2] The nineteenth century has laid basis for development of several International Organisations especially after the World War I, like League of Nations, International Labour Organisations, etc. After World Ward II, the League of Nations was superseded by the United Nations Organisation. Under the umbrella of United Nations Organisation, several international Organisations were come into existence[3]. The total network of International Institutes also comprises more than 100 Intergovernmental agencies out side the scope of the United Nations system. These are supplemented by 1500 nongovernmental Organisations[4]. During late nineteenth and early twentieth centuries several philanthropic individuals and organisations got prominence in the field of Voluntary Sector for their selfless service to the development of mankind. To name some–Ford foundation, Swiss Agency for Development and Cooperation, Oxfam international, Red Cross Society, Action Aid, Inter Cooperation, etc.

The major characteristics of these organisations are: 1. International in nature, 2. Show the supranational characters, 3. Mainly deal with issues related to war, 4. Collective security, 5. Fight against Racial Discrimination, 6. To protect the Human Rights, 7. Poverty alleviation, 8. Fight against Gender discrimination etc.

National Organisations

In the Indian context, the formation of organisation can traced back to pre-historic and Vedic period. However, the reflection of the development of Organisations at the International level during Nineteenth and twentieth centuries is also witnessed in the Indian context. Since the country was under foreign domination, the nature and composition of the organisations were aimed to gain Independence to the country. In addition, one can see a wide range of organisations even under British Rule. They include Political Organisations Religious Organisations, etc. After Independence, in addition to the existing ones several new organisations were emerged keeping their interest in mind. Even the older organisations have modified their objectives to suite to the Independent Indian Context. The fruits of Independence have not percolated to all sections of the society equally. The ruling class which was numerically insignificant started cornering all benefits. It took several years to the general mass to realize the magnitude of the problem. Gradually protests started at various levels with both organised and unorganised. At the organized level the important were the Trade Union Organisations, Peasant organisation, Caste and Community Organisations, Student organisations, Backward Class and Minority Organisations, etc. In addition, the country has witnessed strongly organized protest movements to secure the rights of the downtrodden and neglected lot. These include People's War Groups in Andhra Pradesh, Nexalbar Organisation in West Bengal, Mahoits, in Bihar, Tamil Elam and Dravida Kazagam in Tamil Nadu, Dalit Panthers in Maharashtra, Bodo and Kuki Organisations in Assam and Nagaland, Bheem Sena in Karnataka, Maharashtra, Andhra Pradesh and West Bengal.

Though there are variations across different Organisations, all are to some extent care to the welfare of the community in general and the members of the Organisations in particular. However the history, the development, objectives etc may very from organisation to organisation. In the present context this study address the protest Organisations which emerged to fight against age old evil practice of caste system in India especially among the Hindu social order. Further, these organisations also evolved to secure social justice, equality and fraternity to the oppressed and depressed castes and classes in the society.

Scheduled Caste Organisations

'Discrimination' is a part of human life. Discrimination is found in all societies, at all times, however developed they are. The nature of discrimination varies from society to society. For example in the Western world it is based on occupation, economic status, social position, etc. But in the Indian context in addition to the above, the discrimination and exploitation is mainly based on the Caste. Caste system is the characteristic feature of Indian society. People are grouped on the basis of caste. There are several castes which are arranged hierarchically setup a person in the society pay and get respect based on one's caste. At the top of the hierarchy are the Brahmins who enjoy all privileges and at the bottom of the hierarchy ar the Scheduled Castes who were denied the basics of life and are Scheduled Castes in the society living a condition beyond reporting. In order to bring these Scheduled Castes into the main stream society, several reformists like Raja Ram Mohan Roy, Jyotibha Phule, Mahatma Gandhi, Narayana Guru, Dr. B.R. Ambedkar and others, the governments both the British and the Independent India have brought several policy and welfare measures especially the Constitutional privilege and many voluntary organizations strive for overall development of Schedule Castes. In spite of all these measures for over a century, there is not much improvement in several spheres of Schedule Castes especially in the social and religious aspects.

For several decades due to lack of committed leaders the general mass among the Schedule castes were unable to protest against the illtreatment and other forms of harassment. It was only after Dr. B.R. Ambedkar intervention, the momentum of protest to ascertain their rights took a formal shape. The inspiration from Dr. B.R. Ambedkar to unite and fight has led to the formation of several organisations among the Schedule Castes. These organisations aim to fight against inequality, discrimination, social boycott, inhuman treatment and deprivation. These organisations violently agitate for their legitimate share in social and economic opportunity, educational privileges and political power. Widespread collective mobilization centered on such interests, has led to the rise of several Scheduled Caste Organisations in all states on India including Karnataka State.

Statement of the Problem

The statement of the problem of the present study entitled "Organisations of Scheduled Castes and Social Change: A Sociological Study of Gulbarga", covers various dimensions of Scheduled Caste organisations. The organisations were evolved to resist against the social structure based on inequality. Before going for further analysis of the problem it will be relevant to understand the social structure of Indian society, more prominently, the caste system in India.

Historical Background of Scheduled Castes

Indian society is heterogeneous, wherein people belonging to various castes and communities reside. The people of Indian society are divided on the basis of castes. Caste system is based on Varna system where the Brahmins are at the top of the hierarchy, followed by Vysyas, Kshatriyas and Sudras. Those people who are outside the varna system are known as Avarnas or Antajas or Panchamas or Chandalas[5]. They are external in the sense that they were required to stay outside the village settlement. The concept of pollution attached to them was responsible for treating or categorizing them as Scheduled castes. Those people belonging to the last Varna namely the Sudras and Avarans include many caste groups which have suffered social and economic inequality since the ages.

The census of 1901 identified some castes suffering from disabilities and classified them as 'Unclean Castes'. However, the various official and non-official reports started identifying the 'Unclean Castes' as Depressed Classes'. To identify the 'Depressed Classes' the term 'Untouchables' was first used by the Maharaja of Baroda before the Depressed Classes Mission of Bombay in 1909[6]. These castes were systematically listed in the 1931 census of India. These untouchable castes in India were officially defined as depressed castes in 1932[7]. The then British officials used the term 'Scheduled castes' in 1932 and finally, in 1935 as recommended by the Simon Commission, the term 'Scheduled Castes' was adopted by the British Government as a substitute to all other words hitherto used for identifying the 'Scheduled Castes'[8]. The term 'Harijan' meaning' Children of God' was first used by Narsingh Mehta, a Gujarati saint poet in the 19th century and popularized by Gandhiji to refer to the people of untouchable castes in India[9]. The constituent assembly used the word scheduled castes, while drafting the constitution. The term 'Scheduled Castes' has not been defined anywhere in the constitution. Article 34 of the constitution reads as follows. "Scheduled Castes means such castes, races or tribes, parts or groups within such castes, races or tribes as are deemed under Act 341 to be scheduled castes for the purpose of the constitution of India".

There are more than 3,743 castes and sub-castes in Indian society[10]. The caste system is characterized by a status hierarchy, the scheduled castes or the so-called untouchables are at the base, in fact, at the lowest of the social and ritual status. These sections had, on account of their low social and ritual status, been subjected to a variety of disabilities under the traditional caste system. All through the ages, the Scheduled Castes had suffered from social injustice and exploitation. They were denied all privileges and benefits as had been enjoyed by the upper castes. Their entry into temples of upper castes, public places, educational institutions, etc. were restricted. On account of their being on the lowest rung of the social ladder, they were forced to take up unclean and menial occupations and jobs, which yielded low incomes. They were associated with a variety of specialized traditional occupations such as scavenging, cobbling, disposal of carcass, basketry, etc. As a consequence, these castes have remained socially, economically and educationally, politically and culturally backward for several centuries.

Therefore, the constitution gives special protection to them. Under Article 46 of the constitution, it is the responsibility of the state' to promote with special care the educational and economic interests of the weaker sections of the people in general and the scheduled castes and scheduled tribes in particular and to protect them from social injustice and all forms of exploitation.

Development Initiatives in the Indian Context

Life of Scheduled Castes in contemporary India is faced with many persisting and newly emerging challenges. The crisis in their culture and identity, resulting from sweeping economic changes, political hypocrisy and religious domination continue to paralyse their lives in many open and subtle ways. Despite the several decades of social and economic changes (in the name of development), they are unable yet to understand where they stand in society, or where they lost out. Their efforts to free themselves from a social order characterized by inequality, hierarchy and domination are met with limited success. One often concludes that there is inadequate drive among them to accomplish status mobility and social change in their lives. Over five decades of protective discriminatory policy does not seem to have transformed their lives to the extent expected, while sections of the society continue to question the principles and justification for such policies.

For, it was believed that, with the adoption of a socially sensitive constitution and a system of democracy based on universal franchise, a new social order will emerge and sweep away the old patterns of caste based order of domination and subordination. The intervention by the state in bewildering ways, it is argued, created only new forms of domination and subordination. Rather than creating a condition of developing creative beings and achieving self-reliant outlook to life, there is now a sense of dependence and parasitism. Consequently the Scheduled Castes have succumbed to both the old and new forms of dependence.

There are also contrasts and contradictions. Not all Scheduled Castes have remained backward, passive victims of old and new forms of subordination. Many have moved from such a state to be well off and in a position to challenge the forces of social, cultural, economic or political domination.

Constitutional Guarantee

Although constitutional guarantees are seen as an ideal opportunity to achieve caste mobility, the extent and nature of such mobility varies from one ex-untouchable caste to another. Castes with low in their social status are also those which are economically poor and vulnerable. Untouchability perpetuates at these levels and quite understandably so, in a nation where even attainment of a high position such as Deputy Prime Minister could not avoid humiliation being imposed on the person, only because he was born into an Untouchable caste.

Social mobility among the Scheduled Castes to some extent acts as pressures of control and thereby discrimination against their members has eased considerably: where they persist, there is also resistance and protest, open or symbolic. The latter is most strikingly expressed in many areas by a tendency for leading members of these castes, if they do not move away from the village altogether, to build new houses on their land away from the main village site. The collectivity of village life under their direction has led to a markedly decline in their interest in maintaining it. Whereas village life in the past had focused on village temples and festivals in which the mixture of bottom-ranking and exclusion of such castes was expressed but, today they may adopt their own arrangements for collective festivals and freely patronize temples outside the village.

Social mobility consists here not in any collective revaluing of the status of a caste or a section of it, but in a releasing of old constraints, amounting to a change in the nature of the system itself. Even where discriminations are still exercised and traditional roles still performed, the weight they carried of personal subordination has generally been lifted. Choice has a scope it rarely had before. Legislative support also forms the basis here.

Initiatives for the Development of Scheduled Castes in Karnataka

The status of these communities is determined on the basis of castes. Caste determines not only status but also socio-economic and religious conditions. Another very important aspect while determining the status and economic condition is the criterion of inequality as adopter. On this basis the communities are termed as high and low or upper caste and lower caste. Where as the low caste gets low status in the social hierarchy and is subjected to many kinds of disabilities, atrocities, in human treatment and formed a unique behaviour pattern that alienated them from main stream of the society. Inequality is ubiquitous future of all societies and is true of Indian society as well. But the forms of inequality have engendered certain divisions based on one's birth into a group and on division of labour. Caste based divisions being endemic to Indian Society, there had been many efforts to address the situation arising out of caste inequality.

Karnataka is the premier state in India where the question of inequality and the resultant backwardness of communities or caste groups came to be addressed through protective discrimination. Equal opportunities in the fields of education and employment for people of all castes below the rank of Brahmins (who were considered forward or developed) were envisaged through reservation of seats in educational institutions and in government service. But this move on the part of the then princely government did not come about without the work of leaders from various non-Brahmin communities, which subsequently came to be identified as the Backward Classes Movement.

The rigidity of caste based stratification, the practice of Untouchability in different open and subtle forms, and the processes of transformation of such a system have been a recurring theme of scholarly studies (e.g., Moffat 1979, Mosse 1986, Deliege 1992 & 1993, Nagaraj 1993, Charsley 1996 and Charsley & Karanth 1998, Vincentnathan 1996)[11]. While the Scheduled Castes were denied access to land based occupations, and were condemned to local variant institutions of slavery (Harper and Silverberg, 1968), British impact is stated to have loosened this occupational embargo. Social and economic changes since Independence succeeded in bringing about changes in jajmani relations. This process of delinking caste and occupations forms an important window to an understanding of the status of castes and communities in India today.

Post-independent India has been a witness to many developmental measures for the welfare of the Scheduled Castes. These have been in the form of administrative, political and legal concessions. Popularly known as the policy of reservations, they have been an important constitutional means of attacking inequality between castes. The inhuman practice of Untouchability was also abolished through Article 17 of the constitution. Creation of new institutions like the social Welfare Department, National Commission for Scheduled Castes and Scheduled Tribes and the policy of reservations has succeeded in integrating low caste people into institutions at a higher level. Thus change is thrust both from above and with people's participation from below with the reviving of the Panchayat institutions.

All these gave a further fillip to the already existing process of shift in occupations and the consequent changes in lifestyles of 'low' castes in India. While education, urbanization and urban-ward migration and employment in the emerging industrial and service sectors provided the functional means to caste transformations and mobility in the caste system.

Scheduled castes constitute a sizable population in Karnataka state and the rest of the country. According to census of India, 1991, scheduled castes constitute 16.48 per cent out of the total population of India. Karnataka state scheduled castes population constitute 16.38 per cent of the total population. The scheduled castes population in the division and district of Gulbarga runs as 20.33 per cent and 23.64 per cent respectively. One of the notable features of the scheduled castes population of Gulbarga district, which ranks first among the Hyderabad Karnataka with a population of 23.64 per cent[12].

Basis for Formation of Scheduled Castes Organisations

India is celebrating 50th year of Independence, the condition of the scheduled castes are deteriorating even today. The scheduled castes residing in various parts of India and more particularly in the district of Gulbarga fail to avail all the facilities ensured in the constitution and scheduled castes are subjected to many kinds of illtreatment, inhuman treatment, harassment, humiliation, insult and atrocities which are the order of the day. Even today the upper castes treat the Scheduled Castes worst than animals. This kind of atmosphere forced scheduled castes to form organisations. Organisations come into existence when explicit procedures are stablised to co-ordinate the activities of a group in the interest of achieving specified objectives. Max Weber stated that an organisation as a rational instrument for implementing objectives and policies. Whereas talcott Parsons was of the opinion that organisation as pursuing multiple goals[13].

There has been no political initiation among the scheduled castes. Being more backward, their aspirations are low, lack of education and a general sense of apathy, poverty, and absence of leadership and organisation have restricted their social mobility. Moreover there has been no sense of protest among these people. By forming Scheduled Caste organisations of their own, a process of political, social awakening has been started among the scheduled castes not only in Karnataka state and Gulbarga district but in the nation as well.

Formation of scheduled caste organisations in Karnataka and Gulbarga is an attempt to mobilize the masses, through their castemen, to fight against exploitation of all sorts prevailing within the caste system. An attempt is made in this study as to how the scheduled castes attempted to improve their political bargaining power by forming castes organisation. In this regard Rudolph and Rudolph observe that the caste organisations are para communities or pressure groups to enable members of caste of pursue social mobility, political power, and economic advantage. In Gulbarga district major scheduled castes like Holey, Madiga, Lambani, Bhovi, Chammar, Dhor, Bajantri and Mang-Garudi have also formed caste organisations.

Leadership is a crucial element of organisation. It is one of the major factors which determine the ultimate success or failures of organisation. The strategic move made by the leaders decide the direction, scope and the nature of organisation. Leadership is the product of the social conditions of a given time. Any change in social structure is capable of changing the character of leadership. Due to lack of charismatic leadership and proper organisations, the condition of the scheduled castes more or less remained the same.

It is obvious that the organisations were established to regain self-respect and equal human status for scheduled castes in the society. The means by which it could operate include brining awareness among the scheduled caste masses about their own identity as human beings equal to other human beings, inculcating in them, the attitude of protest against all sort of injustice, oppressions and raising organizational strength as well as pressure against all the forces of inequality in a peaceful manner.

Still higher caste people have been enjoying all political, economic, and social and cultural powers, but the scheduled castes people have suffered all and neglected by higher caste people. Dr. B.R. Ambedkar has rightly said that "We have equality in politics one man and one vote but inequalities in social and economic fields". But there is no equality in any fields, therefore, life of scheduled castes are still in miserable conditions.

Leaders of scheduled castes formed organisations with a specified goal, to place their unfulfilled demands before the Government and bring social awareness among the castes, hoping to bring changes in the socio-economic, political and religious and educational conditions of the scheduled castes. The study focuses to find out the role of the organisations formed by the leaders of scheduled castes in the district of Gulbarga which falls in the state of Karnataka.

The Scheduled Castes and Scheduled Tribes constitute a significant proportion of the population of Karnataka state. Because of their miserable historical background and deeply experienced socio-religious and economic disabilities they have come to receive after independence certain number of special favours, as are made available in the famous constitutional diction known as "protective discriminatory policy", through both the state and the central governments. Naturally, the concern for the upliftment of Scheduled Caste and Schedule Tribes is on the increase in post-independent India. As anywhere else in the country the Government of Karnataka too has launched number of schemes and programmes with a view to uplift the Scheduled Castes and Scheduled Tribes in the state. This has brought about a few noticeable changes in the lives of these sections of the society in Karnataka. However, much remains as yet an incomplete task.

Srinivas (1960) wrote that there is a good case or arguing that the caste consciousness and organisation have increased in modern India. Witness for instance the proliferation of caste-based hostels, co-operative societies, Charities, Marriage Halls, Conferences and Journals etc.

The key question then is: why do some respond in one manner while the others do differently? While there may have been several ways by which answers to this could be sought, this study emphasized the role of organisations among the Scheduled Castes. Some of the research questions attempted to be answered through the study were: Given the persistence of old forms of dependence and emergence of new patterns, how do the Scheduled Castes mould their socio-cultural and economic position in society? What have been the alternative modes of upliftment and tactics of development followed by the organisations? To what extent the Caste organisations brought changes among the depressed castes? Finally, how does the organisations among Scheduled Castes facilitate for their emancipation?

Scheduled caste communities are organizing themselves to fight against socio-religious disabilities, atrocities, caste-based discrimination and the economic exploitations. They agitate for their legitimate right in economic opportunities, educational privileges and political power. Wide spread collective mobilization, centered around such interests, has led to formation of social organisation with defined ideology and leadership. By forming castes organisations of their own a process of social, economic, religious, educational and political awakening has been started among the scheduled castes not only in Gulbarga district but in the country as well. The present book is an attempt to analyse the genesis, growth, dynamic and socio-economic consequences of organisations of scheduled castes and sub-castes along with their achievements and failures. In order to arrive at fruitful conclusion this study has analysed the organisations functioning in Gulbarga District only.

KEY TERMS

Scheduled Castes

Schedule Caste is not just a caste in the Indian caste system but it is a term or a caption given to refer a list or group of castes which more or less subjugated to several forms of inequalities and exploitations like social, economic, cultural, educational, political, religious etc., since generations. In order to improve their conditions and status, the government identified several similar castes and systematically listed them in 1931 Census of India. These castes were officially defined as Scheduled Castes in 1932. the term 'Scheduled Castes' has not been defined anywhere in the constitution. Article 34 of the constitution reads as follows. "Scheduled Castes means such castes, races or tribes, parts or groups within such castes, races or tribes as are deemed under Act 341 to be scheduled castes for the purpose of the constitution of India". The present study also follows the same. However few synonymous terminology is used like Avaranas, Pancahmas, Untouchables, Dalits, depressed castes, downtrodden castes, in the same meaning.

Scheduled Castes Organisations

Scheduled castes organisations means, organisations formed by the members of the scheduled castes or community. For the purpose of the present study, the orgnaisational or institutional efforts made by scheduled castes leaders for the liberation of the downtrodden masses could be termed as scheduled castes organisations.

Organisations are formed by the scheduled caste in Karnataka State and other such orgnaisations of different names, and in Gulbarga district such as Holeya orgnisation, Lamabani organisation, Madiga organisation, Bhovi or Waddar organisation, Samagar organisation, Dhor organisation, Korcha organisation, and Mang-Gurudi organisation are considered as Scheduled Caste Organisations for the present study.

Scheduled Caste Leaders

In the present study, the concept of 'leaders' are used as those persons, belonging to the scheduled caste communities, who endeavoured to liberate the scheduled castes from Untochability, atrocities, social boycott, harassment, customary servitude and superstitions, and tried to uplift them in social economic, educational and political spheres to the level of the caste Hindus. The term includes those persons who by their exceptional abilities, position and efforts had raised the pride and status of the community and boosted up the morale of their brethren. They are considered so, irrespective of their ideological and political affiliations and approaches, irrespective of their sphere of activities and popularity, and irrespective of their success or failure in their mission.

Social Change

In the context of present study author used the term social change, means economic, political, social, education, religious and cultural changes have taken place in the life of scheduled castes communities through the impact of their caste based organisations.

Scheduled Castes Elites

In the present study, author used the term 'elites' means scheduled caste senior people or influential persons in their communities.

Theoretical Framework of the Study

In sociological studies it is necessary to make a reference to theoretical framework with which the research design is contemplated. The experience of sociologists has brought some of the facts that strict adherence to the particular theoretical framework or theory or model becomes difficult as the social phenomenon is complex and dynamic.

Therefore it is suggested to make use of more than one framework, or theory or model, draws inspiration from structural functional framework in the analysis of social structure of scheduled castes and at the same time is open to use other models or frame works which become necessary in the analysis of the organisations of sub caste of scheduled castes. A theory is a set of ideas, which claims to explain how some thing works. A sociological theory is therefore a set of ideas, which claims to explain society or aspects of society work.

The study of structure of a caste/tribe community had been the interest of several social anthropologists. Among them Radcliff Brown, Malinowski, Talcott parasons, R.K. Merton, and Raymond Firth are very important. Evens Pritchard tried to analyse the structure of a society in terms of groups. Raymond Firth tried to understand structure in terms of critical group relations. Radcliffe-Brown analysed social structure in terms of relations between individuals and individuals. Parson treated social structure as norms, status, roles and collectivity as constituent of social structure and social system. Malinowski and Klue-Khonn discussed it at length of the functional nature of each item in a society. They were of the opinion that each relation, is an object or custom has a specific activity and this activity has function and the function being contributing towards the functioning of the system. Nadel emphasized on part of the role of caste or community while analyzing the concept of social structure.

Structural Functional Perspective

Sociological theory in the last few decades has been profoundly influenced by a group of thinkers who have emphasized the so-called functionalist or structural functional approach. Functionalism views society as a system, that is, as a set of interconnected parts which together form a whole. The basic unit of analysis of society and its various parts are understood primarily in terms of their relationship to the whole. Social system refers to the functional aspects of social structure. Social structure is the means through which society functions.

According to Loomis, the social system is composed of patterned interaction of members. It consists of the interaction of plurality of individual actors whose relations to each others are mutually oriented through the definition of and mediation of a pattern of structured and shared symbols and expectations.

Spencer was one of the first writers, who used the term social structure by his biological analogies. Durkheim also left the term vague (Rules of Sociological Method, Chapter IV, Division of Labour, Chapter VI). Radcliffe Brown regards it as a part of social structure. According to him all social relations of person to person in the study of social structure, is the concrete reality with which we are concerned, is a set of actually existing relations, at a given movement of time, which link together human beings. But he goes on to say that the object with which we attempt to describe and analyse the structural from i.e., the general relationship disregarding slight variations and particular individuals involved. His definition is very broad. According to Firth "social structure makes no distinction between the idea of the structure of a society from that of the totality of the society itself.

Ginsberg regards social structure as the complex of the principal groups and institutions which constitute societies. From this point of view, the study of social structure can be undertaken as the terms of institutional arrangements or of the relations between social groups, or of both together and this is helpful in the actual study of societies.

Mannheim writes, the term structure appears already in the writings of Spencer and Durkheim. It becomes simply a synonymous for system, organisation, and complete patterns and indeed does not fall very short of society as a whole.

Levy viewed, the term function here as a condition or a state of affairs, resultant from the operation including the term operation is more persistence of a structure through time.

Merton was of the opinion that functions are those observed consequences which makes for the adaptation or adjustment of a given systems and functions. Those observed consequences which lesson the adaptation or adjustment of the system.

Theory and theoretical frame work are among the more diversely used terms in social sciences. A theory consists of a set of propositions defining the pattern of a relationship among chosen variables comprising a social phenonmenon. The propositions defining constitutions of a theory should enable the observer, to predict events in the relevant field of social existence and should help him to integrate apparently dissimilar observations. The propositions should also allow the possibility of the theory being modified or disproved.

A theoretical frame work consists of either an integrated set of interrelated theories on social phenomenon or a schematic approach to the task of building theory on such phenomenon. In this sense a theoretical frame work for the study of Indian scheduled castes and sub cast communities should help us in identifying the distinctive social characteristics of these communities in Indian society, process of emergence, growth of scheduled castes organisations, specific social settings and the nature of inter relation between these communities and the other segments of society.

Here an attempt is made to apply the structural and functional theoretical frame work for the study of organisations of scheduled castes in Gulbarga. And at the same time institutional framework as conceived by Parsons has been also taken into consideration in the presentation of the data about scheduled castes communities and their organisations.

It is necessary to form organisations to raise the upward mobility of the group as a whole. In the caste based society individual qualifications and achievements have no significance as such. Hence, the Scheduled Castes had to survive to elevate their collective status by a forming organisations and raising the moral and material status of their brethren. Caste organisations are necessary in order to bring some structural and cultural changes even among the Scheduled Castes. It was also essential to narrow down the social distance between the castes among the scheduled castes by coming together and living an association life. This required communications of new thoughts and values to the masses. This process of socioalization was obviously possible through the efforts of the organisations.

Review of the Literature

> "Review of research studies, serves as a buckle between the old and the new, between the known and unknown and between already investigated and investigatd"[14].

In this section, an attempt is made to review important works on scheduled castes, Scheduled Caste Leaders and their organisations in the light of which the finding of the present study could find relevance and lend a meaningful understanding. In a review like this the prime motive would be to thrash out significant theoretical issues which could be brought to bear upon the empirical fact for the purpose of validation of existing knowledge which in turn provides relevance and meaning for the findings of the present scientific inquiry. In addition to these a review provides us with the necessary insights into the current issues and themes under investigation. In the sociological circles the findings of the present study could find a meaningful place. However, the author is aware of the limitation of time and resource which act as constraining factors in making adequate justice to the existing literature concerning the present theme, i.e., organisations of scheduled castes and social change.

During the British period, the British administrators, most of them being officials of the Indian Civil Service, conducted studies on various scheduled caste groups in different parts of the country. Mention may be made of the such accounts as available from Crooke (1986), Steele (1868), Dalton (1872), Sherring (1881), Nesfield (1885), Russel (1916), Hapkins (1901), Baden Powell (1896), Walker (1904), Thurson (1909), Bains (1912), Lillingstone (1913), Risley (1915), Ibbetson (1916), Ethoven (1920), Briggs (1920), Stevenson (1920), Davids (1923), Hennenger and Stevenson (1930), Blunt (1931), Blunt (1931), O'Malley (1932), James (1935-37), Robertson (1938), Fisherman (1941). They provided useful but superficial data about the life, customs, manners and religious belief of scheduled castes[15].

During the post Independence period, a good number of studies were conducted by social scientists who tried to investigate, whether constitutional measures have served to reduce the social disabilities or social discriminations against the scheduled castes in India, and any improvement in their social and economic status. Mention may be made of such studies as those of Rao and Rao (1951), Kuppuswamy (1956), Gupta (1958), Sinha and Sinha (1960), Patwardhan (1965, 1968 & 1973), Beteille (1969), Lynch (1969), Bhatt (1975), Abbassyulu (1978), Malik (1978), etc. These studies reveal the fact that the legal constitutional safeguards provided to scheduled castes has brought a relatively considerable change in their social, economic and political spheres of life[16].

There are studies, which reveals the fact that social inequalities or social discrimination of scheduled castes as a consequence of constitutional safeguards have further accentuated and deteriorated. Mention may be made of studies by Desai and Damle (1954), La Touche (1958), Goyal (1958), Issacs (1965), Anant (1972), Gandhi (1973), Ramu (1977), Ghosa (1980), Kamble (1982), etc among others[17].

Oommen (1984), analysed the social movements among the Dalits, a segment of the Indian population that has suffered cumulative domination, protested several sources of deprivation, including low ritual status, political powerlessness, and poverty. It is argued that nineteenth century charismatic, neo vedantic and conversion movements aimed at remedying degraded ritual status failed because they were initiated by outsiders. Later, protests initiated by Dalits helped to develop self respect and group consciousness, but did not attack the caste system directly. Attempts to gain political power through legislative measures and Dalit organisations resulted in the emergence of a dominant caste and political elite among the Dalits. Measures to remedy the Dalits economic situation through state sponsored development plans led to the creation of a Dalit bourgeoisie. It is concluded that efforts to reduce deprivations in one dimension have failed to bring about the social development of the Dalits as whole[18].

Parvathamma (1986), analysed few important protest movements in India, including anti-caste movements initiated by Basava in the form of veerashaivism, in historical perspective. Some of these movements were anti-Brahmanical, but not anti-Hindu and were assimilated in the mainstream of caste-ridden Hinduism. She also analysed the anti-Brahmanci organisations especially Justice Party, Dravida Munnetra Khazgam and Anna Dravidan Munnetra Khazgam and the SNDP movement in south India. The comprehensive movement of the scheduled castes led by Dr. B.R. Ambedkar is traced from the phase of Scheduled Caste Federation to Republican party of India to Dalit Panthers through Dalits. It seems to indicate the built-in incapacity of the lower castes to effectively combine against the pressure of the dominant upper castes[19].

Krishna (1993), reports that the lower castes in India, who call themselves Dalit are agricultural labour castes, and nearly 20 per cent are from the Sah-Dalit Tribes. They have little share in India's agricultural landholding and even less in the irrigated landholding. The deteriorated civic sanitation and leather work, have low educational levels, and reside in inconvenient localities. While the Untouchability status of the Dalit has been officially abolished, it continues to exist in practice. Quantitative data show that atrocities against the lower castes exist in the form of penal system, crime victimization, agricultural wage rates, and land disputes. The study suggested enforcing official guidelines on Dalits to prevent such atrocities from continuing and provide them good education so that it will empower them to organize and agitate[20].

Mark Juergensmeyer's (1982) study gives a fairly good account of the organisational structure and its role in uniting various factions of Scheduled Castes. He observes, most rural members of the scheduled castes participated in it and the Adi-Dharma was an entirely novel form of organisation. It presented a complete contrast to the closed and parochial society they had always known and as such it stimulated hopes and generated allegiance. But it contained a fatal flaw. For, although its ideological vision spoke of a unity, the organisational reality gave evidence of a sharp difference between the movements, educated progressive leadership and the illiterate traditional following, between Jullunder, Hoshiarpur, and Lyallapur regions and also between the Chamar and Chura castes. The organisational structure was firm enough to obscures these differences during the initial years, but in times the increased tensions and precarious unity showed signs of breakage[21].

Hardgrave, et. al., (1969), in their study highlights the organisations of the Nadar and Irava community which are involved in the process of political mobilisation. Hardgrave observes the Nadar Mahajan Sangam is a voluntary association draw from the ascriptive reservoir of castes. Its actual membership is but a fraction of its potential in full caste recruitment. But the organisation claims to speak for the community as a whole, asserting virtual representation. If this claim is to be accepted as credible in the light of economic differentiation and the diffusion of political support within the community, the organisation must withdraw from active poltical involvement. The organisation has played a vital role, nevertheless, in the political mobilization of the Nadar community serving as the agent of community intergration and as the vehicle for its entrance into the political system of modern India[22].

Omvedt (1990), in her article narrated the protest movements by members of the Scheduled castes in Maharastra, India. The formation of the Dalit movements through the Independent Labour Party (ILP) by Bhim Rao Ambedkar in 1936 and the extent to which mass struggles by peasants and workers have been supported are discussed. Although the Dalit movement has envisioned itself as the movement of all Scheduled Castes and the ILP has attempted to unite all workers, the issue of caste and class continue to undercut one another. The separation of Schedudled Castes and Ambedkar from mainstream Indian nationalism is illustrated through the struggles that pitted the Dalit movement against both prominent caste Hindu reformers and congress nationalists in Maharastra[23].

Barbara (1987), in his article analysed that Dalit protest in India, against the ideology and practice of caste defined Hierarchy and power. Particularly the socio-economic oppression they suffered as a result of their inherited status as "Scheduled Castes" have recently intensified due to increased inter-regional communication and a broadened sense of social identity that cuts across lines of caste, religion and language. The case studies are presented to illustrate both the diversity and common themes of contemporary Dalit mobilization, with focus on the Dalit Panthers and the Bahujan Samaj Party and the earlier BAMCEF organisation from which it evolved, and the Dalit Christian movement[24].

Aslam (1980), analysed the history of neo-Buddhist youth organisations in relation to the protest and reformatory non-Brahmin and Dalit movements of Maharashtra, India. All organisations are representative of the interests of Dalits (untouchable field servants) and other backward classes as well as those of neo-Buddhists. The groups, categorized as socio-religious, political or militant socio-culture, included the Dalit panthers, Vidarbh Republican Students Federation, Republican Yuvak Sanghtan, Samata Sainik Dal and Sarwangini Buddha Vikas Mandal. Chiefly concentrated in urban areas, these groups derive their inspiration from earlier protest movements and gather strength and purpose from neo-Buddhist community consciousness. Their commitment to fight against social injustice in both urban and rural settings is solid, although rural areas have not yet been involved[25].

Parvathamma (1984) has presented a detailed survey of the problems of scheduled castes and tribes. It conclude a comprehensive analysis of the socio-economic conditions of the down trodden communities in Karnataka state. The study has given a picture of the present conditions among the most deprived sections of the population. While examining the main problem emanating from economic and social backwardness of scheduled castes, it brings to light their every day struggle. The constitutional provisions and policy formulations are intended to create conditions conducive for the establishment of equality between people. This study in a way is in evaluation of the schemes provided under the policy of protective discrimination enforced for over 35 years after independence. The study has covered the various aspects of their social and economic conditions including demographic characteristics, caste and sub-caste composition, educational backward residential patterns, economic conditions, occupational structures, political consciousness and awareness of constitutional benefits and the magnitude of untouchability[26].

Viswantham and K. Narshima Reddy (1985) in their study, they have made an explorative attempt to find out the determinants of educational achievement among scheduled castes. Most specifically they have examined whether or not there are class wise variations among them with respect to educational achievement. This research study is based on the assumption that the scheduled castes are no longer homogeneous community and that there perceptive differences among them with respect to class, status and power, parental attitude and its perception as valuable channel of upward social mobility, availability of tradition of education and existence of education oriented sub culture[27].

D. Venkateshwarlu (1990) analysed on Harijan upper conflict, he observes that there is a new level of awareness and consciousness among them that has not only enhanced their aspirations and ambitions but also made them assertive. This is not tolerated by the socially and economically dominant among the caste Hindus. There a situation of conflict develops when the Harijans wish to realize their aspirations or assert their rights, which the dominant among caste Hindus does not concede. Author at the psychological level and also at the manifest level treats such a conflict. The various aspects of both levels of conflict are discussed in detail.

It is thus evident from the preceding review of literature, that there are more studies on the contemporary situation of the untouchables, and measures adopted for their betterment. In other words these studies are broad based and general in the sense that they are pointed towards scheduled castes as a whole. These narrative and empirical studies have made an attempt to study and examine the impact of modernization and urbanization besides the constitutional safeguards and welfare measures on the scheduled castes and their social mobility. Such studies are numerous. But the point however may be noted here is that there are not any significant and detailed studies made on the individual sub caste listed in the scheduled order. In view of this lacuna, the present study has become imperative and important. This study on Malas though purely sociological in character cannot be however under estimated and belittled. It is likely to prove useful it covers all sociological aspects of Malas. This being a limited study in it the author has however made a sincere and honest effort to cover all sociological aspects of Malas and thus, though not to be fullest satisfaction of the sociologists, has fulfilled the minimum requirements that are absent. This study is more a modest beginning would pave the way for further research and social investigation in the field. This may also draw the attention of political leaders, economists, sociologists etc., to frame policies in such manner as to uplift this particular class[28].

Jocob Aikar (1980), analysed the main objectives of the work was to investigate the various factors which had been responsible for general population and that of the scheduled caste in spite of special policies and programmes and larger proportion of funds allocated in plans for the advancement of education to scheduled caste communities. In 1961 the percentage of the literary of the scheduled caste communities. In 1961 the percentage of the literary of the scheduled caste was 10.27 per cent and 1971, 14.71 per cent but the percentage of the general population was 91 per cent. The disparity widened instead of being reduced. Hence, an enquiry in to the reasons was found necessary and the study of the reasons became the chief object of the research. It was also observed that the percentage of enrolment of the scheduled caste students at the primary level was better and much satisfactory but the percentage lowered at the high stages and the proportion of the dropouts increased. Here again the reasons were to be found out the present study probes into the situation and problems of the scheduled caste students at the college level in the city of Bombay. In every aspect of the problem the author gives comparative pictures of the scheduled caste students and the non-scheduled caste of the college in Bombay[29].

Rajani Kotari (1994), author studied the emerging Dalit movement in India and argues that although caste can found the struggle for social justice, it can be oppressive and, when combined with religious communalism, can threaten democratic pluralism, Caste mobilization, however, can be secular and can nourish democratic movements. Many groups left out of India's secular transformation (e.g., The Dalits) are attracted to the new caste based radicalism. It holds more promise for real transformation than the fragmented, often irrelevant politics of the new social movements. The Dalit movement is based on the solidarity of poor and oppressed people in a struggle relatively weak and is flawed (e.g., by a dependence on personalities), it did help reject fascism and fundamentalism in the 1993 elections while simultaneously posing a major challenge to both the state and the traditional effect. It gained sympathizers the upper and middle classes and castes. To increase its strength and support, the Dalit movement should further widen its base and deepen its social and cultural terrain[30].

Yogendra Singh (1958), an eminent sociologist and also made a penetrating study during 1958 on the "Pattern of leadership among the India villages". The study trusted out the upper caste and class still continue to dominate in the village either in direct or manifest form or in an indirect and latent from, although the challenge from the lower caste and class group had substantially increased. The organisation is more on caste-line on caste-line than on class-line and the caste level takes the form of faction alliance leading to increased tension and unrest in the village. Since the rural power structure system tend to favour those who can control the economic expectations of the people, it is obvious that the introduction of economic changes in the rural power system is warranted[31].

Edward B. Harper and Louise G. Harper (1959), authors pointed out that the Brahmins were dominant among the villages because the social, economic, political and religious leadership was vested in them, but following the transformation and with the introduction of democratic decentralization the leadership among Brahmins was getting eroded as passed on into the hands of younger elements coming from other lowest castes of the Indian society[32].

Sachidananda (1974), author analyses the impact of change is more striking among the scheduled castes as they have been comparatively immobile in the past. Changes in status, which may appear limited in absolute terms, acquires different significance when viewed against the background of traditional society. The changes come along three avenues first by reform movements, second by the process of sanskritization, third impacted by the process of westernization. Though they appear separate but they may been seen at work simultaneously. In addition to these three Dr. B.R. Ambedkar through his education, great ability, pugnacity, and political factor. The use of political means to change the condition of status of scheduled castes was first made by him[33].

N.S. Pundir (1993), author analysed on scheduled caste could get education, availed facilities of job reservation, thereby change occurs in their traditional occupation; life-style, working in mixed a cooperative, intercaste, organized relationships. He finds that politics historical geographical conditions of particular region play an important role in the upliftment and social mobility of scheduled castes[34].

Upadhyaya A.K. (1992), author finds that the scheduled castes, despite their numerical preponderance, lack in achieving power positions in the rural power structure. Thought they have got positions of members in panchayat by reservation yet they are unable to make any impact in decision making. There is still a low level of participation. But it is better than in the past. In the name of Ambedkar they could establish an organisation, start a school and a few could emerge as leaders. The scheduled caste people in this area have low social status, low income and low level of literacy, less exposure to mass media and outside situations in comparison to other castes. Thus probably these factors account for their lack of assertion and mobility and the dependency on land owning higher castes for employment[35].

Benjamin, Joseph (1991), author conducted, interview and observation data from 200 members of the scheduled caste of Brah Block of Patna District in Bihar, India are used the examine upward social mobility to escape Barth's backwardness and the atrocities committed by members of higher status castes. A primary concern is whether increased social mobility among the scheduled caste leads to conflict between them and higher castes. Finding reveal that most members of SC's attain only horizontal mobility, which is enough to engender conflict with other members of Barh Society, it is concluded that upward social mobility by members of scheduled castes is viewed by non SC's encroachment on their own share of privileges an encroachment that threatens the traditional normative structure of society[36].

Abbasayulu (1979) author highlights the factors and process, which are responsible for the emergence of scheduled caste elite. He points out that with the dawn of independence, scheduled caste elite. He points out that with the dawn of independence, scheduled caste people have received special attention from government of India. Certain special safeguards for scheduled caste people have been provided in the new constitution of democratic India. These special privileges have opened a channel for that section of people, which was hitherto suppressed socially, economically, and educationally. The new opportunity has been provided for this section to involve them into inner circles of decision-making. An attempt has been made in this paper to analyse recruitment to the elite positions. The author has spelled out the following has the main contributory factors in the rise of scheduled caste elite. Education awareness from within and without, constitutional provision, social service and family reputation. Author suggest that the government might have to pay more attention towards the education of scheduled castes, for education; is seen as the main factor in helping the scheduled castes to come up to elite position. As it has been pointed out by many social reformers, education and education only can help the scheduled castes to come to the level of other forward caste in India. Only them there can be social equality in society[37].

Sachidananda (1977), author stress the point that as a result of the policy of reservations, a new educated elite has emerged in the scheduled caste society and they are taking up leadership roles to the scheduled caste masses. Authors has opined that the policy or reservations has not helped in the integration of Harijans in the mainstream of India society rather it has widened the gulf between scheduled and non-scheduled castes. He has expressed the fear that this policy may accentuate caste tensions. In this very connection it has been pointed out that these cast tensions are generated more by Harijan elites rather that by non-scheduled caste subjects or elites, because it is common knowledge that the Harijan elites have developed a vested interest in maintains a separate identity in order to reap more and more for a small fraction of their relation and friends and those still stepped in poverty, ignorance and unclean occupations would never be in a position to get the benefit of reservations and special privileges. This is likely to create dissatisfaction among a majority of scheduled castes subjects[38].

Chandra Kanchan (2000), narrated the internal organisational structure of a political party determines that party's ability to successfully incorporate elites. Parties that are able to incorporate now elites because of competitive rules regarding intra-party advancement are more stable than those parties with centralized advancement rules. This article builds upon Myron Weiner's (1967) study of India's congress party to prove the validity of the above theory. It beings by modeling the differences between competitive and centralized party rules. It then uses this model to describe the pattern that emerge when scheduled caste elites are incorporated in to both the Congress Party and the BSP. Conclusions are then compared to Duverger's Law. It is of argued that Duverger's Las fails to consider: advancement ruled within the party itself. The articles concludes by exploring the consequences that these findings will have on scholarship pertaining to both democratic stability and electoral system[39].

Natarajan (1959), reviewed the impact of social reform organisation in India occurred in a century some of the deep rooted traditions of the Indian society could be uprooted by creating a new awareness among the people social reforms like Raja Ram Mohan Roy, Justice Mahadev Govind Ranade, Bhandarkar, Dr. Annie Besant and the like developed institutional structures like Arya Samaja, Prarthana Samaja, Brahma Samaja, Ramakrishna Mission to bring about social reform in India[40].

Anita Matto (1991), studied social impact of reform organisation of the recent past in which Arya Samaja, Parathana Samaja, Brahma Samaja, etc., brought about substantial changes in the Indian society. Among the various changes generated by these movements, emergence of new middle class, awareness of cast untouchability, female infanticide and certain endogenous and exogenous sources of poverty are evident. Main agents of social transformation who worked with the reform movements were present leaders, political radicals, entrepreneurs and literary people. Matto also revealed that the reform orgnaisations used religious as a methodology for the eradication of social evils[41].

Shyam Lal (2002), analysed a self-reform organisation formed among the Bairawa caste in Rajasthan. It urged its fellow community men to educate themsevels. It is very significant to mention here that these self reform organisations emphasized the need for internal reform of the community which led to establish its importance of its standing in the Hindu society. These mass actions were intended to secure access to schools as well as non-traditional occupations, and were designed to mobilize the Bairawa community.

Bairawa leadership organized several campaigns for equal rights for them. It enabled its community people to achieve the social, cultural, educational, political consciousness among its community members. The feeling of self-respect and intrinsic dignity had been restored to the community through the organisation[42].

Research Gap

Community (Caste) studies have acquired great sociological significance during the last four decades. Many sociologists and social anthropologists have studied different communities–castes, scheduled castes, and scheduled tribes. These communities were studied with special reference to their social orgnisation and the processes of change which were affecting them, their traditional way of living, difficulties facing in accommodating the changes and at the same time retaining their traditions, values and practices. The foregoing literature clearly highlights the following gaps.

1. No study has attempted to analyse the significance of sub-caste organisations.
2. There seems to be wide gap between the theory and the ground level scenario.
3. The role of the caste leaders and their contribution was restricted to the State or national level neglecting the district and more importantly the grassroots level leaders.

4. The role of multiple organisations at the district level and the interface between these organisations with the state level organisation
5. Implications of factionalism on the development of the community
6. The linkages or the networking of organisations and their positive and negative implications on the community

Objectives of the Study

Based on the above gap in the literature, the present study attempts to fill the gap with the following objectives:

1. To know the flora and fauna of Gulbarga district.
2. To elucidate demographic profile of scheduled castes of Karnataka and Gulbarga district.
3. To know the socio-economic conditions of the respondents.
4. To understand the in depth problems of scheduled castes.
5. To analysis the factors responsible for formation of organisation by the scheduled castes.
6. To study the objectives and programmes undertaken by the scheduled castes organisations.
7. To find out the achievements of the organisations formed by scheduled castes
8. Interactions of elites of scheduled castes towards the performance and changes taking place of organisation formed by scheduled caste
9. To arrive at few policy suggestions for the development of Scheduled Castes through their orgnaisations.

Hypothesis

Kerlinger defines a "Hypothesis is a conjectural statement of relation between two or more variables.

Hypotheses are always in declarative sentence form and they relate either generally or specifically variables to variables. Keeping in view the objectives of the study the following hypotheses are formulated.

1. In spite of the specific policies aimed at the upliftment of scheduled castes by the government there exists backwardness, illiteracy, poverty, ignorance, lack of able leadership, absence of proper organisations among the Scheduled Castes.
2. The leaders of scheduled castes and sub-castes organisations do not show much interest for the upliftment of their community in Gulbarga district, rather than their personal interest.
3. Scheduled castes organisations in Gulbarga district have brought considerable change among the scheduled castes.
4. The changes brought about by the Scheduled caste organisations in Gulbarga district has not percolated evenly among different Scheduled Castes.
5. Scheduled Caste organisations are not utilizing the expert advice of the elites for its proper functioning.

Scope of the Study

It is obvious from the very title of the subject of research that the scope is not narrow and limited. It covers a very wide range of the scheduled caste organisational activities at the higher level. Many and multifarious programmes and activities conducted by the scheduled caste organisations in Gulbarga will also form the part of the research.

Similarly, the author is very much concerned with those organisations, based on sub-caste wise emerging factors, their objectives, achievements, and failures. The study of the respondent's background, their educational, social, economic and religious conditions, political and cultural awareness etc., have to be considered, as man is under the influence of the past as well as the present. In this context it becomes inevitable to recall the historical facts which led to the caste-system and the tradition of Untouchability in the society.

In connection with education of the scheduled castes, the author has to examine how far the facilities and privileges extended to the scheduled castes, how caste leaders try to bring social awareness and social change in their community have to be analysed. The author also elicited the opinions, suggestions, and remarks of the scheduled caste elites on the caste organisations.

Incidentally the author has to take into consideration the historical background and geographical factors, agricultural, industrial and economic circumstances of the district namely Gulbarga. All these aspects formed an integrated which throw sufficient light over the subject of the study and research. Hence the present study aims at investigating the emerging dimensions of caste and sub-caste organisations and the social, economic, political, educational and religious conditions of the respondents in Gulbarga district.

Relevance of the Study

Sociological studies on scheduled castes are numerous. Nevertheless specific studies on individual castes listed in the scheduled order are very few. Particularly in the context of modernisation and urbanisation and in the light of having provided constitutional provisions and safeguards and welfare measures, it is becoming increasingly imperative to study the impact of the scheduled caste and sub caste organisations on the individual scheduled castes against a backdrop of their relative immobility for centuries. Sincere attempt is made to study the socio-economic, political and religious life of the scheduled castes in Gulbarga district of Karnataka. Holeya, Madiga, Lambani, Bhovi, Samagar, Dhor, Bajantri and Mang-Garudi are of the predominant Schedules castes in Gulbarga district.

The purpose of the study is to critically examine, understand and determine the nature and type of changes that have taken place in all spheres and are continually taking place among these castes in Gulbarga district through their organisations. The study is also intended to examine the socio-economic conditions, political, education awareness among these castes. Each caste has tried to establish its own organisation. Caste based organisations are emerging in the present context are on a rise. The need for such a study is imperative and relevant, and is a continuous one and an ever-present challenge to sociologists.

Even today the scheduled castes residing in different parts of India are subjected to various kinds of atrocities, ill-treatment and inhuman treatment. There are quite a few sociologists who have undertaken the present study on scheduled castes and social change in India as well as in Karnataka. The present study is an attempt to fill this gap in literature. This will be a micro level study. This study is of great help to planners, administrators and politicians and become an authentic document to the Government of Karnataka and India, on the eve of Golden Jubilee Celebrations.

Selection Procedure

Familiarity of field is necessary to understand different dimensions of the problem. Further, it will enable the author to focus on issues more sharply and collect the information more accurately. Gulbarga district is chosen for the study just not because of the familiarity of the district but also owing to the specific reasons. They include: 1) In Karnataka state Gulbarga district has higher concentration of scheduled castes, 2) Scheduled castes of Gulbarga are influenced by Dr. B.R. Ambedkar's ideology and philosophy, Sri B. Shyam Sunder's revolutionary thoughts and Jyothibha Phule's principles and 3) Gulbarga district has more number of scheduled castes organisations representing various castes and sub castes within the broader canvas of the 'Scheduled Castes'.

The total population of Gulbarga district was 2,582,169 persons in 1991. Among them 610,681 persons belong to the scheduled castes. While 502,488 persons among the Scheduled Caste population live in rural areas and the remaining 108,193 persons are residing in urban areas. The rural and urban components of the scheduled castes population of the district works out to 82.28 per cent and 17.72 per cent respectively. The proportion of scheduled caste population of the district constitutes 23.65 per cent of the total population which is quite high in comparison to the state average of 16.38 per cent. The rural urban break-up shows that as compared to the overall state averages of 18.17 per cent and 12.40 per cent respectively, the Gulbarga district has 25.47 per cent and 17.74 per cent respectively belonging to the scheduled castes. Thus, the scheduled castes component in both the categories of the population of the district is relatively high.

There are about 101 castes and sub-castes which are listed under scheduled caste category in the Karnataka State[43]. For the present purpose the author has selected the state level Schedule caste organisations DSS and its sub groups which have their units any where in Gulbarga district. In addition, eight sub castes of scheduled castes in Gulbarga district were selected. They are Holeya, Lambani, Madiga, Bhovi or Waddar, Samagar, Korcha or Bajantri, Dhor and Mang Garudi. On an average each taluk in the district has thirteen scheduled castes organisations which were functioning at the time of the commencement of the study. In order to understand these organisations, the author has chosen one of the office bearers as a respondent for the sake of data collection. The office bearers of the organisation constitutions the president, the vice president, the treasurer and the executive member. Thus 118 respondents were selected from the 10 talukas of the district. In addition 32 persons representing the State level organisations located in Gulbarga district were randomly chosen taking the total sample size to 150. In addition, 40 key informants, who are the 'Scheduled Caste Elites', were chosen to have information on not only the functioning of the Scheduled Caste and sub caste organisations but also the holistic picture of the problems of the organisations, issues to leadership, inter and intra organisational relations, the corrective measures required to strengthen these organisations for effective functioning, etc.

Methodology

Research is a process wherein information has to be searched out in a proper and sequential order so as to reach a conclusion. In this process something new may get discovered or old may be rejected or reinterpreted. Keeping these ideas in mind, the study or research on 'Organisations of Scheduled Castes and Social Change' is undertaken. There are various methods and techniques of data collection to be applied for the present study. Unless the methodology is correct, the analysis and conclusions may not be scientific and biased conclusions have no utility for framing definite policies and programmes.

The primary objective of the study is to focus on the causes for emergence of the caste organisations in Gulbarga district. In addition, the study also covers the profile of the leaders, their failures and achievements to lead the organisations and how these organisations are bringing social change among the caste and communities. In order to have a comprehensive understanding of the selected problem, both primary and secondary source of information from different sections of Scheduled Caste population. First type of interview schedule was meant to elicit information from the functionaries or executive members of Schedule Caste and sub caste organisations. This interview schedule intends to elicit information on the nature of organisation, objectives, achievements and failures etc. The second type of interview schedule was canvassed to the Scheduled Caste elites to know their perception towards the functioning of the organisations. First a pilot survey was conducted in order to pre-test the interview schedule. Based on the insights gained in the field, several modifications were made and the consent of the research guide was obtained before the schedule was finally taken to field. In addition, the author used both participant Observation and quasi-participant observation methods to support the data collected through the interview schedules. More emphases have been given to field study due to non availability of literature on scheduled caste organisations. A detailed discussion with the office bearers of each caste organisation was also very useful in understanding the various dimensions of the functioning of the organisations.

Since the approach is holistic in nature, the scheduled castes organisations have been studied in terms of its various aspects of their contribution to the living of the scheduled castes such educational, social, economic, religious and political. In order to substantiate the primary data, an effort is also made to collect secondary data from various sources. The main source of information was available from Gazetteers, Census reports, Articles in Journals and community studies was collected and suitably documented.

According to Becker participant observation is a method in which the observer participants in the day events of the people under the study, either only in the role of the author or in some disguised role[23]. I have participated in every sub-castes and scheduled castes organisations functions, like strikes, Bandh (protest), Jayanti (Birthday celebrations), social gathering, conferences related to their organisations and special functions related to religious, cultural activities, etc.

The data collected through various sources was computerized so as to derive necessary tables. For the sake of analysis only simple percentage and average were used.

Limitations of the Study

The following are the limitations the study:

1. Present research investigation is confined to only Gulbarga district.

2. The study is only confined to scheduled caste organisations, viz DSS, Holeya, Madiga, Lambani, Waddar or Bhovi, Samagar, Korcha, Dhor and Mang-Garudi.
3. The present study has not taken up the other caste organisations like Scheduled Tribes, Backward castes, and upper castes organisations in Gulbarga district.
4. Study selected only one office bearer of every organisations.
5. Study covers only issues concerned with discrimination and the process of addressing them by the scheduled castes organisations.
6. Opinions of the senior citizens and elites of scheduled castes of Gulbarga are specific to the scheduled castes organisations only.

Researcher's Experience

Research is a process of gathering accurate information from others on a particular problem. It is too difficult task and needs special qualities. An indepth knowledge of techniques of field work, training from research guide, an ability to convince and take into confidence of all the respondents. The success of research entirely depends on hard work of the author, a constant visit to the field and a constant guidance of the research guide. In spite of this a author has to face innumerable problems and difficulties in the field because, theory appears to be different from practice. What we read in a book the same techniques always cannot be applied in the field particularly about castes and sub-castes organisations. A author must have an ability to tackle the problems tactfully that may arise in the process of field work. In the process of field work I have come across with many problems. In the beginning it was difficult for me to approaches to the leaders of scheduled castes leaders and sub-caste leaders. Gradually I convince to the all scheduled caste leaders of the objectives of the research. My repeated visits to their house/office made them to extend their co-operation in my field work.

I approached senior citizens/elites of scheduled castes and sub-castes for collecting their opinions, suggestions, advises and negative and positive opinions towards their caste organisations in the taluk and district headquarters. Most of them provided valuable information through questionnaire and orally during the time of field work. Particularly, Lambani, Korcha, and Waddar organisation leaders fear to provide information of their organisation, but I tried to explain the reality of the research work, then they come close to me, provided relevant information of their organisations.

Notes and References

1. David. L. Sills (ed.), (1968), *International Encyclopaedia of the Social Sciences*, Vol. 8, The Macmillan Company and the Free Press, USA, pp. 33-35.
2. *Ibid.*, pp. 36-38.
3. *Ibid.*, pp. 38-42.
4. *Ibid.*, pp. 43-47.
5. Mamtaz Ali Khan (1980), *Scheduled Castes and their Status in India*, Uppal Publishing House, New Delhi, pp. 2-3.
6. Galanter Garc (1972), *The Abolition of Disabilities Untouchability and the Law*, in J. Michael Mahar, (ed.); *The Untouchability in Contemporary India*, University of Arizona Press, Tucson, p. 38.
7. Harold. R. Issacs (1965), *Indian Ex-Untochables*, Asian Publishing House, Bombay, p. 36.
8. Government of India Act, 1935, para. 25, Schedule-1.
9. Murthy. B.S. (1971), Depressed and Oppressed, Asian Publishing House, Bombay, p. 45.
10. Bhatt. S.G. (1977), *Encyclopaedia of District Gazetteers of India*, South Zone, Vol. 1, Gyan Publishing House, New Delhi, p. 454.
11. G.K. Karanth and Charsley Simon (ed.), (1998), *Challenging Untouchability, Dalit Initiative and Experience in Karnataka*, Sage Publication, New Delhi, p. 41.

12. Census of India, 1991, University News, January 1994.
13. David. L. Sills (1968), *International Encyclopaedia of the Social Sciences*, Vol. 2, The Macmillan Company and the Free Press, USA, pp. 297-298.
14. C. Dwarakanath Gupta (1999), *Socio-Cultural History of An Indian Caste*, Mittal Publications, New Delhi, p. 40.
15. Singh. R.K. (1986), *Scheduled Castes Studies in India*, ed. By G.S. Hallen, Survey of Sociological Research in India, M/s. Asha Printers, New Delhi, p. 77.
16. *Ibid.*, p. 77.
17. *Ibid.*, p. 78.
18. Oommen, T.K. (1984), "Sources of Deprivation and Styles of Protest", The Case of the Dalits in India, *Journal of Contributions of Indian Sociology—New Series*, Vol. 18, 1. Jan-June, New Delhi. p. 4561.
19. C Parvathamma (1986), "Role of Protest Movements in Social Transformation" Guru Nanak, *Journal of Sociology*, Vol. 7, 1. Apr, pp. 1-22.
20. Krishna. P.S (1993), "Untouchability and Atrocities", *Journal of Sociology*, Vol. 43. 4, Oct.-Dec., pp. 412-426.
21. Mark Juergensmeyer (1982), *Religion as a Social Vision*, University of California Press, Berkeley, pp. 62-63.
22. Robert Hardgrave and Other (1990), "The Nadar of Tamil Nadu", *The Political Culture of Community in Change*, California Press, Berelery University, p. 114.
23. Gail Omvedt "Ambedkar & Dalit Labor Radicalism" Maharashtra 1936-42, Journal of South Asia Bulletin; Vol. 10. 1, New Delhi, pp. 12-22.
24. Joshi, Barbara, P (1987), "Recent Developments in Inter-Regional Mobilization of Dalit Protest in India", Journal, South Asia Bulletin, Vol. 7, 102, New Delhi, pp. 86-96.
25. Abdullah, Aslam (1980), "Neo-Buddhist Youth Organisations", A Study of Protest Movement, Journal of Youth Affairs, Vol. 2, 1 March, New Delhi.
26. Parvathamma. C (1984), "Scheduled Caste and Tribes", *A Socio-economic Servy*, Ashish Publishing House, New Delhi, pp. 95-100.
27. Vishwantham and K Narashima Reddy (1985), *Scheduled Caste a Study in Educational Achievement*, Nutan Art Printers, Hyderabad.

28. Venkateshwarlu (1990), "Harijan-Uppar Class Conflicts" Cited in p. 14, Dr. K Rathnaih (1991) *Social Change Among Malas*, Discovery Publishing House, New Delhi.
29. Jacob Aikar (1980), "Scheduled Castes and Higher Education", A Study of College Students in Bombay, Dastane Ramachandra & Co., Poona. P-Forword.
30. Kothari, Rajni (1994), "Caste Communalism and the Democratic Process", Journal, *South Asian Bulletin*, Vol. 14, (1), pp. 7-13.
31. Yogendra Singh (1958), "The Changing Power Structure of Village Community", A Case Study of Six Villages in Eastern, U.P." in Desai, *Rural Sociology In India*, (Ed.), Popular Prakashan, Bombay, p. 72.
32. Edward Harper and others (1959), Political Orgnaisations and Leadership in a Karnataka Village, in Park and R.L. Tinker, I, (Eds.), *Leadership and Political Institutions in India*, Princeton University Press, N.J., p. 389.
33. Sachchidanand (1974), "Research on Scheduled Castes with Special Reference to Change" in ICSSR, *A Survey of Research in Sociology and Social Anthropology*, Vol. I. Popular Prakashan, Bombay, pp. 276-310.
34. Pundir J.K (1993), "A Comparative Study of Education Social Mobility and Quality of Life in a Scheduled Caste", paper submitted in the XXXAII Indian Sociological Conference, Mangalore, Dec. 29-31.
35. Upadhyay A.K. (1992), "Scheduled Caste Leader in a Rural Setting in Eastern UP", P. Mhil Project in Sociology Meerut University, Meerut.
36. Benjamin, Joseph (1991), "Social Mobility Among the Scheduled Castes in Bihar", A Case Study of Barh Block, Journal Social Action, Vol. 41, 4, Oct.-Dec., New Delhi, pp. 442-453.
37. Abbasayulu. Y.B. (1979), "The Emergence of Scheduled Caste Elite: Factors and Process" in IJSR Vol. 19, New Delhi, pp. 95-100.
38. Sachchidananda (1977), *The Harijan Elite*, Thomas Press India Ltd., New Delhi, pp. 162-165.
39. Chandra Kanchan (2000), "Elite Incorporation in Multiethnic Societies, Asian Survey, Sept.-Oct., New Delhi.

40. Natarajan, S.A. (1959), *Century of Social Reform in India*, Asia Publishing House, Bombay, p. 8.
41. Anita Matto (1991), *Reform Movements and Social Transformation in India*, The Reliance Publishing House, New Delhi, p. 13.
42. Shyam Lal (2002), *Untouchable Movements in India*, Sublime Publication, Jaipur, pp. 147-149.
43. Scheduled Castes and Scheduled Tribes orders (Amendment) Act, 1976, (No. 108 of 1976) dated 18th 1976, Government of Karnataka.

2

Scheduled Castes in India

This Chapter intends to discuss and assess the status of Scheduled Castes in India. It takes up the caste system in Ancient India. It also focuses on the changes in the life style of scheduled castes i.e., development, changes in social life, culturally and educationally. In this chapter an attempt has been made to evaluate the changes of scheduled castes after independence, particularly through the reservation policies of central governments and state governments.

(A) Caste System in Ancient India

Though the other nations are characterized by social inequality, perhaps nowhere else in the world has inequality been so elaborately constructed as in the Indian institution of caste. Caste has long existed in India, but in the modern period it has been severely criticized by both Indian and foreign observers. Although some educated Indians tell non-Indians that caste has been abolished or that "no one pays attention to caste anymore," such statements do not reflect reality and the caste system has been wide spreading.

Since independence Caste has undergone significant change, but it still involves hundreds of millions of people. In its preamble, India's constitution forbids negative public discrimination on the basis of caste. However, caste ranking and caste-based interaction have occurred for centuries and will continue to do so well into the foreseeable future, more in the countryside than in urban settings and more in the realms of kinship and marriage than in less personal interactions.

Castes are ranked, named, endogamous (in-marrying) groups, membership in which is achieved by birth. There are thousands of castes and sub-castes in India, and these large kinship-based groups are fundamental to South Asian social structure.

Each caste is part of a locally based system of interdependence with other groups, involving occupational specialization, and is linked in complex ways with networks that stretch throughout the nation and cross regions.

The word caste derives from the Portuguese caste, meaning breed, race, or kind. Among the Indian terms that are sometimes translated as caste are varna, jati, jat, biradri, and samaj. All of these terms refer to ranked groups of various sizes and breadth. Varna, or color, actually refers to large divisions that include various castes; the other terms include castes and subdivisions of castes sometimes called sub-castes.

All castes are traditionally associated with an occupation, such as high-ranking Brahmans; middle-ranking fanner and artisan groups, such as potters, barbers, and carpenters; and very low-ranking "Untouchable" leatherworkers, butchers, launderers, and latrine cleaners. There is some correlation between ritual rank on the caste hierarchy and economic prosperity. Members of higher-ranking castes tend, on the whole, to be more prosperous than members of lower-ranking castes. Many lowercaste people live in conditions of great poverty and social backwardness.

According to the Rig Veda, sacred texts that date back to oral traditions of more than 2,000 years ago, progenitors of the four ranked varna groups sprang from various parts of the body of the primordial man, which Brahma created from clay. Each group had a function in sustaining the life of society—the social body. Brahmans, or priests, were created from the mouth. They were to provide for the intellectual and spiritual needs of the community. Kshatriyas, warriors and rulers, were derived from the arms. Their role was to rule and to protect others. Vaishyas landowners and merchants sprang from the thighs, and were entrusted with the care of commerce and agriculture. Shudras artisans and servants came from the feet. Their task was to perform all manual labor.

Later conceptualized was a fifth category, "Untouchable" menials, relegated to carrying out very menial and polluting work related to bodily decay and dirt. Since 1935 "Untouchables" have been known as Scheduled Castes, referring to their listing on government rosters, or schedules. They are also often called by Mohandas Karamchand (Mahatma) Gandhi's term Harijans, or "Children of God." Although the term Untouchable appears in literature produced by these low-ranking castes, in the 1990s, many politically conscious members of these groups prefer to refer to themselves as Scheduled, a Hindi word meaning oppressed or downtrodden. According to the 1991 census, there were 138 million Scheduled Caste members in India, approximately 16 percent of the total population.

The first four varnas apparently existed in the ancient Aryan society of northern India. Some historians say that these categories were originally somewhat fluid functional groups, not castes. A greater degree of fixity gradually developed, resulting in the complex ranking systems of medieval India that essentially continue in the late twentieth century.

Even though a varna is not a caste, when directly asked for their caste affiliation, particularly when the questioner is a Westerner, many Indians will reply with a varna name. Pressed further, they may respond with a much more specific name of a caste, or jati, which falls within that varna.

The Members of a caste are typically spread out over a region, with representatives living in hundreds of settlements. In any small village, there may be representatives of a few or even a score or more castes.

Among castes Inequalities-are considered by the Hindu faithful to be part of the divinely ordained natural order and are expressed in terms of purity and pollution. Within a village, relative rank is most graphically expressed at a wedding or death feast, when all residents of the village are invited. At the home of a high-ranking caste member, food is prepared by a member of a caste from whom all can accept cooked food (usually by a Brahman). Diners are seated in lines; members of a single caste sit next to each other in a row, and members of other castes sit in perpendicular or parallel rows at some distance. Members of Dalit castes, such as Leatherworkers and Sweepers, may be seated far from the other diners—even out in an alley. Farther away, at the edge of the feeding area, a Sweeper may wait with a large basket to receive discarded leavings tossed in by other diners. Eating food contaminated by contact with the saliva of others not of the same family is considered far too polluting to be practiced by members of any other castes. Generally, feasts and ceremonies given by schedules castes are not attended by higher-ranking castes and sub-castes.

Among Muslims, although status differences prevail, brotherhood may be stressed. A Muslim feast usually includes a cloth laid either on clean ground or on a table, with all Muslims, rich and poor, dining from plates placed on the same cloth. Muslims who wish to provide hospitality to observant Hindus, however, must make separate arrangements for a high-caste Hindu cook and ritually pure foods and dining area.

Castes that fall within the top four ranked varnas are sometimes referred to as the "clean castes," with Dalits considered "unclean." Castes of the top three ranked varnas are often designated "twice-born," in reference to the ritual initiation undergone by male members, in which investiture with the Hindu sacred thread constitutes a kind of ritual rebirth. Non-Hindu caste like groups generally fall outside these designations.

Each caste is believed by devout Hindus to have its own dharma, or divinely ordained code of proper conduct Accordingly, there is often a high degree of tolerance for divergent lifestyles among different castes. Brahmans are usually expected to be nonviolent and spiritual, according with their traditional roles as vegetarian teetotaler priests. Kshatriyas are supposed to be strong, as fighters and rulers should be, with a taste for aggression, eating meat, and drinking alcohol. Vaishyas are stereotyped as adept businessmen, in accord with their traditional activities in commerce. Shudras are often described by others as tolerably pleasant but expectably somewhat base in behaviour, whereas Dalits—especially Sweepers—are often regarded by others as followers of vulgar life-styles. Conversely, lower-caste people often view people of high rank as haughty and unfeeling.

Within castes explicit standards are maintained. Transgressions may be dealt with by a caste council, meeting periodically to adjudicate issues relevant to the caste. Such councils are usually formed of groups of elders, almost always males. Punishments such as fines and out casting, either temporary or permanent, can be enforced. In rare cases, a person is excommunicated from the caste for gross infractions of caste rules. An example of such an infraction might be marrying or openly cohabiting with a mate of a caste lower than one's own; such behaviour would usually result in the higher-caste person dropping to the status of the lower-caste person.

Activities such as fanning or trading can be carried out by anyone, but usually only members of the appropriate castes act as priests, barbers, potters, weavers, and other skilled artisans, whose occupational skills are handed down in families from one generation to another. As with other key features of Indian social structure, occupational specialization is believed to be in accord with the divinely ordained order of the universe.

The existence of rigid ranking is supernaturally validated through the idea of rebirth according to a person's karma, the sum of an individual's deeds in this life and in past lives. After death, a person's life is judged by divine forces, and rebirth is assigned in a high or a low place, depending upon what is deserved. This supernatural sanction can never be neglected, because it brings a person to his or her position in the caste hierarchy, relevant to every transaction involving food or drink, speaking, or touching.

In past decades, scheduled castes in certain areas (especially in parts of the south) had to display extreme deference to high-status people, physically keeping their distance—lest their touch or even their shadow pollute others—wearing neither shoes nor any upper body covering (even for women) in the presence of the upper castes. The lowest-ranking had to jingle a little bell in warning of their polluting approach. In much of India, Dalits were prohibited from entering temples, using wells from which the "clean" castes drew their water, or even attending schools. In past centuries, dire punishments were prescribed for Dalits who read or even heard sacred texts.

The degrading discrimination was made illegal under legislation passed during British rule and was protested against by pre-independence reform movements led by Mahatma Gandhi and Bhimrao Ramji (B.R.) Ambedkar, a Dalit leader. Dalits agitated for the right to enter Hindu temples and to use village wells and effectively pressed for the enactment of stronger laws opposing disabilities imposed on them. After independence, Ambedkar almost single handedly wrote India's constitution, including key provisions barring caste-based discrimination. Nonetheless, discriminatory treatment of Dalits remains a factor in daily life, especially in villages, as the end of the twentieth century approaches.

(B) Caste System in India

India has a hierarchical caste system in the society. Within Indian culture, whether in the north or the south, Hindu or Muslim, urban or village, virtually all things, people, and groups of people are ranked according to various essential qualities. If one is attuned to the theme of hierarchy in India, one can discern it everywhere. Although India is a political democracy, in daily life there is little advocacy of or adherence to notions of equality.

Castes systems in India and caste like groups—those quintessential groups with which almost all Indians are associated—are ranked. Within most villages or towns, everyone knows the relative rankings of each locally represented caste, and people's behaviour toward one another is constantly shaped by this knowledge. Between the extremes of the very high and very low castes, however, there is sometimes disagreement on the exact relative ranking of castes clustered in the middle.

In India, castes system are primarily associated with Hinduism but also exist among other Indian religious groups. Muslims sometimes expressly deny that they have castes—they state that all Muslims are brothers under God—but observation of Muslim life in various parts of. India reveals the existence of caste like groups and clear concern with social hierarchy. Among Indian Christians, too, differences in caste are acknowledged and maintained.

In India, individuals are also ranked according to their wealth and power. For example, there are "big men" (bare admi , in Hindi) and "little men" (chhote admi) everywhere. "Big men" sit confidently on chairs, while "little men" come before them to make requests, either standing or crouching down on their haunches, certainly not presuming to sit beside a man of high status as an equal. Even men of nearly equal status who might share a string cot to sit on take their places carefully—the higher ranking man at the head of the cot, the lower-ranking man at the foot.

Within families and kinship groupings, there are many distinctions of hierarchy. Men outrank women of the same or similar age, and senior relatives outrank junior relatives. Several other kinship relations involve formal respect. For example, in northern India, a daughter-in-law of a household shows deference to a daughter of a household. Even among young siblings in a household, there is constant acknowledgment of age differences: younger siblings never address an older sibling by name, but rather by respectful terms for elder brother or elder sister. However, an older sibling may address the younger by name.

Even in a business or academic setting, where colleagues may not openly espouse traditional observance of caste or class ranking behaviour, they may set up fictive kinship relations, addressing one another by kinship terms reflecting family or village-style hierarchy. For example, a younger colleague might respectfully address an older colleague as chachaji (respected father's younger brother), gracefully acknowledging the superior position of the older colleague.

(C) Purity and Pollution

Many status differences in Indian society are expressed in terms of ritual purity and pollution. Notions of purity and pollution are extremely complex and vary greatly among different castes, religious groups, and regions. However, broadly speaking, high status is associated with purity and low status with pollution. Some kinds of purity are inherent, or inborn; for example, gold is purer than copper by its very nature, and, similarly, a member of a high-ranking Brahman, or priestly, caste is born with more inherent purity than a member of a low-ranking sweeper (Mehtar, in Hindi) caste. Unless the Brahman defiles himself in some extraordinary way, throughout his life he will always be purer than a Sweeper. Other kinds of purity are more transitory—a Brahman who has just taken a bath is more ritually pure than a Brahman who has not bathed for a day. This situation could easily reverse itself temporarily, depending on bath schedules, participation in polluting activities, or contact with temporarily polluting substances.

Purity is associated with ritual cleanliness—daily bathing in flowing water, dressing in properly laundered clothes of approved materials, eating only the foods appropriate for one's caste, refraining from physical contact with people of lower rank, and avoiding involvement with ritually impure substances. The latter include body wastes and excretions, most especially those of another adult person. Contact with the products of death or violence are typically polluting and threatening to ritual purity.

During her menstrual period, a woman is considered polluted and refrains from cooking, worshiping, or touching anyone older than an infant. In much of the south, a woman spends this time "sitting outside," resting in an isolated room or shed. During her period, a Muslim woman does not touch the Quran. At the end of the period, purity is restored with a complete bath. Pollution also attaches to birth, both for the mother and the infant's close kin, and to death, for close relatives of the deceased.

Members of the highest priestly castes, the Brahmans, are generally vegetarians (although some Bengali and Maharashtrian Brahmans eat fish) and avoid eating meat, the product of violence and death. High-ranking Warrior castes (Kshatriyas), however, typically consume non-vegetarian diets, considered appropriate for their traditions of valor and physical strength.

A Brahman born of proper Brahman parents retains his inherent purity if he bathes and dresses himself properly, adheres to a vegetarian diet, eats meals prepared only by persons of appropriate rank, and keeps his person away from the bodily exuviate of others (except for necessary contact with the secretions of family infants and small children).

If a Brahman happens to come into bodily contact with a polluting substance, he can remove this pollution by bathing and changing his clothing. However, if he were to eat meat or commit other transgressions of the rigid dietary codes of his particular caste, he would be considered more deeply polluted and would have to undergo various purifying rites and payment of fines imposed by his caste council in order to restore his inherent purity.

In sharp contrast to the purity of a Brahman, a Sweeper born of Sweeper parents is considered to be born inherently polluted. The touch of his body is polluting to those higher on the caste hierarchy than he, and they will shrink from his touch, whether or not he has bathed recently. Sweepers are associated with the traditional occupation of cleaning human feces from latrines and sweeping public lanes of all kinds of dirt. Traditionally, Sweepers remove these polluting materials in baskets carried atop the head and dumped out in a garbage pile at the edge of the village or neighborhood. The involvement of Sweepers with such filth accords with their low-status position at the bottom of the Hindu caste hierarchy, even as their services allow high-status people, such as Brahmans, to maintain their ritual purity.

Members of the Leatherworker (Chamar) caste are ascribed a very low status consonant with their association with the caste occupation of skinning dead animals and tanning the leather. Butchers (Khatiks, in Hindi), who kill and cut up the bodies of animals, also rank low on the caste hierarchy because of their association with violence and death.

However, castes associated with ruling and warfare—and the killing and deaths of human beings—are typically accorded high rank on the caste hierarchy. In these instances, political power and wealth outrank association with violence as the key determinant of caste rank.

Maintenance of purity is associated with the intake of food and drink, not only in terms of the nature of the food itself, but also in terms of who has prepared it or touched it. This requirement is especially true for Hindus, but other religious groups hold to these principles to varying degrees. Generally, a person risks pollution—and lowering his own status—if he accepts beverages or cooked foods from the hands of people of lower caste status than his own. His status will remain intact if he accepts food or beverages from people of higher caste rank. Usually, for an observant Hindu of any but the very lowest castes to accept cooked food from a Muslim or Christian is regarded as highly polluting.

In a clear example of pollution associated with dining, a Brahman who consumed a drink of water and a meal of wheat bread with boiled vegetables from the hands of a Sweeper would immediately become polluted and could expect social rejection by his caste fellows. From that moment, fellow Brahmans' following traditional pollution rules would refuse food touched by him and would abstain from the usual social interaction with him. He would not be welcome inside Brahman homes—most especially in the ritually pure kitchens—nor would he or his close relatives be considered eligible marriage partners for other Brahmans.

Generally, the acceptance of water and ordinary foods cooked in water from members of lower-ranking castes incurs the greatest pollution. In North India, such foods are known as kaccha khana , as contrasted with fine foods cooked in butter or oils, which are known as pakka khana . Fine foods can be accepted from members of a few castes slightly lower than one's own. Local hierarchies differ on the specific details of these rules.

Completely raw foods, such as uncooked grains, fresh unpeeled bananas, mangoes, and uncooked vegetables can be accepted by anyone from anyone else, regardless of relative status. Toasted or parched foods, such as roasted peanuts, can also be accepted from anyone without ritual or social repercussions. (Thus, a Brahman may accept gifts of grain from lower-caste patrons for eventual preparation by members of his own caste, or he may purchase and consume roasted peanuts or tangerines from street vendors of unknown caste without worry).

Water served from an earthen pot may be accepted only from the hands of someone of higher or equal caste ranking, but water served from a brass pot may be accepted even from someone slightly lower on the caste scale. Exceptions to this rule are members of the Water bearer (Bhoi, in Hindi) caste, who are employed to carry water from wells to the homes of the prosperous and from whose hands members of all castes may drink water without becoming polluted, even though Water bearers are not ranked high on the caste scale.

These and a great many other traditional rules pertaining to purity and pollution constantly impinge upon interaction between people of different castes and ranks in India. Although to the non-Indian these rules may seem irrational and bizarre, to most of the people of India they are a ubiquitous and accepted part of life. Thinking about and following purity and pollution rules make it necessary for people to be constantly aware of differences in status. With every drink of water, with every meal, and with every contact with another person, people must ratify the social hierarchy of which they are a part and within which their every act is carried out. The fact that expressions of social status are intricately bound up with events that happen to everyone every day—eating, drinking, bathing, touching, talking—and that transgressions of these rules, whether deliberate or accidental, are seen as having immediately polluting effects on the person of the transgressor, means that every ordinary act of human life serves as a constant reminder of the importance of hierarchy in Indian society.

There are many Indians, particularly among the educated urban elite, who do not follow traditional purity and pollution practices. Dining in each other's homes and in restaurants is common among well-educated people of diverse backgrounds, particularly when they belong to the same economic class. For these people, guarding the family's earthen water pot from inadvertent touch by a low-ranking servant is not the concern it is for a more traditional villager. However, even among those people whose words and actions denigrate traditional purity rules, there is often a reluctance to completely abolish consciousness of purity and pollution from their thinking. It is surely rare for a Sweeper, however well-educated, to invite a Brahman to dinner in his home and have his invitation unself-consciously accepted. It is less rare, however, for educated urban colleagues of vastly different caste and religious heritage to enjoy a cup of tea together. Some high-caste liberals pride themselves on being free of "casteism" and seek to accept food from the hands of very low-caste people, or even deliberately set out to marry someone from a significantly lower caste or a different religion. Thus, even as they deny it, these progressives affirm the continuing significance of traditional rules of purity, pollution, and hierarchy in Indian caste system.

(D) Unsociability and the Caste System in India

Unsociability has its roots in India's caste system, which is supposed to be more than 1,500 years old. A Hindu can belong to a particular caste by virtue of his/her birth and the lower caste or the out-cast Hindus can never escape this tortured ordeal till his/her death. The caste system in India is often described as the longest surviving social hierarchy, a defining feature of which involves complex stratification of social groups based on ritual purity. There are four basic caste groups, also known as 'varna', and in order of precedence they are the Brahmins (priests and the teachers), Ksyatriyas (rulers and soldiers), Vaisyas (merchants and traders), and Shudras (laborers and servants). Shudras, the lowest caste of the four, are supposed to serve the higher castes. Besides these principal castes, there are thousands of subcastes also known as Jatis'. These are all endogamous (marrying within the same caste only) groups that are further divided along occupational, sectarian, regional, and linguistic lines.

A fifth category falls outside the four broad vama groups; people too 'impure' to rank as worthy beings were known as the 'Achuts' or Untouchables. They were (and still are) often assigned tasks like sweeping, cleaning up filth, disposing of dead animals, leather work and other 'polluting jobs' that were beyond the purview of the caste Hindus. Mahatma Ghandi gave them the name 'Harijan', meaning Children of God, and he also launched a campaign to have 'Untouchables' be renamed 'Harijan'. However, nowadays the word 'Dalit' is the most acceptable word used to address this section of society. It is a Sanskrit word that means 'broken, discriminated or shattered people '. Dalits are also further divided into more than 70 sub-castes.

Unsociability was abolished in India in 1950 under Article 16 of the Constitution. Interestingly, Dr B.R. Ambedkar, himself a Dalit, played a major role in drafting the Constitution. He is also known as the father of the present Dalit movement, which is questioning the whole caste structure. Even though 50 years have passed since the abolition of untouchably, the practice continues in many forms throughout the country. In many places Dalits are not permitted to draw water from common wells and hand pumps, separate utensils are used to serve them in many tea and food stalls, they are not allowed entry to the temples and Dalit children are made to sit at the back of the classroom. The situation is even worse in rural areas where the majority of the population as well as Dalits reside. In its book, 'Broken People: Caste Violence Against India's "Untouchables"', the Human Rights Watch reports that most Dalits in rural areas live in segregated colonies away from the caste Hindus. In a specific case from the Villupuram district in the state of Tamil Nadu, villages have segregated Dalit colonies; basic supplies like water are also set apart and medical facilities and the better thatched houses exist exclusively in the caste Hindu colonies. Unsociability is also observed at the highest judiciary level. In July 1998 a judge from the Allahabad High Court in Uttar Pradesh had his chambers cleaned with the 'sacred waters of the river Ganges' as it had been earlier occupied by a Dalit judge.

The constitution also grants Dalits certain privileges that include reservations (meaning quotas) in education, government jobs, and government bodies. The Scheduled Castes and Scheduled Tribes (Prevention of Atrocities) Act, 1989 was enacted to prevent abuses against members of the Scheduled Castes and the Scheduled Tribes. The law, however, has benefited few as its implementation is weak. The National Commission for Scheduled Castes and Scheduled Tribes in its 1997 report highlighted: "Whenever Dalits have tried to organise themselves or assert their rights, there has been a backlash from the feudal lords resulting in mass killings of Dalits, gang rapes, looting, and-arson etc. of Harijan (Dalit) bastis (villages)". According to government statistics, in 2001 there were 24,792 registered criminal cases that included murder and rape committed against Scheduled Castes. Yet, it is believed that this is only a tip of the iceberg as the majority of cases are not reported, especially in rural areas. Even registering a case does not ensure conviction of the culprits. Every year, even though more than 1,000 cases are registered, actual convictions are just a meagre one to three.

Dalit women are often sexually harassed and assaulted by men of the upper castes. A government investigator told the Human Rights Watch in Tamil Nadu, "No one practices unsociability when it comes to sex." There are many reports where Dalit women have been stripped and even paraded naked for showing dissent, demanding more wages from landowners, or even for crossing the path and not bowing in front of the men of upper castes.

(E) Caste System in Modern India

The leaders of independent India decided that India will be democratic, socialist and secular country. According to this policy there is a separation between religion and state. Practicing unsociability or discriminating a person based on his caste is legally forbidden. Along with this law the government allows positive discrimination of the depressed classes of India. The Indians have also become more flexible in their caste system customs. In general the urban people in India are less strict about the caste system than the rural. In cities one can see different caste people mingling with each other, while in some rural areas there is still discrimination based on castes and sometimes also on unsociability. Sometimes in villages or in the cities there are violent clashes which, are connected to caste tensions. Sometimes the high castes strike the lower castes who dare to uplift their status. Sometimes the lower caste get back on the higher castes.

In modern India the term caste is used for Jat and also for Vama. The term, caste was used by the British who ruled India until 1947. The British who wanted to rule India efficiently made lists of Indian communities. They used two terms to describe Indian communities. Castes and Tribes. The term caste was used for Jats and also for Varnas. Tribes were those communities who lived deep in jungles, forests and mountains far away from the main population and also communities who were hard to be defined as castes for example communities who made a living from stealing or robbery. These lists, which the British made, were used later on by the Indian governments to create lists of communities who were entitled for positive discrimination.

The castes, which were the elite of the Indian society, were classified as high castes. The other communities were classified as lower castes or lower classes. The lower classes were listed in three categories. The first category is called Scheduled Castes. This category includes in it communities who were untouchables. In modern India, unsociability exists at a very low extent. The untouchables call themselves Dalit, meaning depressed. Until the late 1980s they were called Harijan, meaning children of God. This title was given to them by Mahatma Gandhi who wanted the society to accept untouchables within them.

The second category is Scheduled Tribes. This category includes in it those communities who did not accept the caste system and preferred to reside deep in the jungles, forests and mountains of India, away from the main population. The Scheduled Tribes are also called Adivasi, meaning aboriginals.

The third category is called sometimes Other Backward Classes or Backward Classes. This category includes in it castes who belong to Sudra Varna and also former untouchables who converted from Hinduism to other religions. This category also includes in it nomads and tribes who made a living from criminal acts.

According to the central government policy these three categories are entitled for positive discrimination. Sometimes these three categories are defined together as Backward Classes. 15% of India's-population are Scheduled Castes. According to central government policy 15% of the government jobs and 15% of the students admitted to universities must be from Scheduled Castes. For the Scheduled Tribes about 7.5% places are reserved which is their proportion in Indian population. The Other Backwards Classes are about 50% of India's population, but only 27% of government jobs are reserved for them.

Along with the central government, the state governments of India also follow a positive discrimination policy. Different states have different figures of communities entitled for positive discrimination based on the population of each state. Different state governments have different lists of communities entitled for positive discrimination. Sometimes a specific community is entitled for rights in a particular state but not in another state of India.

In modern India new tensions were created because of these positive discrimination policies. The high caste communities feel discriminated by the government policy to reserve positions for the Backward Classes. In many cases a large number of high caste members compete for a few places reserved for them. While the Backward Classes members do not have to compete at all because of the large number of reserved places for them compared to the candidates. Sometimes in order to fill the quota, candidates from the lower classes are accepted even though they are not suitable. Sometimes some reserved positions remain unmanned because there were few candidates from the lower classes causing more tension between the castes. Between the lower castes there are also tensions over reservation.

In the order of priority for a reserved place of the Backward Classes, candidate from the Scheduled castes is preferred over a candidate from the Scheduled Tribes who is preferred over a candidate from the other Backward Classes. As stated earlier Other Backward Classes are about 50% of India's population but only 27% of the Other Backward Classes are entitled for positive discrimination according to central government policy. Some Other. Backward Classes communities are organizing politically to be recognized as Backward Classes entitled for positive discrimination.

The Scheduled Tribes who are seen as the aborigines of India got ownership and certain rights over Indian land. Many communities in India claim also to be aborigines of India and they are claiming the same rights as the Scheduled Tribes. The caste identity has become a subject of political, social and legal interpretation. Communities who get listed as entitled for positive discrimination do not get out of this list even if their social and political conditions get better. In many cases the legal system is involved to decide if a certain person is entitled for positive discrimination.

But with all this positive discrimination policy, most of the communities who were low in the caste hierarchy remain low in the social order even today. And communities who were high in the social hierarchy remain even today high in the social hierarchy. Most of the degrading jobs are even today done by the Dalits, while the Brahmans remain at the top of the hierarchy by being the doctors, engineers and lawyers of India.

In view of this position, the framers of the Indian Constitution incorporated in the Constitution itself provisions for affirmative action or compensatory discrimination as some people call it. This was done by providing for reservation of jobs for dalits in government employment and reservation of seats for them in educational institutions [see Articles 15(4) and 16(4)].

The Constitution of India provides for reservation of seats for scheduled castes and scheduled tribes (dalits) in the Lower House of Parliament and in the state legislatures (Article 330 and Article 332 respectively). When the Constitution was enacted in 1950, the reservations were to cease after 10 years. However, having regard to the conditions of scheduled castes and scheduled tribes, the Constitution has been amended from time to time, and the period of 10 years has been extended to 20 years, then to 30 years, then to 40 years and then to 50 years. At present it provides that the reservation will cease after 60 years, i.e., after 2010 (see 79th Amendment Act, 1999 in Article 334).

Article 338 provides for the constitution of a National Commission for the Scheduled Castes and Scheduled Tribes. Article 338(5)(b) makes it the duty of the commission to enquire into specific complaints with respect to deprivation of rights and safeguards of the dalits. 1294 complaints were received in the year 2000. After examining them, action has been taken by requiring competent authorities of the states to take cognizance under the penal acts. This has been done in a majority of cases. The Constitution further provides that the Union and every state government shall consult the commission on all major policy matters affecting scheduled castes and scheduled tribes.

With the increase in the quantum of reservations of jobs and seats there were court challenges. The Supreme Court of India ruled that as a general rule reservation should not exceed 50%. The court also held that whilst there can be reservation up to 50% in the case of initial recruitment there should be no reservation in respect of promotions.

In order to further protect and promote the fundamental rights of the dalits, the Constitution has been amended to get over and neutralize these Supreme Court judgments. An act of the state of Tamil Nadu providing for reservation up to 69% has been the subject of a constitutional amendment (see 76th Amendment Act, 1994). Articles 16(4A) and (413) have been added to the Constitution by way of amendments in order to get over the aforesaid judgments (see 77th Amendment Act, 1995 and 81st Amendment Act, 2000). These articles have escaped the attention of the author of the working paper.

Article 335 of the Constitution provides that in the making of appointments in public employment, 'the claims of the members of the scheduled castes and the scheduled tribes shall be taken into consideration, consistently with the maintenance of efficiency of administration.' In order to further advance the rights and claims of the dalits there has been a constitutional amendment, viz. 82nd Amendment Act, 2000 which provides for 'relaxation in qualifying marks in any examination or lowering the standards of evaluation' for reservation in matters of promotion for dalits. This significant constitutional amendment finds no mention in the working paper.

There have been protests from other sections of the society and complaints of reverse discrimination. There is lot of heart-burning that a student who has secured 90% cannot get admission to a college whereas a dalit student who has secured much lower marks can get admission. The government's view is that for centuries dalits have suffered worse and more severe discrimination and these measures are felt necessary at the present stage for their advancement. Is that apartheid? Is that racism or racial discrimination?

Unsociability, which is abhorrent, has been abolished by the Constitution. Its practice is made a penal offence and stringent punishment is provided, like mandatory minimum prison sentence and also forfeiture of property in some cases. This act also contemplates formation of special courts for trial of such offences, which are enumerated in the act. Many district headquarters have a separate special court to try the offences under the 1989 Act. Eighty exclusive special courts have been set up in various states. Other states have conferred upon the existing sessions courts the powers of special courts for trial of offences under the 1989 Act.

The rate of convictions is also growing. Of course, there could be and should be more convictions but remember that India's criminal jurisprudence is based on the presumption of innocence and proof beyond reasonable doubt in criminal cases. Partial or ineffective enforcement cannot amount to impunity, unless there is a deliberate official policy of non-enforcement. The number of people convicted in 1996 was 1827. For the year 1997 it was 2017.

The Parliament has also passed another law, Employment of Manual Scavengers and Construction of Dry

Latrines (Prohibition) Act, 1993 whereby members of the disadvantaged sections of society are to be prevented from doing manual scavenging. The government has formulated a scheme for liberation and rehabilitation of scavengers and their dependents. A national Safai Karamcharis Finance and Development Corporation is being constituted to provide credit at confessional rates to ameliorate the plight of the scheduled castes/scheduled tribes. From 1997-98, 1998-99, 1999-2000, over Rs 600 million have been spent for this purpose.

It is a fact that discriminatory practices against the dalits do persist. An absence of effective enforcement of the legal provisions is one of the causes. Urgent action in this regard is necessary and the same is engaging attention of the authorities. But non-implementation of legal provisions is not confined to dalits. In a vast country like India beset with several problems, regrettably there is non-implementation in other cases also like labour legislation, legislation for protection of children and women, environmental laws and so on.

India has a free and independent media, which also exposes and condemns discriminatory practices against dalits. Articles by dalit groups and those espousing their cause and which are severely critical of the government are widely published in several newspapers. There is no restriction or interference with the fundamental rights of the dalits to organize conferences and seminars in which their grievances are ventilated and demands are made for further measures and initiatives.

(F) Social Change and Legislations

The cure is part of the cause in this case; as Dalits avail themselves of the advantages of reservation in India, and awareness of rights increases, the status quo of inter-caste relations in villages faces severe challenges. Increased violence, and increased reporting of incidents of violence, is a natural product. Although Dalit groups have had great success in gaining publicity for their cause, they have consistently failed to hold the Indian government to the standards of existing national and international legislation.

There is, in fact, a law in place to fight the violence being visited upon Dalits, but it suffers from neglect.

In 1989, the Government of India passed the Prevention of Atrocities Act (POA), which delineates specific crimes against Scheduled Castes and Scheduled Tribes as "atrocities," and describes strategies and prescribes punishments to counter these acts. The Act attempts to curb and punish violence against Dalits through three broad means. Firstly, it identifies what acts constitute "atrocities." These include both particular incidents of harm and humiliation such as the forced consumption of noxious substances, as well as the systemic violence faced by many Dalits, especially in rural areas. Such systemic violence includes forced labour, denial of access to water and other public amenities, and sexual abuse of Dalit women. Secondly, the Act calls upon all the states to convert an existing sessions court in each district into a special court to try cases registered under the POA. Thirdly, the Act creates provisions for states to declare areas with high levels of caste violence to be "atrocityprone" and to appoint qualified officers to monitor and maintain law and order.

Unlike its predecessor, the 1955 Civil Rights Act, which only concerned itself with superficial humiliations such as verbal abuse of the lower castes, the POA was a tacit acknowledgement by the government that caste relations are defined by violence, both incidental and systemic. The POA gives Dalits vital ammunition in the form of legal redress for this violence.

Although the POA is a powerful and precise weapon on paper, in practice the Act has suffered from a near-complete failure in implementation. Ironically, the primary obstacles to implementation are the primary enforcers of the Act-the lowest rungs of the police and bureaucracy that form the primary node of interaction between state and society in the rural areas. Policemen have displayed a consistent unwillingness to register offences under the act. This reluctance stems partially from ignorance.

In most cases, unwillingness to file a First Information Report (FIR) under the Act comes from caste-bias. Upper caste policemen are reluctant to file cases against fellow caste-members because of the severity of the penalties imposed by the Act; most offences are non-bailable and carry minimum punishments of five years imprisonment. Hard work by human rights defenders has slowly begun to decrease this problem. Nevertheless, the staggering scope of the problem demands government intervention before cases can be properly registered under the Act.

A bigger obstacle faces victims who actually manage to lodge a complaint. Failure to follow through with cases is alarmingly apparent at the lowest echelons of the judicial system. The statistics speak for themselves: out of 147,000 POA cases pending in the courts in 1998, only 31,011 were brought to trial. Such delay is endemic to the Indian judicial system. Although the POA mandated the creation of special courts precisely to circumvent this problem, only two states have created separate special courts in accordance with the law. In other states, existing sessions courts have been designated special courts, while still being asked to process their usual case loads. Since many different Acts require the creation of special courts, such sessions courts are often overloaded with a number of different kinds of "priority" cases, virtually guaranteeing that none of these cases receive the attention they are mandated to receive.

Even if cases make it to trial, the POA also suffers from abysmal rates of conviction. Out of the 31,011 cases tried under the POA in 1998, only a paltry 1,677 instances or 5.4 per cent resulted in a conviction and 29,334 ended in acquittal. Compare this to the conviction rate in cases tried under the Indian Penal Code: in 1999, 39.4 per cent of cases ended. In a conviction and in 2000, 41.8 per cent. Judicial delay is just one cause of this low conviction rate; the time lapse between the case being registered and the trial means that witnesses who are often poor and face intimidation in the interim, turn hostile and the case becomes too weak for a conviction. The long wait also results in many plaintiffs losing interest. Judicial bias against Dalits is rampant and unchecked, and court decisions frequently bear the mark of such bias.

Although the Prevention of Atrocities Act is a powerful weapon on paper, in practice it has suffered from a near-complete failure in implementation.

(G) Reservations and Development SC/ST

The Depressed Classes, as the SC&ST Dalits were known those days, during their long struggles were demanding not for a token foothold, but a formal Representation in the Administration, due Presence in the Bureaucracy, full Participation in the Govt. and for their Share in the Governance of the Country. They were ably led by the well-learned indomitable Baba Saheb Dr Ambedkar. It is because of Dr Ambedkar's Struggles, even in the face of severe threats to his life and that of his followers, and in spite of the presence of strong oppositions to his demands and scheme of thinking for the good of the Country, well-being of the People including the Dalits, and better future of the Society including his own Dalit Sections that we find the SCs & STs present here and there, at times noticeably even if not prominently, in the visible segments of the Society, in the notable layers of the Bureaucracy, and in important places in the Govt. like the Central Secretariat of the Govt of India at Delhi.

The presence of some SCs & STs in Services, including the Central Secretariat at Delhi is a fact, even though the SC&ST Communities have not yet really got their Dues, or a real and true Share of Power or Responsible Part in the Governance of the Country. Even this small presence, has now become possible, only because of Dr Ambedkar's Statesmanship Vision Foresight, and his Insistence for Preserving and Continuing in Free India, if not more, at least the moth-eaten Reservations for the Depressed Classes, to which he was forced to agree by Gandhi in 1932, and entered into a formal Pact, a written and signed Solemn Agreement with the caste Hindu leaders, on behalf of the Depressed Classes. It is this Agreement, the Poona Pact, which formed the basis of the Govt of India Act 1935, and the Foundations of our Constitution. And it is these, and particularly because of Dr Ambedkar and his Reservations-that while the Anglo-Indians, Other Christians, Muslims, Parsis etc of the British

India, have either faded or vanished from the Central Secretariat, the then rare SCs & STs have gained some presence in Free Independent India, the caste Hindu dominated India, as many Minority and Backward Class Leaders of those days including Dr Ambedkar also, rightly predicted and feared Even this small presence of SCs & STs in the Central Secretariat today, is not a small achievement. And this, in short, is what the Policy of Reservation has achieved.

Many poor Backward Castes with Social Conditions, Economic and Political Standards, comparable or at times at least in some ways bad if not worse than that of the SCs, who in the early days of Independence of the Country refused and fought bitterly against any proposal or suggestion or even an idea to include the names of their Castes into the list of SCs, when the Governments in the States were considering and enumerating various Castes to compile and declare the Lists of the Scheduled Castes for the States, have come around and made a complete about turn, clamoring for their respective individual Castes to be included in the List of Scheduled Castes. They were primarily interested in getting the advantages of Reservations and Special Development Programmes for the SCs & STs, particularly in the spheres of good Education, especially Professional and University Education, Employment and Promotions in Services, Financial Assistances for Education and Development, such as the Grant of Scholarships Fellowships Free ships Exemptions from Payment of tuition/hostel/mess/ examination Fees and to start Business/setup Shops/ Factories/Industries etc, Grants for Studies Abroad, Admissions to General or Special Students' Hostels, allotments of Surplus Agricultural and even Fallow or Waste Lands, Building Sites, Houses or Flats and Industrial Plots/ Sheds, Political Representations etc, through the Schemes of various Reservations and Development Programmes meant for the SCs & STs.

The demand by the Other Backward Classes and also many others, and their claim to be declared as a SC, or at times at least as a ST, even by hook or crook was going on silently almost all the times. This, even though they were all otherwise publicly opposed to the SCs & STs, and were running the SCs & STs down badly as if they were outsiders and their enemies. They were also denigrating the SCs & STs, calling them names and humiliating them openly. The others were opposing all forms of Reservations, specifically any assistance or help by the Govt. to the SCs & STs. And they were the bitter critics of the whole Scheme of Reservations, particularly Caste based Reservations. They were arguing that the Reservations should not be on the basis of Castes, even though they were specifically asking for inclusion of their Castes in the List of SCs, only and in order to get the benefits of Reservations for themselves and their own Castes. In the public, they were always critical of Reservations, even when demanding Reservations for themselves. Such were and still are, the double standards of the Hindu society. They were claiming that the Reservations were there, and in fact were conceived only to please the SC&ST Dalits, with an eye on the hustings. They were, as the caste hinds today still are, cribbing that the Politicians upheld Reservations only due to the compulsions of electoral necessities. They were all complaining that the Political Parties and the Govts. in Power supported and sustained the Reservations, just for the sake of getting the votes of the SCs & STs, and to preserve them as their Party's solid Vote Banks. Thus, they were and others are, so foolish even to criticise and blame Democracy, and the processes of choosing the Peoples' Representatives for sending them to the Panchayats, Legislatives and the Parliament through Adult Franchise. In the end, finding the doors of entry and inclusion of their Castes into the List of the SCs closed, or at least closed tight, some of them came around to open a new front or line of similar Reservations in the name of Backward Classes.

Constitution facilitates the Govt to provide for, Reservations to Other Backward Classes, who are not Represented in Govt. But the dominant castes who appropriate everything and take all good things in life for themselves, 'have been effectively and systematically blocking the Reservations for the Backward Classes all these years.

Many caste Hindus, with a criminal bent of mind and crooked attitudes, also began to impersonate themselves as SCs/STs to mislead the authorities, just to take the benefits meant for the SCs & STs. Many of them had gone up in the offices and in their lives. Many others, with the connivance of the officials themselves, even today appropriate and continue to enjoy the benefits meant for the SCs & STs, with the help of bogus SC/ST Certificates they manage to obtain falsely, and or by falsification of facts, about their birth or that of their parents, or just by paying bribes to the caste Hindu peons, clerks and the Caste Certificate Issuing Authorities in the States and UTs. This, only because of the all round realizations that Reservations really help, and help even the lowly placed, despised, marginalized, socially suppressed, culturally physically politically, educationally and economically oppressed weaker sections and communities like the SCs & STs. This also, in spite of all the negative steps taken against the SCs & STs as well as the Reservation Policy, and the severe oppositions and silent hurdles mounted in the way of implementation of the Reservations by almost most those who are in offices and positions of power and authority. Almost all the authorities and other officials are totally opposed and are against the SCs & STs and their Development, or are jealous and intolerant of the SCs & STs getting even an iota of Progress, little Liberation, inch of Freedom, or at least a bit of Justice.

Reservations are really and truly beneficial not only to the people concerned like the SCs & STs and OBCs, but also to the whole Nation and the Society for the overall and just Development. Also, the Country's Economy gets benefited, and can achieve better and quicker results through all-round Growth and Progress. Whatever may be the shortcomings and oppositions, or behind the screen scheming that go against Reservations, the Reservations had served well, the Nation and the Indian Society. With the part acceptance in 1990, of Reservations for the Backward Classes recommended by the Mandal Commission, Reservations have come to stay, in spite of all the fury and all-round oppositions. Reservations now have become permanent. Nobody in the Country now has the courage or the guts to scrap them, however much they may dislike Reservations and or hate the SCs & STs and OBCs. Now, there is a flurry of rush by individuals and castes to include themselves and their castes as Backward Castes. This is an ample proof, for the reality that Reservations have at last come to stay in our Country also. Reservations have been accepted by all, as the sure means to develop even the badly disadvantaged despised and marginalized sections of the society. In fact, the Reservations for long have been recognized as a reliable mechanism to help the Weaker Sections of the Society anywhere in the World. And there is no better Model, to Uplift the Backward the Helpless the Marginalized and the Neglected Communities. It is only for this reason that, there is so much of fury and oppositions to Reservation Policy on the one hand, and the silent sabotage and subversions that we see on the other in the actual implementation. The specific details of Reservations, the mechanisms and processes of operating and enforcement of the Reservations, are silently and cunningly derailed by those who are jealous and intolerant of the Growth Development and Progress of the SCs & STs.

The Reservations for OBCs had multiple effects. They are yet to be felt or realised in full. But the immediate effects are that the dominant castes had lost their control over the OBCs, and thus an effective tool to oppress the SCs & STs, and focus their tirade against the Reservations for the SCs & STs. They had lost an effective excuse to keep the OBCs captive anymore. They could no more blame the Reservations for the SCs & STs and their growth, for all the Backwardness of the OBCs, and the lack of Opportunities for the OBCs, which they had deliberately not created or allowed to be made available. They could no more turn the attention of the OBCs away from the fact that, they have always been taking away the opportunities, shares and dues of others including the OBCs, and thus have all along deprived the growth development and progress of the OBCs. They could no more divert the anger of the OBCs against the SCs & STs, to escape from the same. Hence they could no more succeed in keeping the OBCs and the SCs & STs—the Deprived Sections of the Society-divided, and hold down the SCs & STs by using the OBCs to keep the SCs & STs suppressed.

The dominant castes till now had only contempt for the SCs&STs, and had only occasionally shown their intolerance and hatred for the Reservations They were only Jealous of the Development of some SCs & STs in spite of all the oppositions and hurdles for growth. They rarely had to deal directly with the SCs & STs, or oppose Reservations by themselves. That task, they had effectively managed to put on the OBCs. They were only operating from the back, by manipulating the Details and the Methodologies of Reservations, and the actual Processes of Implementation. Now, for the first time, they had to handle the SCs & STs directly, and not only that have to face the OBCs fully, that too almost on the side of the former. With the Reservations for the OBCs, their hatred had increased, and the targets of hatred had enlarged from the just hopeful expectant SCs & STs, to the restless and aggressive but at the same time unorganized OBCs also. Now they had to confront both, almost at the same time and on the same issues. At the same time, they had to also carry on by themselves on their shoulders the burden of opposing the Reservations, and also keep manipulating the Reservations, so that the Reservations don't actually benefit either the SCs & STs or the OBCs. They are thus actually playing with fire. What will happen when the OBCs fully wake up, organize themselves and get united? What will they do to face the fury of the organized OBCs? And what will happen if the SCs & STs also join them? The dominant castes apparently are not thinking beyond the immediate, and are making a great mistake. They should quickly and amicably settle themselves in a just manner, while they still hold the levers of power, without attempting to play one caste or tribe against the other, the SCs against the STs, the SCs & STs against the OBCs, or any such combination to buy time.

The significant is the fact that the caste Hindus have developed in their minds a great fear about the grouping, coming together, possible unity, and combination of the OBCs and the SCs & STs, at least as the Beneficiaries of Reservations. But instead of finding a practical and lasting solution, they still want to play their games. They don't want change or mend their ways. They want to continue with their manipulations. That is the reason why they have Administratively and through the Courts, limited the Reservations for the OBCs, to only Appointments in Public Services by Direct Recruitments alone, and not in Promotions. Therefore, they want to avoid the OBCs and the SCs & STs joining hands, and prevent them from fully coming together. Hence, they want to preserve many areas of divergence between the OBCs and SCs & STs, and thus the disunity and conflict, particularly in Admissions to higher and professional education, at least in the Central Institutions and in Promotions in Services.

Today, the fear in the minds of the caste Hindus had grown so intense that all the dominant castes, almost without any exception, feel threatened that their days are counted, and that their dominance now is really at stake. Therefore, even some of those well placed fellows, and happy satisfied comfortable and self contented individuals, who had in the past shown some sympathy for the poor bright or the helpless and needy or capable and promising individual SCs & STs, have no more empathy left in them for the later. Their fear is now so great, intense and total. They are no more willing to help even the most needy and deserving poor SC/ST. They are now totally opposed to the SC&ST Communities, the Reservations for the SCs & STs, and the whole Scheme of Reservations. As they are in power, and in full control of the Govt, Bureaucracy, and the Administration of Public Affairs, the heat is increasingly being felt now, by most of the SCs & STs.

(H) What have the Reservations for the SC's & ST's Achieved?

Many things! And at the same time the Reservations had failed to achieve much more essential things! They have proved to be a great disappointment to the SC&ST Communities as a whole! They have failed the SCs & STs almost in all the fronts and every walks of the life! It is not that Reservations are bad, but those who have been called to work them have proved to be really bad! The learned officials, the Public Servants of the Country, in whose hands the responsibility of implementing the Reservations rest, have deliberately let down the still poor and helpless SCs & STs! They really have no heart, neither any compassion or concern for the poor helpless and the weak, nor any interest in the Welfare Growth and Development of the People, the Society, the Country and the Nation!

We have adequate and reasonably reliable data on the Reservations for SCs&STs, and there are lots of Reports and other Writings on their actual effects. But sadly, after five decades of operations of Reservations for SCs&STs in free Indian Republic-even if.we neglect the period between 1935 Govt of India Act and 1950 when the Constitution with Special Provisions for the SCs&STs including various Reservations for the SCs&STs, in different and related spheres of Politics Education Employment and Economic Activities, like Development Growth Housing Welfare etc came into force-the achievements are not really worth recounting. For, the Reservations have never been seriously or sincerely enforced, except in Politics for Electing the Representatives of the People to the Lok Sabha in Parliament at the Center, and the Legislative Assemblies in the States. As a result, in the significant areas of Education and Employment, there is nothing we can talk of proudly, or the Govt can take credit of.

Today, fifty years after Independence of the Country, there are only two SC Secretaries to the Govt of India-one an IAS Officer, and the other the Law Secretary to the Govt of India. There is no ST who is a Secretary to the Govt of India. Not very long ago, there were about ten SC&ST Secretaries to the Govt of India-about six or seven SCs and two or three STs, and nearly half a dozen Additional Secretaries as well as more than a dozen Joint Secretaries in the Central Secretariat. This situation instead of showing an improvement to reflect the actual presence of the SCs&STs in Public Services all over the Country, and development of an unbiased tolerant Civil Society without any prejudices and biases or contempt against the poor and the weak, had rapidly detoriated to the present sad situation of hardly two Secretaries at the Center. And what is worse, there is no worthwhile effort to improve the situation. On the other hand, there is a strong animosity against SC&ST Officials, particularly against the intelligent hardworking honest capable and result oriented ones. Practically every one of them are suffering, have suffered and will suffer more and more problems in the days to come.

Why is this so?

The answers are not far difficult to find. One need not even search for them. They are readily available before us, and are clearly visible. They are obvious to everyone. Both the Bureaucracy and the Judiciary have been gunning for the SCs & STs, and the Reservations for them. They are aggressively intolerant, jealous and have been openly working against the Development Growth and Welfare of the SCs & STs. For reasons they can not clearly explain to themselves, or honestly speak out, or perhaps out of total ignorance, or shear stupidity and bull headedness, they are still opposing the Reservations for the SCs & STs and OBCs. And what is worse, there is no more empathy towards the SCs & STs.

Today's Political Party Leaders don't have any concern, or even show any lip sympathy towards the SCs & STs, even for public and political reasons. They feel that they need not bother at all, or show any concern for the weak and the helpless, like the SCs & STs, Backwards and Minorities. Hence they just don't care now for anyone. They are very sure that they can manage all of them with out really doing anything good or positive for them. They think that, with the help of a few captive leaders in their parties from these marginalized groups, or by some clever manipulations of the different leaders, weaker sections and their votes, and also by other devious methods and dubious means of managing the elections, they can win and capture power. Under these circumstances what else or what more can then we find?

(I) Representations of SC's & ST's in Public Services

SCs & STs taken together form nearly 26% of the Indian Population. In absolute numbers they are more than 260 million today. It is not only significant, but is a very large Population. Most of the Nations, barring China and India are not that big. But such a large People have no place or Representation in the Country even today. In fifty years of the Indian Republic, there was only one Vice President, and only just now we have a President from the SCs. There has never been anyone in these Offices from the STs. During the same period, there were hardly two or three Tribal Cabinet Ministers at the Center. There has never been a SC or ST Prime Minister. Able, capable, efficient, intelligent, honest, hardworking, sincere, very senior and prospective Ministers, and probable or sure SC/ST Candidates, who would have perhaps proved to be the best/most successful and deserving Prime Ministers the Country could have ever produced, have been pipped or pulled down and sabotaged at the final moments of reckoning many a times. Hardly ever been there any SC/ST Chief Minister in the States and UTs, and the rare ones also were not allowed to stay in office evén for one or two years. The only exceptions have been in the inevitable North Eastern States. There too, the SCs&STs of Manipur and Tripura have a very bad experience to narrate.

In thirteen Planning Commissions that we have seen so far, there never was a regular SC Member, and only one ST was a Member, twice with tenures of less than one year and five years, from 1990 to 1991, and again from 1991 to 1996. The Planning Commission of India at the Center, surprisingly does not yet have a Separate Department or even a small Cell for either the SCs & STs taken together, or for the larger group of the SCs, or for the special groups of STs, even though the conditions of the SCs & STs are pitiable all over the Country, and is going from bad to worse with each passing day,-as the overall Planning and Development of the Country, Market Forces, as well as the growing numbers of greedy social elements are squeezing and forcing the SCs & STs out, even from their own traditional lands and homes. This may be surprising and strange, given their population of more than 26.0 million now, almost evenly spread all over the Country, save for the North Eastern States and the Tribal Concentrated Belts and Pockets here and there on the sub-continent, and their abject poverty of homelessness, landlessness, assetlessness, powerlessness, massive illiteracy, extensive superstition, systematic suppression and planned oppression. But this is not at all shocking, given the still prevailing prejudices and biases in the Indian Society, particularly in the Hindu mind against the SCs&STs.

The Representations of the SCs&STs in the Judiciary are woefully poor, and that again shows the prevailing awful animosity against the SCs&STs in the minds of the so called learned Judges, and other highly placed Jurists Authorities and the Govt, who choose consider select recommend and make appointments of the Judges, especially to the High Courts in the States and also to the Supreme Court of India. Some of them are not only against the SCs&STs as Judges, but are openly and blatantly against the SC&ST Communities as a whole. With such animosities biases and prejudices, what type of Justice can they do or what sort of Judgments will they deliver? No one has yet made any study of the damages they have done to the creative hardworking SCs&STs, and thus to the Country. In fifty years, there were only three SC Judges in the Supreme Court at different points of time, and not even one ST. Now no one is there, and hardly anyone is likely to be allowed to come in there in the near future. Such is the opposition against them. Hence, it is no wonder that the Courts these days are openly intolerant towards SCs&STs, or to hear their pleas. They throw out their Cases, don't have patience or want to listen anything from the SC&ST Lawyers, even for the sake of appearing to be just and show off that they have heard the Case, and are doing and would do Justice, both to the Lawyers and the Parties they represent in the Case before the Court.

(J) SC's&ST's in Academics and Education

The Representations of the SCs&STs in Academics, either as Students or Employees in Schools, Colleges, Universities, other Autonomous Institutions or Centers of Higher Learning are still very poor. Thousands of qualified Job-Seekers are deliberately refused employment in the Schools Colleges Universities etc. Hundreds and hundreds of SC&ST Students aspiring for higher studies are turned out every year denied admissions, or even after admissions are thrown out or forced to get out under some pretext or the other from the Colleges, Universities, Autonomous Institutions and other Centers of Higher Education. The caste Hindu Lecturers and Professors are both unwilling and are actually incapable of teaching the SC&ST Students, unlike the British who produced the likes of Dr Ambedkar during those days itself.

The Opportunities for Studies Abroad available to Indian Students are by and large still kept as a secret from the SCs&STs, even though hundreds of Indian Students are to be found in many Foreign Countries with various Scholarships and other Schemes that help them to pursue their studies abroad, without taxing their families. Even Dr Ambedkar's Dream of educating select SC&ST Students Abroad, accepted by the then British Indian Govt, has been badly twisted beyond recognition by the Welfare Ministry over the years. A similar Scheme of Dr Ambedkar Overseas Fellowships for Students to study abroad, through Dr Ambedkar Foundation has been in the cold storage for quite sometime, and many students already selected for the Award of the Fellowships have not been permitted to avail of the Fellowships. A silent effort is said to be in the offing, to turn it as a facility only for SC&ST University and College Teachers already in job. Thus, the Scheme meant for the Students is being distorted, and at the same time, the UGC and other authorities would be washing off their responsibilities in providing opportunities to Train Abroad, the SC&ST Lecturers and Professors working in the Colleges and Universities. Thus by one change, two opportunities available to SC&ST Students and the SC&ST Teachers are now being cleverly and silently closed.

The numbers of SC&ST Lecturers, Senior Lecturers, Readers, Assistant Professors, Associate Professors, Professors etc in the Colleges, Autonomous Colleges, Universities, Deemed Universities, Research Centers and other Institutions of Higher Learning in the Country are extremely poor. One can have a taste of this, when we find that in the whole of Delhi, the Nation's Capital, barring the Govt Engineering and Medical Colleges to which Recruitments are made by the Union Public Service Commission and the

Appointments by the Govt. today there are only five Professors-One SC and One ST, a respectable total of Two SC&ST Professors in Delhi University, Two SC Professors in JNU, and one SC Professor in the Indian Institute of Technology Delhi. This in spite of the fact that, Delhi attracts professionals scholars and teachers from allover the Country. Yet, the authorities have managed successfully so far to keep the SCs&STs at a very far distance away from Delhi. In this, the negative role being played by the University Grants Commission etc. cannot ever be discounted or forgotten.

The UGC is not even allowing or facilitating the SC&ST Students to acquire the requisite Higher Qualifications of M Phil and Ph D essential for Teaching in the Universities and Colleges. They do not provide them any Scholarships and Fellowships to pursue these long and costly studies. The Govt. and the Ministry of Social Justice and Empowerment is not helping the poor SC&ST Students wanting to go for such essential higher studies. The caste Hindu Professors and Universities are also doing their best and contributing their shares in denying the SCs&STs admissions to these courses, and also in rating them deliberately lower so that they do not become eligible for teaching, even if the SC&ST Students manage to do these essential higher Courses. Such is the situation in the Country today.

Perhaps India is the only Nation in the World where the Teachers instead of teaching the poor are denying them education, instead of equipping them with knowledge are condemning them, turning them as unfits and deliberately rating them low. In fact this has been the history of India. One could not ever afford to forget Egalivya.

(K) SC's & ST's in Government Services

The Representations of the SCs&STs in Govt Services, even on the overall reckoning is extremely poor, in spite of operating the Reservation Systems for the last fifty years. And this, with so many brilliant and highly educated and qualified SCs&STs, duly examined and certified so, by all those caste Hindu controlled Universities and Educational Institutions, always knocking at the doors of the Govt Offices and various Recruiting and Appointing Authorities for Jobs and Employment. The overall Representations of the SCs&STs in the Central Govt Services allover the Country, as on 1st January 1995 are-

10. 15% SCs and 2.89% STs in Group A (Class I) Services and Posts

12.67% SCs and 2.68% STs in Group B (Class II) Services and Posts

16.15% SCs and 5.69% STs in Group C (Class III) Services and Posts

21.26% SCs and 6.48% STs in Group D (Class IV) Posts

Even in the Group C (Class III) Services and Posts, the Representations of the SCs and STs in the higher grades are very very poor. Even these small Representations of the SCs&STs in Services, most of the caste Hindu authorities are unable to tolerate and digest. They therefore, go after the blood of even these small numbers of SCs&STs in Service.

All the observations and empirical data available today indicate that, on an average more than 90% of Vigilance Cases are against the Employees and Officers who are weak, susceptible and are vulnerable, such as those about to retire, due for promotions, and are SCs&STs. And what is more surprising is that, more than 60% of the Employees and Officers facing Vigilance Cases, or are under Suspension, caught up in Inquiries, suffering Punishments of loss of increments, reduction in pay or pay scales, withheld increments, withheld promotions, denial of promotions, downgrading in rank or termination, are the helpless and godfather less SCs&STs. Since these are Vigilance Cases, none is generally forthcoming or are in a position to extend any helping hand to them. The Departments and senior officials are also in a position to casually and carelessly brush aside their pleas and representations, without even taking a cursory look at them and their cases. But, the losses, being suffered by so many SC&ST Employees and Officers all around, and their Families in Physical, Psychological, Mental, Social and Financial Terms are immense and colossal: In fact it is a serious and major economic loss to the Country and a criminal wastage of well qualified highly trained productive responsible and useful manpower. And only this caste ridden Country can afford the luxury of wasting so much of scarce valuable assets and resources, that too deliberately.

Those who get poor Assessments, Reports, Gradings, and hence as a result miss their Promotions often times and repeatedly, are almost exclusively the SCs&STs. This, in spite of the fact that, many of them have been recruited through All India Competitive Examinations by the UPSC or other Commissions/Agencies. It is often an humiliating experience for them, which get further compounded, when they find that they have lost the race for promotions and seniority, to those who are far far juniors to them in service, and many times to those who are not even qualified and are from the ranks, but have managed the promotions only because they are caste Hindus and hence are well connected having direct access to their seniors who matter, either directly by themselves or through their families or with the help of other relatives, friends, or the ever important caste circles.

In the sphere of Sweeping, a category of cleaning jobs as Sweepers, an area and occupation exclusively Reserved by the Hindu society for the SCs, others are today making inroads edging out the poor SC Sweepers, even when they are unwilling to work as Sweepers. They are coming in as Sweepers, not to Sweep and work as Sweepers, but to take by hook or crook a well paid Govt Job in Govt Offices, where they can easily and safely avoid work, if they even otherwise choose not to work or don't want to work. These others, are coming in dubiously as Sweepers, to get into Govt Service with a clear intention and motive of quickly migrating into other areas or cadres of Service within the Office. For them, the job of a poor Sweeper is a convenient backdoor entry into Govt Offices, which they are otherwise, unable to enter for want of requisite education, training, experience, intelligence, capabilities and such other qualifications required for direct recruitment to the jobs they desire to take. Hence their attempts to take jobs of Sweepers is farce, and is a fraud on the Sweepers and Govt. They therefore, always refuse to work as Sweepers even for a second, and avoid touching the broom ever, even though they had applied for and joined service as Sweepers, hold the job of Sweepers, mark attendance as Sweepers, take salaries as Sweepers, ask for special facilities as Sweepers and promotions as Sweepers. Once in the Govt Offices as Sweepers, these others with the open support help and connivance of their caste Hindu superiors hold for namesake the job of Sweepers. They are never asked to do any work as Sweepers. Even when they are allotted or have to do the work of Sweepers, they become benami Sweepers. They get their work done through other Sweepers in the office, or act informally as Sweeping Contractors or Suppliers of Casual Manpower for Sweeping on their behalf the offices as also for keeping clean the premises and the areas allotted to them for cleaning, for a paltry token payment which they pay from out the full Govt Salaries they take as Sweepers.

In many offices, the system of exploiting and cheating both the Govt and the poor lowly paid Sweepers has been formalized, and the caste Hindu Contractors are given regular Contracts to Supply Casual Sweepers regularly to the office, or get the sweeping done on a regular basis on Contract. These Contractors, employ a very small number of Sweepers, fully exploit and force the Sweepers to do the work of many, and pay them far less wages for carrying out the day to day job of sweeping and keeping the premises clean.

It is because of the ingenious dubious practices, cheating and exploitation of the helpless Sweepers, by the educated and well employed superior officials, and the realization of the same by the regular Sweepers, the regular Sweepers are on an unnoticed continuous strike, and they are now adopting a non-cooperative go slow tactics, that they don't take their work anymore seriously. Thus, the quality of their work is poor. Hence the sweeping work suffers. It is because of these that, the maintenance of Cleanliness and Hygiene in Govt Offices and their surroundings are very poor, and the Corridors awfully stink even many paces away from the toilets and waste bins anywhere, that sensitive and conscious individuals cannot pass by them easily.

Unless the Govt makes peace with the Sweepers, genuinely and sincerely look into their grievances, end all forms of cheating and exploitations, and put a complete stop to the present dubious methods of employing others, the overall cleanliness and hygiene not only in the Govt Offices but in the Country will suffer very very seriously, particularly when we take into consideration the peoples lack of consciousness and attitudes of not maintaining general cleanliness in their places of work/living and surroundings. They require a separate class of people to work as Sweepers, and maintain their homes, work places and surroundings clean, on behalf of themselves and the whole society.

With acceptance of some Reservations for the OBCs, consolidation of the OBCs which was inevitable and taking place even before the Reservations for them was accepted, and the growing consciousness of the SCs&STs, the caste Hindus are today a worried lot. Even then, they don't want to rest, or change and mend their ways. They don't want to adopt reasonable just and fair Civilized Methods of working, and managing the affairs of the society. Since the caste Hindus are still in positions of power, and always speak for the Nation, on behalf of the Nation, as if they are the Nation, they adopt such policies and practices that it appears the Nation is hitting back at the SCs&STs, the OBCs and the Reservations. Yes, they are under attack, and the attacks though systematic severe and total, are meted out silently. They are being hit below the belt and in the back at unexpected times.

It is the considered opinion of the SCs&STs and the OBCs that, the Country had adopted the path of Liberalization, Globalization, opted for opening up the Economy, and had slowly begun the privatization and selling of the Public Sector Govt Enterprises built up so laboriously over a long period, with the hard earned money and great savings of the people, only because they want to avoid Reservations at any cost, and are unwilling to part with the Jobs and Employment there, rightly due to the SCs&STs and OBCs. The caste Hindus are palming off, as if on silver platter even the profit making PSUs. Thus the PSUs which have formed the core of the Nation's Economy, the base of the Country's Self Reliance, the Pride of the People and the Foundations of National Development, are either being dismantled or passed off into private hands and to the Indian or Foreign Multi-National Corporations, only to reduce the Govt's Role and eliminate the PSUs, and hence the availability of the Jobs therein, which were till now available to the Public, and would therefore now be subjected to Reservations to the SCs&STs and OBCs. It is to avoid this, and still deny jobs with a decent salary and livelihood to the OBCs and the SCs&STs, that caste Hindus are wanting to close, sell off, hand over the PSUs to the private sector, including foreign Multi-National Companies.

As a result of the above, the SCs&STs and OBCs today are foxed. There are in principle, on paper, Reservations for them in Employment and Jobs, but in practice there is no Employment Opportunities and no Jobs! The Govt. Offices and PSUs themselves are vanishing! Employment and Job Opportunities are shrinking sharply and abruptly for the Public. Private Sector Companies do not believe in Public Employment. They make recruitments silently and privately, with out any knowledge or information to the public. Even if there is any information, the claims of the public are crudely brushed off and set aside. For, they make appointments based on personal contacts and through their own private and secret arrangements.

(L) Steps to Integrate SC's & ST's into the main Stream

The SCs&STs are now at the Cross Roads. Their hopes and aspirations are getting frustrated. Their sufferings and miseries are on the increase. They don't see any signs of change. And there is no such possibility in the near future. The atrocities against them, the crude criminal premeditated oppressions and offences in the Rural Areas and Urban Slums, the sophisticated silent planned white collar suppressions by the educated superiors in Educational Institutions, Govt. Offices etc. are rapidly on the increase. Their patience is already running out. They may now go in any direction, and take any path. One side, they want to stick to the Path of Peace and Constitutional Methods, shown to them by Baba Saheb Dr BR Ambedkar, and follow his ways. They clearly remember his exhortions-

> If we wish to maintain Democracy, not merely inform but also in fact, what must we do? The first thing in my judgement we must do, is to hold fast to Constitutional Methods of achieving our Social and Economic Objectives. It means, we must abandon the bloody methods of Revolution. It means that, we must abandon the method of Civil Disobedience, non-Cooperation and Satyagraha. When there was no way left for Constitutional Methods for achieving Economic and Social Objectives, there was a great deal of justification for Unconstitutional Methods. But, when Constitutional Methods are open, there can be no justification for these unconstitutional methods. These methods are nothing but the Grammar of Anarchy, and the sooner they are abandoned the better for us.

On the other hand, will the SCs&STs stray away in future from the Constitutional Methods of achieving the Economic and Social Objectives of the People, the Aspirations of the Society, the Goals of the Nation and the Dreams of the Founding Fathers of the Constitution pointed out by their Messiah Dr Ambedkar, and opt out in frustration to Unconstitutional Methods of Change and bloody Revolutions warned by Dr Ambedkar himself many a times? The signs of these are already in air, in various pockets in almost different parts of the Country. Will SCs&STs radically choose to alter the Economic, Social and Cultural Orders of People in the Society, and the Political Structure of the Country, or go for balkanizing and break away from the Nation, as we see many frustrated impatient Sections of various societies are already doing in different parts of World? Will there be Social Unrest endless Law and Order Problems, as we already experience, in our Cities and Metropolises? Will there be an avoidable Civil War? We don't know! The real answers to these unanswered potentially dangerous and virtually explosive questions, ultimately depend upon the choices the Society makes and the Govt. Leaders now take, to establish a just fair and equitable Economic Order and build an Egalitarian Social Structure. And it needs to be thought as to what can We the People or the Govt, the Country, the Society and the SC&ST themselves do? We have to find an answer, and find it quickly. For, the time is really running out for all of us and the Country as a whole.

What we need more urgently now, is not Liberalization of the Economy but Liberation of the People, the downtrodden the weak and the marginalized; not Globalization of our Economy but Universalisation of Human Rights in favour of the poor and the helpless like the SCs&STs.

The SCs&STs are poor weak marginalized and powerless. They need Education and Employment. They want Development and Growth. They are still to get their Independence and Freedom. They are eagerly looking forward to the Day of their Deliverance. They are seeking Liberty and Equality. They have waited all these days with great hopes and patience. They are now demanding Justice and Human Rights. They want Human Rights and Life with Dignity. They are thirsting for Individual Recognitions and Equal Opportunities. They are asking for Self Respect and Fairness in Social Lifc. They need Good Jobs and Decent Salaries. They look for Helping Hands and Respectful Wages alright. But they may not wait for long. They cannot afford to pay bribes or bring in influences and recommendations in their favor. Hence, there is a need to implement the Reservations honestly fairly and in full. There is also a need to force the private sector companies and the Indian and Foreign Multi-National Companies, to make their Recruitments and Appointments public and fair, through open advertisements and without any secrecy. They should be asked to give Representations to different Sections of the Society. After all, these are the ways of any Civilised Nation and all Civil Societies of the World. Secret Selections and Private Appointments based on personal contacts and private considerations are not the ways of a decent World.

If Reservations here in the Country are the due Rights and Shares of the SCs&STs and the OBCs in the Nation

Building, Administration and Governance of the Country, even in the Mecca of the Free World and the fountainhead of all the new waves of Liberalization and Globalization sweeping the World now, there is Affirmative Action for the Blacks enforced by the Govt. This Affirmative Action has now been proudly accepted by the Private Sector there. The American Educational Institutions, Universities, Seats of Higher Learning and Centers of Research, and also the big powerful and rich MNCs there, are vying with each other to show to their Society and the World their achievements in this respect. Why should the caste Hindus here then not honourably accept their own educated sisters and brothers from the SC&ST and OBC Communities? Why should they resent the SCs&STs and the OBCs even today, or feel jealous of the alters' progress or become envious of their development? And why should there be oppositions to the Reservations that only seek to provide the SCs&STs and the OBCs their proportionate share of Education, Jobs and other Opportunities in Life in the Country? Why should anyone, any reasonable or rational individual crib? One really does not know.

The caste Hindus are now forcibly taking away, what they used to silently steal all these days. Now they are openly grabbing the shares and dues of the SCs&STs and also the OBCs, in the name of Excellence, National Interest, National Security, Defence, Science, Technology, Research, Higher Studies, Super Specialties, Development of Excellence to International Standards, rapid or accelerated Economic Development, Opening up the Economy, Privatization, Liberalization, Globalization, Structural Adjustments, Financial Discipline, and the frauds of their Special Merits and Efficiencies. These are nothing but an open fraud to cheat the people, shield and cover up all their inefficiency, blatant nepotism, shameless favoritism, violation of rules and regulations as well as the norms and procedures/ precedence's, open corruption, lack of respect for fair open honest selections/recruitments/promotions and appointments. The repeated jokes they are trying to play on the Country is the Superiority and Respect to, as well as the need and compulsions of having to abide by the decisions of a pack of caste Hindu individuals, who have reached their positions due to their closeness proximity and compromises with those they were and are in positions of power, with the right political authority to select appoint patronize backup and promote them all along the line.

The latest cruel joke of caste Hindus is that, they are all now waking up after fifty long years, to talk about the need to produce and support the specialists in the making, comparable to International Standards, but only from the dominant castes. What were they doing all these five decades? What happened to all those meritorious sons and daughters of theirs, whom they freely selected all these years, saying that no suitable SC/ST was available, and without giving any Reservations to the OBCs? Why should they get this urge now, when the SCs&STs have already grown up to become Specialists, and are doing extremely well in Serving the Country with out fleeing to foreign shores, and as the OBCs are getting their Opportunities? Even now, why don't they produce such International Class Specialists from their top most meritorious scholars? Why do they need to grab or take so blatantly the Opportunities of the SCs&STs and OBCs? Why do they want to deny the poor SCs&STs and OBCs admissions to higher studies, professional courses and super specialities, and give these admissions to their third rate scholars who could not make their grade by themselves, competing with their own fellow colleagues freely and fairly, but come at the last, much behind their own caste individuals? Do they have no faith in their most meritorious fellows, who come at the top in the assessment of merits as per their own methods, standards of evaluations and the scheme of norms and scales? Do they want to play a game of choices, and gamble on those who miss out in the race, that they want to bring them in the places of the SCs&STs and OBCs? Would they then wait, hope, pray, or dream that at least one of their third-rate scholars, who had come in through the back doors, to the professional and super-speciality courses, in place of the poor SCs&STs and OBCs, to become an International Expert par-Excellence? Should we or can anyone believe them? Still, they try to fool the Country the SCs&STs and the OBCs? Have they gone crazy, or are they such big fools or so stupid to think that the SCs&STs and OBCs are such fools that they can buy their arguments and keep quiet?

Govt. should now come out with a Comprehensive Reservation Policy for the whole Country covering Govt., Public Sector Enterprises, Banks, Financial Institutions, Colleges, Universities, Centers of Higher Learning and Research, other Educational Institutions, Autonomous Bodies, Non-Governmental Organisations, Voluntary Organisations, and Private Enterprises including Indian and Foreign Multi-National Companies in the Country.

(M) Efforts of Central and State Governments in bringing the Social Change of SC/ST

It is high time that the Govts. take some specific steps and positive action beyond Reservations. Fifty-three years of Independence had already passed. Fifty years after the establishment of the Republic, had also rolled by. We have wasted precious long time. We can not afford to sleep any further. Otherwise, the poor people would soon lynch us all alive. It is necessary to think what we need to do, and at the sometime act fast. Honestly speaking, we have not yet really started thinking of Development of the Weaker Sections. We have only been playing soft balls with them all these days. Let us get serious now, at least a bit. The Govt. of India therefore, should bring in the learned SCs&STs and thinkers amongst them, to chalk out real Plans and Action Programmes for their Social, Economic and Cultural Development. It is only they, who can understand the needs and aspirations of the SCs&STs. As Baba Saheb Dr Ambedkar had long ago rightly said, it is only the servile class who can lead them. Definitely not their antagonists, nor the class room city products of just the Universities, or those with foreign education, or WB and IMF trainings and mandates. The Govts. at the Center and the State/UTs should at least now establish-

National and State Level Administrative and Professional Training Establishments for the SCs&STs, to develop and improve their Administrative and Professional Competence and Capabilities

National SC&ST Housing Finance and Development Corporations

National and State/UT Level Centers for SC&ST Development

National Level Centers for Planning for, SC&ST Education and Employment

National and State/UT Level Task Forces, for Entrepreneurship Development amongst the SCs&STs

Separate Tribunals to look into and expeditiously dispose off the Cases of SC&ST Employees.

Separate District Level Courts to expeditiously hear and decide the Cases of SC&ST Lands taken away by others.

A Special Judicial Commission to exclusively look into the Judgments of the various Judges, who have a tendency to decide cases against SCs&STs, and make specific recommendations to the Govt. to protect the interests and Welfare of the SCs&STs

A Special Committee to visit and look into the working of SC&ST Student Hostels and make appropriate Recommendations to the Govt. to improve the Conditions and Working of these Hostels

1. The Govt. at the Center should also Institute

Awards for Selection, Recruitment and Promotion of SCs&STs, similar to those for the physically handicapped.

Recognition of Individuals and Institutions, working for the Development and Integration of the SCs&STs

Special Insurance Schemes, to protect and also provide succor and help to the SCs&STs, from suspensions terminations and non-payment of salaries and wages

A Cadre of Rural Welfare and Labour Officers, to look into and expeditiously solve the Grievances of the Workers in the Rural Areas and in the Unorganized Sectors

Special Social Security Schemes, for the SCs&STs, especially the educated and unemployed

Special Tax Concessions, to SCs&STs to educate their Children, and for sending them for Higher Studies or Studies Abroad, and or for Specialist and Advanced Courses and Trainings

Special Concessions, to SCs&STs for building their own homes, to eliminate the slums and the growing problems associated with them that dehumanizes the people

Special Schemes and Concessions to SC&ST Entrepreneurs taking up self-employment, starting their own business, and setting up their own industries

Special Programmes, to harness and utilise the talents, knowledge and experiences of retired SC&ST Professionals, for the Development and improving the Standards of Life of the SC&ST Communities

2. The Govt. should also regularly Constitute an High Power Committee, at least every two years, to review the Allocation, Utilisation, Appropriation and Diversion of the Funds meant and Budgeted for the Education Welfare and Development of the SCs&STs both in the States/UTs and at the Center.
3. Similarly, in the STATES and UTs also, appropriate Committees should be constituted, to look into the Funds earmarked, actually made available, utilised, surrendered and or diverted by the STA TEXT Govts. Zila Parishads and down at the Village Panchayats.
4. GOVT. SHOULD REGULARLY REVIEW, ASSESS and CHANGE from time to time, both the LONG TERM and SHORT TERM SC&ST Schemes and Programmes to EVOLVE better Schemes and Programmes. There should also be Schemes and Programmes, evolved and structured to suit Specific Communities/Castes/Tribes, and also sub-Castes, sub-Tribes and Part of the Castes and Tribes living/settled in different areas. This is absolutely necessary, in view of Large Scale Migrations due to Education, Employment, Search of Livelihood and for Survival; and also the Uprooting/Shifting/Relocation of whole Villages,

Communities and the people of different Regions, particularly the STs and also the SCs of many small pockets, as a result of Development Programmes and Mega-Projects.

Here are some ideas and facts about reservations in India from Sowell's book that I found interesting. The information I'm passing on isn't slanted either proreservations or against them. I do provide my own interpretations in parentheses, but other interpretations of the facts might be possible:

(1) **Caste violence still occurs.** Sowell cites a 1991 *India Today* article on the public lynching of cross-caste lovers in a village 100 miles from Delhi. But more importantly, Sowell cites government statistics: "Government statistics on atrocities against untouchables never fell below 13,000 per year during the decade of the 1980s and reached well over 16,000 in 1984. Far from abating with time, these officially recorded atrocities escalated to more than 20,000 a year in the 1990s. "That's 20,000 a year. Most atrocities occur in a small number of states (Sowell cites Bihar and Uttar Pradesh especially). They are primarily rural occurrences; Sowell acknowledges that strong caste feeling the kind that can lead to violence is rare in India's big cities.

(2) **Unfilled seats.** Reservations for Scheduled Castes (SC) in schools and government posts remain largely unfilled, whereas reservations for Other Backward Classes (OBCs) are generally filled to capacity. Sowell cites a 1997 study that indicates that nationally preferential policies only benefit 6 per cent of Dalit families. Moreover, the same study reported that "none of India's elite universities and engineering institutes had filled its quota for members of scheduled castes."

(3) **Continued under representation.** People from the scheduled castes and scheduled tribes continue

to be absent from white collar positions. "For the country as a whole, members of the scheduled castes and scheduled tribes—combined—did not receive as much as 3 per cent of the degrees in engineering or medicine, though together they add up to nearly one-fourth of the population of India."

(4) **Other economic and practical factors.** The government provides scholarship to SC students to attend school, but sometimes that is not enough: "Even when the government provides primary schooling free of charge, the costes of books and supplies may not be affordable by very poor people. For secondary education, rural students especially may not always find a school nearby, so that those whose parents cannot afford the costs of commuting or relocating and paying for housing and boarding have little realistic prospect of attending, regardless of preferential admissions policies."

References

1. https://www.ambedkar.org/NHRC Report/prelim.pdf
2. https://www.censusindia.net/scst.html-6k-2 Apr 2005-
3. https://www.vedamsbooks.com/no11739.htm
4. https://www.hrw.org/reports/1999/india/India994-16.htm-
5. https://www.indianchild.com/caste_system-india.htm-
6. https://www.countrystudies.us/india/116.htm
7. https: www.karnat.com/indica/caste/
8. https:/www.indianngos.com/issue/other/caste/govtschemel.htm
9. https://www.dalitchristians.com
10. https://www.supremecourtonline.com/
11. https://wwwl.umn.edu/humanrts
12. https://www.friesian.com/caste.htm
13. https://www.countercurrents.org/dalit-sikander200903.htm

14. https://www.freerepublic.com/focus/f-news/1367740/posts
15. https://www.pucl.org/Topics/Dalit-tribal/2002/harisingh.htm-14k
16. https://www.dalitawaz.com
17. https: www.answers.com/topic/scheduled-caste-18k
18. https://www.hrw.org/reports/1999/india/-5k
19. https://www.yourrights.org.uk/cgi-bin/
20. https://www.lehigh.edu/-amsp/2004/05/thomas
21. http://www.columbia.edu/itc/m-ealac/pritchett
22. https://www.amrc.org.hk/5304.htm-46k.

3

Universe of the Study

Historical Background

In order to provide a holistic understanding of the research problem or issue, it is necessary to know in detail the background of the study area. In this chapter the author has made an attempt is made to provide a brief account of the physical, historical, social and demographic background of the State and the district. In addition an overview of the historical background of the Macro and micro level organisations of the Scheduled Castes is also provided. The area of the present study constitute the Gulbarga district. Gulbarga district forms a part of the Karnataka State in India.

Karnataka State

Karnataka State has a geographical area of 191,791 square kilometers and constitutes 5.83 per cent of the total area of the country. It is situated in the southern part of Indian peninsula stretching from 11° 19° North latitude and 74° to 78° East longitude. It is one of the 28 States and 4 Union Territories of India. Karnataka is bounded by Maharashtra in the North and north-west, Andhra Pradesh in the east, Tamil Nadu in the south-east and Kerala in the South-West.

As per the 1991 census, Karnataka State has a population of 44,817,398 persons constituting 5.31 per cent of the total population of the country. It ranks 8th among the

22 states and 9 union territories in the Indian Union in respect of both the total area and the total population.

The decadal growth rate of Karnataka was 26.75 per cent in 1981, which was above the national average growth rate of 24.66 per cent. In 1991, the growth rate fell down to 20.69 per cent, which is contrastingly below the national average of 23.50 per cent. During the last 90 years period from 1901 to 1991, the population of Karnataka has increased by 24.3 per cent (1991 census).

In 1991 the density of population was 23.4 as against 194 persons per square kilometer in 1981. on both the counts the density of state's population is less than the national average of 26.7 and 21.6 respectively. Of the total population, 55.98 per cent are literates in Karnataka in 1991, as against 46.20 per cent in 1981. Both the figures are higher than the national averages of 52.11 per cent and 43.56 in 1991 and 1981 respectively. The male literacy rate in the state has increased from 58.72 per cent in 1981 to 67.25 per cent in 1991. Among females, the literacy rate is 33.16 per cent and 44.34 per cent in 1981 and 1991 respectively. All these figures are above the levels of literacy in the country as a whole.

In 1991, the sex ratio in Karnataka is 960 females pcr 1000 males, which is also higher than the national average of 929. The rural and urban differentials of sex ratio show that rural areas have a higher sex ratio (975) than the urban counterparts (930).

Karnataka has 27 districts spread over three agro-climatic regions namely Malnad or Coastal region, Southern Maidan or Plateau region and Northern Maidan or Plateau. The Malnad and Coastal region consists of six districts, namely, Chickmagalore, Dakshina Kannada, Udupi, Kodagu (Coorg), Shimoga and Uttar Kannada. The Southern Plateau comprises of ten districts, namely, Bangalore, Bangalore Rural, Chitradurga, Davanagere, Hassan, Kolar, Mandya, Chamarajanagara, Mysore and Tumkur. The Northern Plateau has eleven districts, which includes Belgaum, Bellary, Bidar Bijapur, Bagalkot, Dharwad, Haveri, Gadag, Gulbarga, Koppal and Raichur.

For administrative convenience, these districts are grouped under four divisions. They are: (1) Banglaore Division comprising Bangalore Urban, Bangalore rural, Chitradurga, Davanagere, Kolar, Shimoga and Tumkur districts; (2) Mysore division comprising Mysore, Mandya, Chamarajanagar, Kodagu (Coorg), Hassan, Dakshina Kannada, Udupi, and Chickmagalur districts; (3) Belgaum division comprising Belgaum, Bijapur, Bagalkot, Dharwad, Haveri, Gadag and Uttar Kannada district; and (4) Gulbarga division comprising Gulbarga, Koppal, Raichur, Bidar and Bellary districts.

History of the Karnataka can be traced from 3rd century B.C. onwards. Several edicts in the northern plateau of Karnataka, particularly, in the Raichur, Bellary and Chitradurga districts date back of Emperor Ashoka. Chandragupta Maurya is said to have spent his last years of his life at Sravanabelagola in Hassan district. Later on, the Satavahana dynasty rose to power and ruled this area for four centuries. With the emergence of the Sakas, the Satavahana dynasty came to an end. With the rise of Gauṭamiputra Satakarni of Satavahana dynasty, again, the Sakas lost their prominence. Later on, the Satavahana dyanasty was split into several branches such as Kuntala Satakarni, belonging to one branch that ruled a major part of Karnataka.

The other prominent dynasties which ruled the State were Vakaṭakas (4th Century A.D.), Kadambas, Chalukyas, Pallavas, Rastrakutas, Hoysalas, Yadavas of Devagiri, Sangama, Saluva and Tuluva dynasties of Vijayanagar and others. Prior to and during the British rule in India, the State was under the rule of Wodeyar dynasty of Mysore. Hyder Ali and Tipu Sultan also ruled some parts of the state, before the British brought Mysore State under their domain.

Prior to Indian Independence, a large part of the present Karnataka State was under the British ruled provinces of Madras and Bombay, and Hyderabad State ruled by Nizam. Coorg was a separate state. The Karnataka State, as it is today, came into being on 1st November, 1956, with the merger of Kannada speaking areas from the neighbouring territories with the then Mysore State. Though there is a linguistic admixture in the state now, a majority of its people speak Kannada, which is also recognized as the official language of the State (along with English).

The civilization of a population depends on the nature of infrastructure facilities available to the people. The infrastructure of any state depends on the network of roads, railways, communication facilities like posts and telegraph, human resource aspects like medical, educational, health etc., and natural factors such as favourable monsoons and climatic conditions.

Karnataka is one of the premier states of India with regard to education. Apart from numerous primary and high schools, the State has 631 professional institutional including teacher's training institutions and nine Universities in addition to several research institutions. The State has more private educational institutional from pre-primary or Nursery to the professional level. Particularly, the private medical and engineering colleges attract a large proportion of students from other states.

Karnataka has good medical facilities provided by both government and private organisations. The State has fairly good source of drinking water facilities. Though Karnataka has good source of hydro-electricity, electricity in rural areas is still at a lower level. But, the urban areas and the industries have fairly good supply of electricity.

The State has 2,944 kilometers of railways lines. Most of the railways lines are in the meter gauge section. Efforts are on to convert the meter gauge into broad gauge in a big way. However, compared to railways the road network seems to be better connected between the towns, cities and villages.

Infrastructural facilities available in the State have facilitated the establishment of many gigantic industries like Hindustan Machine Tools, Hindustan Aeronautics Limited, Bharat Electronics, Bharat Heavy Electronics, Bharat Earth Movers, Sandal Soap Factory etc. besides, a number of major, medium and small industries (of government, co-operative and private sectors) have come up in and around Bangalore city (State capital) as well as in different districts.

In spite of many industrial establishments, the main source of livelihood for a majority of the people (64 per cent) continues to be agriculture. The main food crops grown in the state are paddy, ragi and jowar which are also the staple food of its people. Along with these crops minor millets like wheat, bajra, maize etc., and pulses like tur, green gram, red gram etc., are also grown. The main oilseeds grown in the state are groundnut, sunflower, Kusebe (rapeseed), Castor etc. Cash crops like sugarcane, mulberry and cotton, pepper, cardamom, coffee, cocoa, and tea are grown in the State. In addition to the above, coconut, arecenut, mango, banana, cashew, jackfruit and the like are important cash crops grown in the state. Karnataka is famous for its sandalwood. Forest resources like teak, cane, bamboo predominate its forest produce.

On the irrigation front, the state has achieved tremendous success by utilizing the available resources. Even in the pre-Independénce era, as for back as the first quarter of the century, the State had major irrigation projects like Vanivilas Sagar, Krishna Raja Sagar and medium projects such as Anjanapur, Marconahalli, Kanva, Byramangala reservoirs etc., which irrigated thousands of hectares of land. If we compare the progress made in other states in the Country now, Karantaka's share is low, despite its long history of irrigation.

Of the total geographical area in the State (in 1985-86), 3,057 thousand hectares were forests, another 1,961 thousand hectares were not available for cultivation, 1974 thousand hectares were uncultivated lands and 1,883.9 thousand hectares were fallow lands. About 11,146.4 thousand hectares and 10,172.2 thousand hectares were under gross cropped and net sown areas respectively. There were about 1,675 thousand hectares of land under irrigation accounting for 16.5 per cent of the sown area. Coming to the sources of irrigation, canals form the major source irrigating 734.7 thousand hectares, which is followed by wells (480.9 thousand hectares), tanks (242 thousand hectares) and others (217.4 thousand hectares).

According to the 1981 census, a majority of the population (85.77 per cent) were Hindus. Muslims constituted 11.21 per cent followed by Christians with 2.08 per cent, Jains (0.77 per cent), Buddhists (0.11 per cent), Sikhs (0.02 per cent) and others (0.04 per cent).

Among the Hindus, the Scheduled castes constituted 15.07 per cent, and the Scheduled tribes 4.91 per cent which is less compared to many states. Karnataka provides a great spectacle with its varied regions and salubrious climate. Karnataka has ancient and historical places like Udupi, Tala Cauvery, Sravanabelagola, Belur, Halebedu, Hampi, Mysore, Dharmasthala and so on. Apart from above, the Brindavan Gardens in Mysore, Vidhana Soudha in Banglaore, Golgumbaz in Bijapur etc., are some of the noteworthy visiting places in Karnataka[1].

GULBARGA DISTRICT

Physical Environment

In the present study an attempt is made to know in-depth characteristics of the physical, historical, demographic and social background of the Gulbarga district which constitutes the field of the study.

Gulbarga is both a district and a divisional headquarter comprising the five district viz., Bellary, Bidar, Gulbarga Raichur and Koppal. It is also a revenue headquarter. Geographically, Gulbarga division is in the south western corner of Hyderabad Karnataka and is known as southern division. It lies between 76° 04' and 77°42' longitude and 16°12 and 17°46' latitude. The district shares its boundaries with Sholapur and Osmanabad district of Maharashtra and on the east it is bounded by the district of Medak and Mahaboobnagar of Andhra Pradesh. On the other side of Gulbarga district is surrounded by territories belonging to Karnataka state itself. Bidar district is in the north, Raichur district in the south and Bijapur district on the west. The district is situated in the region which is generally known as the Deccan plateau. According to 1991 census the area of Gulbarga district is 1730 sq km.

There are two versions available regarding the origin of the name of the city as 'Kalburgah' and 'Gulbargah'. During the Chalukyan period the city is named as 'Kalumberge', which means in Kannada 'a stony land' or 'stone roofing' or heap of stones'. It was during the regime of Muslims the city was named as 'Gulbarga', in the Parsian language to connote a leaf with flower. It signifies a place of beauty like a flower with a leaf. It is certain that it was known as 'Kalburgi' in earlier days and later changed to 'Gulbarga' during the Muslim regime. But is not uncommon to hear that rural people still call Gulbarga city by its previous name 'Kalburgi'. It is also Muslim regime; the same has been retained by the Government of Karnataka soon after the reorganisation of Indian states[2].

Gulbarga district is situated in the dry climatic zone. The summer heat is some what excessive as compared to other several districts of the state. The temperature begins to rise steadily with commencement of summer season from about the middle of the February. Simultaneously humidity decreases day by day. This season lasts till about first week of June. Usually, May happens to be the hottest month of the year and maximum temperature would up to 45°C. The district lies in a region where the rainfall is moderate low besides being quite capricious. The average annual rainfall is 715 mm[3].

Gulbarga District is also known for its limestone at huge quantity. The varieties of limestone industries and cement factories attracted the attention of the people of the country. The city is also known for its location on south central broad gauge railway line running from Mumbai to Chennai. It is also known for its rivers flowing in the districts. The river Bheema and its tributaries flow in the district.

Historical Background

Chalukyas of Badami (515 A.D–785 A.D.)

With the fall of the Satavahana Empire, and the consequent disintegration, the Chalukyas of Badami undertook the superme political task of consolidation and unification. In this mighty endeavour, they did succeed to a remarkable degree and all the credit of consolidation goes to Pulikeshi-II who brought peace and order in the troubled land. The origin of the Chalukyas is obscure in detail ever since many myths and legends are associated with their emergence. There is reason to believe that the Chalukyas of Badami were indigenous and belonged to Karnataka. Among the prominent rulers of Chalukya dynasty were Pulakeshi-I, Kiritvarma and Pulalkeshi-II they ruled this area for about 250 years.

If one can glance on the rulers of this region or part, one may come to know that the Rastrakutas were the prominent rulers in this part of the state and they flourished during the sixth and the seventh centuries A.D. as feudatories of the Chalukyas of Badami.

Rashtrakutas (785 A.D. to 983 A.D.)

The dynastic rule of the Rastrakutas begins with their elevation of sovereignty under Dantigurga in 753 A.D. The Rastrakutas were of the Kannada origin, as has been proved by Dr. Altekar. They professed to be the descendants of the Rathikas, a clan which inhabited western Deccan, since the time of Ashoka. Dantidurga's family originally belonged to Lattulura or Latur in Osmanabad district of Maharashtra state. He ascended the throne in 753 A.D. This king was able, ambitious, and courageous and became thelord of the Deccan in less than fifteen years.

Among the predominant rulers of the Rashtrakuta Dynasty were Krishan-I, Govinda-II, Dhruva, Govinda-III, Amoghavarasha-I, (814-878), Krishna-II, Indra-III, Amoghavarahs-III, Amoghavarasha-III, Krishna-III, Khottiga and Karka-II. The region between the Cauvery and Godavari river is called the Kannada country, came under the control of the Rastrakutas. So, the period of Rashtrakuta in the Deccan from about 753 A.D. to 973 A.D. constitutes, perhaps the most brilliant chapter in its history.

No other ruling dynasty in the Deccan played such a dominant role in the history of India till the rise of the

Marathas as an important power in the 18th century. Some of the rulers of Rashtrakuta carried their victorious arms in to the heart of Northern India and by inflicting severe defeats upon its most powerful rulers, and changed the course of history. Their success in the south was equally remarkable and literally advanced as far as Rameshwaram in the course of their victorious carrier. All the great powers of India, the Prathiharas, the Pallas, of the north, the eastern Chalukyas and the Cholas of the south were subjected (defeated) by them at one time or the other. They, no doubt suffered reverse at times but on the whole their military campaigns against powerful adversaries were repeatedly crowned with brilliant success.

The Rastrakutas befriended the Muslims and gave them all facilities for setting in their territory. They allowed them to build mosques and to be ruled by their own governors. They manifested their spirit of religions tolerance which characterized India, but was rare in that age elsewhere in the world. It may be safely said the Rashtrakuta of Manyakheta were the heirs of the Chalukyas of Vatapi in the imperial sovereignty of the Deccan.

Chalukyas of Kalyana (973 A.D. to 1285 A.D.)

After the Rastrakutas era, the Deccan area was ruled by the Chalukyas of Kalyana during the period 973 A.D. to 1285 A.D. The Chalukyas of Kalyana are considered descendants of Badami Chalukyas. The Chalukyas (Taila-II. 973-1997 A.D.) first established their seat of Government at Manyakheta (Malkhed) which is 22 miles away from Gulbarga towards the east and then changed their seat of Government to Kalyana which is 1200 kms away from Gulbarga towards the north.

The most illustrious king among the later Chalukyas of the Kalyana was Vikramaditya-VI, the famous poet, Bilhana, who flourished in his court has given a glowing description of the life and achievements of this great monarch. The great Jurist Vijnaneshwar lived during the same period at Kalyana. Perhaps the greatest name in the sphere of legal literature

(Dharma-Shastra) is that of Vijnaneshwar, who adorned the court of Vikramaditya-VI. His Mitakshara, commentary on Yajnavalkya's Smriti is an important treatise on law accepted in south India.

Numerous inscriptions of that time found in Mysore, Andhra and Madras states testify to the accuracy of the statements made by Bilhanas about his patron. With the permission of his father Someshavara-I, Vikramaditya is said to have repeatedly attacked the cholas and plundered Kanchi, and to have lent his assistance to the king of Malwa who came to him for help to regain his kingdom. Inscription of his time claim that he conquered, Gujarat, Dahala, Konkana, Maru, Nepala Barbura, Kashmir, Sindh, Turushka, Abhira, Nallura, vidarbha and other places.

Vikramaditya, immediately after he had firmly established himself on the throne, began a new ear bearing with his own name as era of "Chalukya Vikramavarsha" in the year 1706 A.D. (The era was previously called as Saka Varsh in all records). Vikramaditya VI, had a long and brilliant reign of over 50 years. None of his successors was as powerful as he was. Consequently about 1155 A.D. one of the feudatories of the Chalukya's Kalachurya Bijjala usurped (conquer) the Chalukya throne and he and his descendants continued to hold it till about 1184 A.D. Subsequently, two subordinates of the Chalukyas, the Yadavas of Devagiri and the Hoysalas Dwarasamudra, gradually grew powerful and occupied the Chalukya territories. Art, architecture and sculpture, temples of Aihole, Pattadkal, Gadag, Haveri, Lakkundi and Kuruvatti and the Channakeshva Temple at Gulbarga and Mannur may be cited as the examples of the famous styles of the Chalukyan architecture. Some of the famous literary giants of Kannada, such as Pampa, Ponna, Ranna, Durgasimha and Nagachandra, were lived during this period.

Kalchuryas of Kalyana, who conquered the throne of Chalukyas, claimed their descent from the Kalachuris of Central India. The Bijjala the greatest of this line, usurped the throne of the Chalukyas is evident from two inscriptions found at Harsoor and kalgi of Gulbarga district. During this period inter caste marriages also appear to have been common between the Kalachuris and the Chalukyas, the Rastrakutas and the later Chalukyas. Bijjala seems to have ruled from about 115 to 1167 A.D. from Kalyana. The period though was short, is an event full of interest prominent throughout the Kannada speaking territories. The Veerashaiva renaissance under Basaveshwara ushered in a new era in the religious and philosophic literature of Karnataka.

After Vikramaditya-VI, the Chalukyas could not survive for a longer period. Two new dynasties came into power were Yadavas of Devagiri (also called Sevunas) in the north and Hoysalas in the south. There were severe struggles between the Hoysalas and the Yadavas for the possession of the Chalukya Kalachurya dominions. The Yadavas in course of time, became masters of all the western Deccan (Including the district of Gulbarga and its neighbourhood) having their capital at Devagiri of modern Daulatabad. The continuous struggle between the Hoyslas and Yadavas on the one hand and with the Kakatiyas of Warangal on the other hand weakened the Mohammedan invader to conquer the whole area of South India.

Bahamani Dynasty

Gulbarga was the capital city of Bahamani dynasty from 1347 to 1924 A.D. Alla-Ud-Din Bahaman Shaha was responsible for making Gulbarga as their capital city in 1347 and continued it as the capital city up to 1924 A.D. Later on Ahmad Shah wali (1422-1436) shifted the capital from Gulbarga to Bidar. Gulbarga continued its status as an important even during the Nizam and Mughals. Nizam Mulk Asif Jah made it districts headquarter in 1873. Gulbarga was ruled by Nizam dynasty. The district was an integral part of the Hyderabad Karnataka state known as Hyderabad Karnataka Area. It became apart of Karnataka state in the year 1956.

In the middle of the 14th century the revolt of the Muslim officer appointed by Delhi resulted in the establishment of the Bahamani kingdom in 1347 A.D. Hassan Gangu Bahamani, the founder of the Bahamani kingdom, selected Gulbarga as his capital and remained its ruler till his death in 1358 A.D. After Bahaman Shah, the area was ruled by Mohamed-I (1358 A.D.–1397 A.D.) and other rulers of the same dynasty.

It was during the rule Ahmad Shah, that the capital of the Bahamani kingdom was shifted from Gulbarga to Bidar, a neighbouring district Headquarters in 1429 A.D. with this Gulbarga lost its importance and remained only as a provincial center. When Yusuf Adil Shah became the ruler of Bijapur, Gulbarga came into his possession and remains with the Adi Shah Kings until the Mughal conquest of the Deccan in 1656 A.D. It would be of interest to know that the heroic exploits of Krishnadevaraya of Vijaynagar also included a campaign against Bijapur in 1523 A.D. and invaded Bijapur territory and captured Gulbarga and razed its fortress to the ground.

The storm of Mughal invasion having blown over termporarily, the Bijapur state next showed revival of power for some time under Ali Adil Shah-II. But with his death in 1672 A.D. and the consequent crowning of his son, Sikanda, a boy of four, the gory of Bijapur started declining. The incapacity of responsible persons to take action against the Nizam and measures to disband the Razakar organisation fell on deaf ears. The Razakas even committed aggression against the Indian Union. The Government of India could no longer sit silent. It tried negotiations, but this proved fruitless. By the beginning of the year 1948, it became clear that the Nizam was actually on the war path and hence in 1948 late Sardar Vallabhbhai Patel ordered police action and included the Nizam provinces to the Indian territory.

Social Background

Gulbarga is a center of religious place. Every year fair (Jatra) of Shri Sharanabasaveshwara is held in the month of March wherein devotees from the Gulbarga district and various parts of Karnataka attended with great devotion.

The Gulbarga is known for a Hindu temples and a Muslim Dargahs. The former is a Shrine of Shri Sharanabasavaeshwara saint of the 19th century which attracted the attention of the Sharanas, bhaktas and devotees residing in various parts of the Karnataka State. The latter was the Muslim Dargah, a great pilgrimage center for Muslims of south as well as north. Every year 'Urs' is held in which Muslims from various parts of the country attend the 'Urs' with great enthusiasm and devotion.

Gulbarga is also famous for the fort, a unique monument. The fort of Gulbarga was said to have been originally built by Raja Gulchand of Wrangal and subsequently strengthened by Ala-ud-din Bahamani. It is an extensive work which has fifteen towers. But the outer walls and gateway of the fort are now in a dilapidated condition. The only remarkable building in the fort remained intact is the mosque which is considered as a significant contribution of Bahamani Kings. Feroze Shaha (1397-1422) built the huge mosque in the fort in 1397 and it resembles the great mosque of Cardova in Spain, measuring 216 ft east to the west and 176 ft north to the south covering an area of 38016 sq ft. It is a unique mosque in India which is completely roofed. Rufi from Quasvin in Iran was its architect. This has attracted the attention of the Muslims of the country in particular and Hindus in general[4].

Gulbarga was under the administration of Nizam dominions even after India became independent. With the enactment of the State Reorganisation Act in 1956, the long cherished andardent desire of the people of Hyderabad Karnataka region was fulfilled and the three Kannada speaking districts of Gulbarga, Raichur and Bidar formed part of the new Mysore State with effect from November 1, 1956. Gulbarga is a multi-religious district of Karnataka state having unique characteristics. It is interesting to note that there has been through the ages a kind of interplay of Muslim and Hindu culture in Gulbarga each influencing the other and enriching it. The Muslim rulers over the years had its influence on the habits and customs of the people who are mostly Hindus. Quite a number of Muslims themselves were descendents of Hindu converts. Even the Muslims who claimed descent from foreign immigrants lived in closeness with the Hindus for generations. It was inevitable and there was a reciprocal influence. Many social practices of the Muslims such as marriage were closely influenced by the Hindu society. Even the caste distinctions characterizing Hindu society spread to the Muslim aristocracy. In matters of dress, food, language, music art and architecture there was considerable mutual influence even in religious matters. There was this mutual influence perceptible as is indicated by Sufism on the one hand and the doctrine of the Medieval Hindu society on the other. The Muslim saints were respected by the Hindus and the Hindu saints were held in high respect by the Muslims. In the field of scholarship and literature Muslim scholars studied Hindu philosophy and sciences such as yoga, Vedanta, medicine, astrology, arithmetic and chemistry. Some Muslim rulers were great patron of Hindu scholars and a few Muslim scholars wrote in the Indian languages. Gulbarga played a memorable role in the development of what is known as 'Deccani Hind'. A few Hindus wrote in the Persian language. This led on to conclude that, insofar as scholarship in the field of science and humanities are concerned there was a great inter-play between influence touched mainly the external elements of life. The Hindus continued to retain their habits of social exclusiveness and the Muslims their religious zeal.

Influence of Mahammedan Sufi

The Muslim mystics were men of deep religious feelings. They led ascetic lives and laid great stress on the practices of self discipline as preparing the human being for the intuitive knowledge of god. This doctrine was not only widely propagated in the Islamic world outside the country but was also further developed on Indian soil. Nizam-du-din Auliyas was one of the greatest sufi in the country. He laid emphasis on the elements of faith as a means of the realization of the god. It has been widely believed by some that the views, beliefs and practices of the Sufi sect of Islam had some influence on Hinduism in the Deccan. The moderate wings of two religious groups, i.e., Hindus and Muslims might perhaps prove a common meeting ground.

Gulbarga is a land wherein even Jain relgion had a great influence on the life of the people of Gulbarga district. The Jain temple found in the Malkhed, Sedam, Hansi-Hadagalli and Several other places in Gulbarga district bear testimony to the fact that the whole of the district was under the influence of the Jain faith once upon a time. But it must be said that during Vikramaditya's time there was catholicity in religious outlook. Jainism, Shaivism, Vaishnavism and even Buddhism which still claimed a few votaries received support at his hands. The Buddhists seemed to have also held either places in the Gulbarga equally with the other religions.

Demographic Features

According to the surveyor General, India, the total geographical area of Gulbarga district is 16224 sq. km. Amongst the 27 districts of Karnataka state, Gulbarga happens to be the second largest and ranks next to Bijapur. According to the village records, as reported by local officers, the aggregate area of the villages and towns of the district is 16,174 sq. km. a figure which is smaller by 50. sq. kms. than the figure furnished by the surveyor General, India. The slight difference between the two agencies is attributable to the difference between the two agencies is attributable to the difference in the methods employed by the two agencies for measuring the area of the district. Incidentally, it may be mentioned that the smallest unit for which the area figures are furnished by the surveyor general is the district. As a result at the district is the district as a result.

The total area of the district is unevenly distributed among the ten talukas. In terms of area, Jewargi and Surpur talukas together account for 22.52 per cent of the total area of the district. The talukas of Chitapur, Aland, Gulbarga, Yadgir, and Shahapur–each of which has an area slightly more than the taluk average are medium sized and the remaining three talukas of Chincholi, Afzalpur, and Sedam are small sized with an area of 1025 sq. km. (6.34 per cent of the total area of the district). Sedam taluk happens to be the smallest taluk of the district.

According to the 1991 census, the total population of Gulbarga district is 2,582,169 persons and since there are ten talukas in the district the average population of a taluk comes to 258,217 persons. In terms of population size, Gulbarga ranks first and Chitapur follows as a poor second while Afzalpur occupies the bottom most, i.e., the tenth place. The population of Gulbarga taluk alone which is 253,481 accounts for 20.29 per cent of the total population of the district where as the population of Chitapur taluk (309,481) constitutes 11.99 per cent. The other talukas which are fairly large and have above average population are Surpur, Yadgir and Aland. These three talukas are fairly large in geographical size as well and area wise, Surpur is in fact the second largest taluk. The population of these three talukas forms 31.62 per cent of the total population of the district. The remaining 36.10 per cent of the population of the district is shared by five talukas including Jewargi, the taluk with the largest area. In terms of population size, Jewargi holds the eight place while Sedam and Afzalpur hold the ninth and the tenth places. The population of these three talukas constitutes 7.32 per cent, 6.32 per cent and 5.84 per cent of the district total. Gulbarga which is the most populous taluk holds the eighth rank in terms of population size. Area wise, Afzalpur and Sedam hold the ninth and the tenth rank respectively. In the terms of population size also these talukas are quite small whole Afzalpur occupy the bottom-most, i.e., the tenth place, Sedam occupy the penultimate place[5].

Scheduled Castes

In a total population of 2,582,169 persons enumerated in Gulbarga district at the 1991 census, 610,641 persons have turned themselves as belonging to the scheduled castes and, of them, while 502,488 persons are residing in rural areas, the remaining 108,183 persons are residing in urban areas. The rural and urban components of the scheduled castes population of the district work out to 82.28 per cent and 17.72 per cent respectively. In terms of population, scheduled castes constitute 23.65 per cent of the total population of the district. It may be incidentally noted that this figure is quite high in comparison to the state average which is 16.38 per cent. The rural urban break up shows that as compared to the overall state averages of 18.17 per cent and 12.40 per cent respectively, in Gulbarga district 25.47 per cent of the rural population and 17.74 per cent of the urban population belong to scheduled castes. The scheduled castes component in both the categories of the population of the district is relatively high.

According to 1991 census, different scheduled castes found in the district, Holeya–1, 51, 109, Lambani–1,21,842, Madiga–87,755, Bhovi or Waddar–27,569, Samagar–6, 114, Dhor–4, 95, Korma or Bajantri-2, 893, Mang-Garudi-612. The total number of scheduled castes in ten talukas as follows: Afzalpur–28,104, Aland 63,813, Chincholi–62,466, Chittapur–92,673, Gulbarga–1,12,006, Jewargi–37,840, Sedam 40,057, Shahapur–54,591, Surpur–53, 354 and Yadgir–65,737[6].

Gulbarga is a multi-linguistic district consisting of a large number of people speaking different languages namely, Kannada, Urdu, Hindi, Telugu and others. Kannada is the principal language spoken by more than half of the district population. Telugu and Urdu were next in importance. Since Gulbarga was under the rule of the Nizam for quite a long time Urdu became prominent for a large section of the population of the Gulbarga. Marathi, Gujarati, Tamil, Tulu or Konkani are also spoken by respective families of these areas. English is also a popular language, adopted by most of the students as the medium of instruction in school and colleges. A part from these main languages dialectical languages of the Waddar, Korcha, Lambani are also among the languages.

Life Style

In the matters like food pattern, clothes and fashions, social customs and conventions, ceremonies and celebrations, hobbies and entertainment's, the city of

Gulbarga is no exception to any big city in Karnataka. Politically the district is far advanced and the people of Gulbarga district represent several political parties and a large number of them play important role in the reconstruction of the district and State in addition to the nation.

Organistions of Scheduled Castes in India

In the based society individual qualifications and achievements have no significance as such. Forming caste organisations by the low castes in India was an attempt to mobilies the masses, through their caste's men, to fight against exploitation of all sorts prevailing within the caste system. Powerful organisations began to emerge among certain non-Brhamin castes during the end of the last century. Such organisations addressed themselves to social reform within the caste and sought to secure better position for the caste in the wider society.

Scheduled castes organiasations have emerged throughout the country. Organisations of scheduled castes attempted to improve their educational level, social conditions, religious conditions, economic conditions, cultural conditions and political by forming caste orgnaisations in society. Rudolph and Rudolph observe that the caste organisations are para-communities or pressure groups to enable members of caste to pursue social mobility, political power, and economic advantage. Caste organisations are necessary in order to bring some structural and cultural changes among the scheduled castes. It was also essential to narrow down the social distnce between the castes among the scheduled castes by coming together and living an organisational life. This required communication of new thoughts and values to the masses. This process of socialisation was obviously possible through organisations. Some of the important organisations are analysed below.

Satanami Organisation was formed by Shri Ghasi Das at Chhattisgarh region in the year 1830. the objectives were: to bring Dalit upliftment, by preaching against consuming liquor and tobacco, to maintain high moral and cultural standards[7].

South India Buddhist Association was founded by Pandit Iyodhi Dass at Madras in the year 1890. objectives were: free and compulsory eduction facilities for scheduled caste, to review Buddhism in India[8].

Adhi-Dravida Mahajan Organisation was formed by group of Pariahs at Madras in the year 1890. objectives were: agrarian concessions to the scheduled caste, separate electorate for the Depressed classes[9].

Dravid Kazhagham was formed by John Rathnam at Madras in the year 1892. Objectives were: to unite the Depressed classes in Madras, to act as a pressure group in order to get the demands of the untouchable's fulfilled[10].

All India Ramnami Organisation was founded by Shri Parashu Ram Bhardwaj at Chhattisgarh region in the year 1901. objective were: not to believe in idol worship, not to believe in any magic and not believe in holiness of Ganga water for purification of the sins, not to go Hindu temples for worshipping their goods, not to accept Brahmin supremacy and their holy books including Manusmriti and Rama Charit Manas, to believe in equality and human brotherhood[11].

Sanmarga Bodhak Nirashrit Samaj was founded by Shri Kisan Fagu Bansod at Nagpur in the Year 1903. objectives were: to spread education among all the scheduled castes, to preach against drinking spurious liquor and against beef eating, to oppose conversion to other religion, to organize all the scheduled castes under one banner, to propagate moral and religious principles, to reform the untouchable society, to struggle for human rights[12].

Sadhujan Paripalan Yogam was formed by Shri Ayyan Kali at Kerala in the year 1905. objectives were: Organisation to protect the poor, organise untochables, preach congregations to maintain cleanliness and maintain high moral standard[13].

Jagan Mitra Mandal was formed by Shri. M.V. Bhagya Reddy at Hyderabad in the year 1906. objectives were: to create awareness among scheduled castes towards their backwardness, new awakening among the people[14].

Sadu Jana Paripalana Sangham was formed by Sadantha Swami at Travancore Tamil Nadu in the year 1907. objectives were: it was prevent mass exodus of pulays to Christinaity, education for puliya, to establish Harijan hostels, organise cultural programmes like music, drama, etc., which brought them cultural awareness and organisational sprit[15].

Pratyaksha Raksha Deiva Sabha was founded by poyakayil Yohannan at Keral in the year 1908. Objectives were: to reject Christinaity and Hinduism, to believe that God will incarnate to liberate the untouchables, to believe in liberty, equality and fraternity, to pray in the name of the Creator, but not to offer sacrifice, to pray in separate temples[16].

Adhi-Hindu Social Service League was founded by Shri Bhagya Reddy Varma at Hyderabad in the Year 1911. Objectives were: to eradicate social evil of intemperance, to eradicate the system of animal sacrifice, to eradicate the custom of dedicating girls to deities, to prevent child marriages, to create friendly relations between all the untouchable castes and the people of the high castes[17].

Depressed India Association was founded by Ganesh Akkaji at Pune in the year 1917. Objectives were: to spread education among the scheduled castes, to develop their moral and material condition, to introduce social reforms, to protect the interests of the industrial and agricultural labourers, to safeguard the political interests of the scheduled castes[18].

Jatav Veer Mahasabha was formed by Prabhutanand Vyas at Agra in the year 1917. Objectives were: to motivate the Jatavas towards education, sanskritisation of their ways of life and change of their identity and it demanded representation for the Jatavas in the legislature[19].

Adi-Hindu Organisation was founded by Sri Arigaya Ramaswamy at Hyderabad in the year 1922. Objectives were: Uplifting scheduled castes to the main stream, to settle internal disputes among the scheduled castes, to bring moral and cultural development of the untouchables[20].

Jat-Pat Todak Mandal was founded by Shri Sant Ram at Punjab in the year 1922. Objectives were: to break caste system, arranging and promoting inter caste marriages[21].

Bahishkrit Hitkarini Sabha was founded by Dr. B.R. Ambedkar at Bombay in the year 1924. Objectives were: Promote the spread of education among the Depressed classes by opening hostels or employing such other means as may seem necessary or desirable, to promote the spread of culture among the Depressed classed by opening libraries, social centers and classes or study circles, to advance and improve the economic conditions of the Depressed classes by starting industrial and agricultural schools, to represent the grievances of the Depressed classes, the founding principles of the sabha were "Educate, Agitate and organise"[22].

Ad-Dharm Mandal was founded by Shri Mango Rama at Jullunder city in Punjab in the year 1926. objectives were: Adopted non-theistic notion of divinity, nature has created human beings from the original source Adi, the philosophy of Ravidas ought to respectfully follow[23].

Vidarbha Asprushya Samaj Sudharka Seva Mandal was founded by Shri Sambhji Ansuji Khandare at Akola on 1st December 1927. Objectives were: to struggle for religious equality, and to reconvert those who had converted to Islam or Christianity, to propagate against sub-casteism among the untouchables, to encourage inter sub-caste marriages, to propagate against drinking and beef eating, to spread education amongst the untouchables by opening schools, hostels and to spread technical education, to work for getting due representation on the District Boards and legislature"[24].

Adi-Kerlotharana Sangham was formed by Kelappan and C. Krishnan at Calcutta in the year 1927. Objectives were: education to the Dalit, freedom to walk along public roads, and starting hostels for the Dalit students"[25].

Bharat Sant Samaj was founded by Shri Patit Pawan Das at Ankola in the year 1927. Objectives were: to propagate

Dr. Babasaheb Ambedkar's thoughts, to preach against superstitious habits and traditions, to stress the importance of education[26].

Khet Mazdoor Sabha was founded by Shri Jagjivan Ram at Bihar in the year 1930. Objectives were: to protect the interests of the agricultural labourers[27].

Hyderabad State Depressed Classes Association was formed by P.R. Venkataswamy and B.S. Venkatrao at Hyderabad in the year 17th May 1936. Objectives were: to organise the youth of the Depressed classes under one banner, to support Babasaheb Ambedkar in his mission to lead the community out of Hinduism, to enlighten the community on the evils of Hinduism, to obliterate existing caste differences among different sections of population, to start a vigorous campaign to ameliorate their social and economic disabilities[28].

Marwar Mehtar Sudhar Sabha Organisation was formed by Shri Prabhu Das Gharu at Rajasthan in the year 1945. Objectives were: they wanted to be treated as permanent servants, they wanted to get brooms for sweeping, they demanded one month's leave in a year with full salary, they wanted to have pucca houses and separate wells to be dug for them[29].

People's Education Society was founded by Dr. B.R. Ambedkar at Bombay on 8th July 1945. Objectives were: to provide facilities for education secondary, collegiate, technical, physical and the like, to establish education institutions such as schools, colleges, hostels, libraries, play grounds, etc., at suitable place in the state of Bombay as well as any other part of India, and give aid to such institutions, to create and foster a general interest in education amongst the scheduled caste and in particular to give them special facilities, and scholarship for higher education in India and abroad, to provide facilities for the education of the poor[30].

Dalit Harijan Samaj was formed by Muldas Vaishya at Ahmedabad in the year 1948. Objectives were: to Organise Dalit Communities in Gujarat, to revive traditional occupation like tanning and weaving, to improve their economic conditions, to remove untouchability within dalit or scheduled castes and abolish social customs which degenerated them[31].

Rajputana Mehatar Sudhar Sabha was founded by Shri Gopal Chand Maharaja at Rajasthan in the year 1948. Objectives were: to promote the spirit of unity among the community members, to promote social and material welfare of the members of the Bhangi community, to preach importance of education they aimed to promote social change by way of sanskritisation[32].

Buddhist Soceity of India was founded by Dr. B.R. Ambedkar at Nagpur in the year 1955. Objective were: to spread the knowledge of Buddhism in India, to build Vihars at as many places as possible in order to strengthen the faith of the new converts, to establish schools and colleges where education will be provided in Buddhist literature and philosophy, to establish orphanages and hospitals and undertake other social work, to train workers to carry the message of Buddhism to all parts of India and to establish study circles for the purpose[33].

Bombay State Inferior Village Servants Association was formed by Dr. B.R. Ambedkar at Bombay on 31st August 1955. Objectives were: the Vatan land should be given to the inferior village servants, the inferior village servants should be treated as government servants for the purpose of salary and other benefits, the duty time and particulars of their work should be decided[34].

All India Backward SC/ST/OBC and Minority Committee was formed by Kashi Ram in the year 6th December 1978. Objectives were: to pay back to the oppressed and exploited society to which they belong[35].

Keral Pulaya Maha Sabha was founded by P.K. Chathanin at Kerala in the year 1976. Objectives were: extension of reservation for scheduled caste for another ten years, distribution of 50 per cent of surplus land to scheduled castes, minimum wage, allocation of small scale industries, provision for loan facilities[36].

Dalit Panther was formed by Mahar Youths at Sidhartha Nagar Bombay in the year 1972. Objective were: the wages of landless laborers must be increased, Dalits must have allowed to draw water from public wells, Dalits must live, not outside the village in a separate settlement but in the village itself, all means of production must belong to the dalits, exploitation by private capitalists must cease, social, cultural and economic exploitation must give away to a true introduction of socialism, all dalits must be assured of daily wages, unepmployed dalits must be given unemployment benefits, all dalits must be given free education, medical facilities, housing and good quality cheap grains, religious cateist literature must be banned[37].

Organisations of Scheduled Castes in Karnataka

Karnataka Bahiskrit Sangh was founded by Swami Deoral Ramji Ingle at Belgaum in the year 1922. Objectives were: to propagate among the scheduled castes people, especially those living in the villages that they should struggle for the human rights, to propagate among all the untouchables including Mahar, Mang, Chambar, and tried to unite them for all social activities[38].

Adi-Jambava Organisation was formed by Justice Shankar Narayana Rao at Bangalore in the year 1920. Objectives were: to improved cultural life of the Madiga, to giving up the custom of child marriage, and buffalo sacrifice, to avoid consumption of carrion, payment of bride price and serving liquor at engagement ceremonies[39].

Bhim sena Organisation was founded by Shri B. Shyama Sunder at Gulbarga in the year 1968. Objective were: to Surrender of twenty five per cent of villages in every taluk, a separate electorate for scheduled castes, a separate University for scheduled castes in each state and strong political organisation for untouchables.[40] He proclaimed: "We will rather die on our legs than live on our knees", "We are not Hindus", Hindu names[41]. "We will burn Hindu Gods With us", "We will throw off our".

Scheduled Caste Organisation (Macro Level Organisations) in Gulbarga

Organisational structure of scheduled caste organisations has a district identity on location, caste and the alliance to a leader. Accordingly we find same type of organisations with common objective functioning at several levels like State, District, taluk and the village. At times there will be two or three factions of the same organisation working at a place. Here a brief analysis of these organisations is done for the purpose of clear understanding of the similarities and variations.

Karnataka Dalit Sangharsha Samiti: The Objectives were: to fight against deep rooted social, cultural, and economic inequality towards scheduled castes. To try to build the casteless and class less society through abolition of monopoly of production process, to honour the national and international persons and freedom fighters who support to protest against communal attack on minority people, to open meals center for the orphanage old age persons, to start Adult educational schools for dalit community, to impart education, songs, dramas and art of dalit kala mandals to fight against the blind belief and slavery system, to promote compulsorily education, cultural unity, community dinning in marriages, simple and inter-caste marriage etc. to facilities for basic needs like food shelter, clothing, water and other economic assets, to protect against atrocities, social boycott etc. on dalit people especially women. To establish Janatha Courts for dealing with dalit cases, to promote abolition of customary duties and sale of liquior and other alcoholic beverages in the residential localities of dalits. To popularize the ideas, thoughts, and principles of Lord Buddha, Dr. B.R. Ambedkar Phule, Ramabai and Savitribai Phule[42].

Karnataka Dalit Students Federation (KDSF): The objectives were: to promote education free from the monopoly of upper castes from primary school to university level, to bring unity among the dalit students, to fight for vocational training to downtrodden students based on their caliber, skill and cultural values based education, to fight for free education and educational expenditure should be borne by government, to fight against caste, religion, language, and gender differences. To bring equality, liberty and fraternity in society, to fight for the employment to the unemployed educated dalits, to support all revolutionary movements and organisations which fight against unjust practices of the society, to support to caste based reservation and fight against upper castes conspiracy of merit and economic reservation slogans, to agitate distribution of sub-caste reservation and support to enhance from 18 per cent to 22 per cent to dalit reservation, to fight against social evils like caste, dowry, communal clashes, in society and tray to bring social awareness to fight against involvement of communal syllabus or Kesari Karana syllabus in education, to create political awareness, self-respect, and self-confidence in the mind of dalit students. It helps to get equal status to other upper castes people in the society. To support the other Backward caste reservation provided it don't affect to the dalit reservation[43].

Sub Caste Organisations (Micro-Level Organisations) in Gulbarga

Dalit Panther Gulbarga: The organisation's main objectives are to secure land to landless people belonging to depressed castes, fight against feudal system and atrocities on dalits, Caste System, Untouchability, and other social, cultural and economic exploitation. Special Provision for these castes in education, employment, development schemes, etc.[44]

Dalit Sahitya Parishad, Gulbarga: The Objectives were: to conduct special lectures about dalit literature, art and culture all over the districts dalit literature conference and awards and honours to the distinguished dalit literates in various disciplines, Encourage dalit cultural literature, publications of books, conduct seminars, conference, endowment lecturers etc. on Dr. B.R. Ambedkar, Jothi Rao Phule and others[45].

Karnataka Dalit Sahitya Sansad, Gulbarga: The objectives were: to promote Dalit literature education, science and fine arts, to promote education and development of Dalit community, fostering the feeling of a unity and brotherhood[46].

Kranti Jyoti Savitrabai Phule Mahila Organisation: The objectives were: to achieve the overall development of Dalit women, to fight against injustice, encourage literature, art, culture, vocational education, training in handicraft and other small scale industries, to emancipation from poverty, blind beliefs and practice of blind faiths, customs and traditions of dalit women, to provide educational facilities in the rural and urban areas. To popularize the ideas, thoughts, and principles of Lord Buddha, Dr. B.R. Ambedkar Phule, Ramabai and Savitribai Phule[47].

Lambani Caste Organisation: The objectives were: to works for the overall development of community and create awareness. To facilitate rural development programmes, establish, schools, colleges, training institutes, hostels. To promote women development and child welfare programmes. To propagate the traditional culture[48].

Madiga Community Organisation: Akhil Karnataka Adi Jambhav Jagrata Organisation represents the Madiga Caste. Objectives were: to develop Adi Jambava community, to protect from exploitation and rehabilitate the labourers, physically handicapped, destitute women and, Dumb and Deaf people, to promote educational facilities through schools, colleges, training centers, hostels etc. To facilitate socio-economic development programmes for the community in general and women in particular[49].

Waddar or Bhovi Caste: The objectives were: to provide educational facilities, to provide financial and technical assistance to the unemployed persons for of self employment, like crushing machines, stone industries, to promote self employment schemes for the women, and to propagate the traditional culture[50].

Samagar Caste Organisation: The objectives were: To provide Vocational training in leather technology for both men and women and to facilitate financial and technical assistance to promote leather industry, readymade shoe market etc., to start schools and colleges, hostels, etc., to establish Mahila Banks for the sake of women, to establish orphanage home for destitute children and old age persons and to propagate the traditional culture[51].

Dhor Organisation: The name of the caste organisation is Veerashaiva Kakaiyya Dhor Organisation. The objectives were: promotion of professional education, hostels for old age persons and poor Dhor students, to facilitate economic developmental activities, to promote social, religious and cultural activities of the community[52].

Korcha Seva Organisation: The objectives were: To promote social, educational religious, economic, development programmes, to facilitate self employment schemes to establish credit cooperative society, to promote women development programmes[53].

Mang-Garudi: The objectives were: To facilitate to remove the social and economical backwardness of the members of the Mang-Gaurdi community, to promote education, training, hostel facilities for their children, to promote employment opportunities, through the vocational, scientific Industrial and commercial training camps, to introduce cooperative cottage industries. To eradicatc illitcracy, superstition and provide opportunities for the development of women, to provide security against all sorts of exploitations[54].

The Scheduled Castes in Gulbarga District

It is generally believed that the caste plays dominant role in shaping the destinies of a person. In the Indian context, caste is indispensable. A person is born in one or the other caste. Society normally recognizes every person as belonging to also with the occupations, ownership of assets, education, employment etc. It is undisputed and foregone conclusion to say that there exist a direct relationship between the ritual status of caste and social or economic development. In this section an attempt is made to describe a brief history of major scheduled castes in Gulbarga district.

Holeya

Holeya also known as Holeya or Holer, they are distributed in Bidar, Dharwad, Gulbarga, Belgaum, Bijapur and Raichur districts of Karnataka. They are largely distributed in rural areas. They speak Kannada with the family and kin group. They are also conversant with the Indo-Aryan languages, Marathi. They are non-Vegetarians and eat chicken, mutton and beef, but do not eat pork.

The traditional occupation of Holeyas was to work as servants in the agricultural land belonging to the headman (patil) of the village. At present, both men and women work as agricultural and casual wage labourers and industrial workers. Many of them work as masons. Some of them are employed in the government service. It is evident from the census report that out of their total population, 42.29 per cent were workers. Among them 53.30 per cent were male and 31.07 per cent females. The composition of working population reveals that majority of the workers (64.40 per cent) work as agricultural labourers and as cultivators (17.51 per cent). Another 4.65 per cent of the workers engaged in livestock, etc., 1.73 per cent in the household industries and 2.30 per cent in other than household industries. The remaining 9.41 per cent work in various other services.

The Holeyas follow Hinduism and celebrate all Hindu festivals. They celebrate Dasara, Deepavali and Holi. Caste elder of their own community officiates at their marriage and death ceremonies. Their attitude towards formal education is favourable for boys and partly favourable for girls. Boys usually up to the secondary level but a few of them drop out due to economic reasons. Girls discontinue their studies after the primary level for economic and social reasons. Their literacy rate was 19.08 per cent which is lower than the general literacy rate of 20.59 per cent of the scheduled castes in the state (Census 1991). The male and female literacy rates were 29.21 per cent and 8.77 per cent respectively[55].

Lambani Community

They are also referred to as Lambani Lamani, Lambadi, Banjaras, they are predominantly found in rural areas. Lambani spoke an Indo-Aryan language within their family and kin group and the Dravidian language, Kannada is spoken with others. Kannada is the script used by them.

A few of the Lambani own land, but majority are landless labourers. Their traditional occupation was trade and liquor manufacture. According to 1991 census, 43.76 per cent of them were workers. The proportion of male and female workers was 55.27 per cent and 32.50 per cent respectively. Of them, 36.41 per cent work as cultivators, 48.88 per cent as agricultural labourers, and 4.52 per cent work in livestock, forestry, etc., 2.78 per cent engaged in manufacturing, processing, etc., and 1.87 per cent in trade and commerce. The latter refers to their traditional occupation of manufacturing and trading liquor. The remaining 5.54 per cent of the workers are engaged in various other services. Child labour exists in their community. Their traditional caste council deals with cases like adultery, rape, elopement, etc. the council imposes cash fines on offenders.

The Lambani follow Hinduism and celebrate Ugadi, Dassara, Deepavali, Kar-Hunnime, etc., they worship family, village and regional deities of the great tradition. Priests from other communities as well as from their own community perform various rituals. Formal education is favoured for both boys and girls. Boys study up to college level and girls study up to the secondary level. However, many of them belonging to rural areas, remain illiterate because of social and economic reasons. Their literacy rate, according to 1991 census, was 13.54 per cent, which indicate that they are still lagging behind in the filed of education. The sex-wise literacy rates show that 21.54 per cent males and 5.02 per cent females are literate[56].

Madiga Community

The Madiga are concentrated all over Karnataka and considerably high in Gulbarga district "The Madiga who are also known as left-hand caste or Edagaiyavaru, among them selves". The traditional occupation of the Madiga is to make or repair leather footwear and any ancillary work associated with skin and hides which they continue to the present day. Besides, they are sweepers, drumbeaters and wage labourers. As per the 1991 census, only 28.65 per cent of them were workers (41.82 per cent males and 15.59 per cent females). Workers among them were classified mainly as workers in other services (42.68 per cent) followed by workers in other than household industries (22.61 per cent). A mere 0.98 per cent was reported as cultivators, and 5.12 per cent as agricultural labourers. The remaining 28.61 per cent workers are engaged in services such as livestock, forestry, mining, quarrying, construction, etc. They are Hindus and their main deities were as Mariyamma, and other goddess. They are the followers of Vaistnavism and worship Lord Venkateshwara and others. Festivals like Ugadi, Dassara, Deepavali, etc., are celebrated.

Among the Madiga community the boys usually study up to the secondary level, while girls discontinue after the primary level. Their literacy rate was 36.74 per cent, out of which 46.36 per cent were males and 26.47 per cent were females (Census 1991). The literacy level of Madiga was higher than the general literacy rate for the scheduled castes in Karnataka (20.59 per cent). The female literacy rate among them is indicative of the progress achieved by them in the field of education[57].

Bhovi Community

The word Bhovi is seems to be a corrupt from of bhavi, meaning a well; in Kannada, it also means earth-digger. They are also called as Vadda, Waddar. They are the people who engage themselves in sinking wells for agricultural and other purposes. They are mainly concentrated in rural areas of Bangalore, Kolar, Chitradurga, Tumkur, Dharwad and Gulbarga districts. They are predominatly distributed in rural areas. However, 20.97 per cent of their total population lives in urban areas. The Dravidian languages of Telugu and Kannada are spoken in the family and with other community members.

Earth works (digging), stone-cutting and daily-wage labour are their traditional occupation. Agriculture is a secondary occupation of those settled in villages. According to 1991 census, 41.96 per cent of them were reported as workers and among them 57.32 per cent were cultivators, 37.12 per cent were agricultural labourers and 2.19 per cent engaged in livestock rearing, forestry etc., Another 4.42 per cent of the workers were engaged in mining and quarrying and 10.42 per cent as construction workers which is indicative of their minimal involvement in their traditional occupation. The remaining 16.91 per cent of the workers were engaged in various other services. Child labour was a common feature among them. The traditional council of the community is no longer functional. There is a district level of caste organisations which look after their socio-economic interests.

The Bhovi are Hindus by faith, Muneshwar is the patron deity, but many of them are devotees of Anjaneya. They also worship Mariyamma and other gods and Goddesses. They celebrate all Hindu festivals especially Dasara, Diwali etc. The Bhovis prefer to impart formal education to their children irrespective of sex. Their boys study up to the college level while their girls study only to the secondary level. The literacy rate, according 1991 census, was 17.92 per cent which is indicative of their moderate progress in the field of education. The male and female literacy rates were 26.90 per cent and 8.55 per cent respectively[58].

Samagara Community

Samagaras are also known as the Chamagars or chamabars. They are distributed in the entire Karnataka state. They speak the Indo-Aryan language, Marathi, within the family and Kannada with others. The Devanagari and Kannada scripts are used for writing. 44.30 per cent of their population lives in urban areas.

Their traditional occupation is leather work. Even today the Samagaras engage in footwear making. They also make bridles and whips besides engaged in skilled labour. Of the total population 34.58 per cent of the Samagaras are workers constituting 50.44 per cent males and 18.19 per cent females (Census 1991). Among the total workers 33.94 per cent are engaged in manufacturing, processing, servicing, etc., 21.27 per cent in the household industry and 12.67 per cent in other than household industries i.e., their traditional occupation of leather work, 5.91 per cent are engaged in trade and commerce which includes the workers engaged in their traditional occupation of the sale of leather goods. However, a considerable number of them, i.e., 46.45 per cent, are engaged in the primary sector of the economy, i.e., 17.40 per cent cultivators and 29.05 per cent as agricultural labourers. The remaining 13.70 per cent of the workers are engaged in various other services.

The traditional community council settles their disputes. Their modern caste association or the organisations works for their community welfare. They profess Hinduism. Ugadi, Dasara and Deepavali are the festivals celebrated among them. They worship all deities of the wider Hindu pantheon. They participate and celebrate festivals like Gajanna Utsava, Haralayya Jayanthi, Basaveshwara Jayanthi, etc. along with members of other communities. Samagaras send their children to schools and colleges. Boys study up to the college level and girls study up to the secondary level. Their boys discontinue studies largely due to social and economic reasons. Their literacy rate of 33.45 per cent (1991 census) seems to be very moderate. The male and female literacy rates are 45 per cent and 21.52 per cent, respectively[59].

Korama or Bajantri

The caste or Bajantri is also referred as Korama setty. The word Korama is derived from kuru, meaning fotune-telling. They are largely concentrated in Bangalore, Tumkur, Chitradurga, Kolar and Chikamangalur districts. Thurston (1909) writes that Korama or korava are known by different names in different localities. They are known as koracha in areas of North Aroct and in few other districts they become Yerukula. Their mother tongue is a dialect of Tamil Nadu, but all are bilingual and are also conversant with Kannada. Korama are non-vegetarians who consume pork. Mat-weaving, rope-making and tattooing. A regional association oversees the welfare and upliftment of the community. They are Hindus and are mainly the followers of Lord Vishnu. They employ their own priests but in cities they employ a Brahman to perform their rituals. They celebrate all Hindu festivals like Ugadi, Dasara, and Deepavalli. Their principal deity, Nulichannaya, is propitiated along with other gods and goddesses like Hanumanta, Karewwa, Dyammavva, Durgavawwa and Ellawwa. A Brahman priest (jangam) conducts their rituals. Nowadays, they have from group orchestras, known as kardimailu, to play music[60].

Dhor Community

The Dhor in Karnataka and Gulbarga are synonymously called Dhor or Kakkayya or Kankayya and the latter is not a subgroup in the state. The word Kakkayya is derived from their Lingayat preacher and Dhor means cattle. According to 1991 census, 46.03 per cent of them were reported as settled in urban areas. The Indo-Aryan language, Marathi language is spoken within the family and kin group and Kannada is spoken with others. Both the Devanagari and Kannada scripts are used.

Tanning is the traditional occupation of the Dhor community. They purchase raw hide from slaughter houses and tanned it suitable and sold to cobblers. Wage labour is the secondary source of income. In the recent past, a few have taken up white-collar jobs. Of their total population, 32.89 per cent were reported as workers (47.53 per cent males and 17.96 per cent females). Of them, 25.14 per cent were engaged in manufacturing, processing, servicing, etc., 15.38 per cent in the household industry and 9.76 per cent in other than household industry indicates the extent of the involvement in their traditional occupation of leather tanning. However, in recent years, a change is observed where there is a movement towards the primary sector of the economy. Of the workers, 18.96 per cent were cultivators and 32.56 per cent were agricultural labourers. The remaining 23.34 per cent were engaged in various other services (Census 1991).

The Dhor community professes Hinduism and worship Renuka, Yellamma, Karewwa, Hanuman and Rama. Their literacy rate, according to the 1991 census, was 33.23 per cent (50.29 per cent among males and 15.82 per cent among females). However, many of their children discontinue their studies in the primary level only due to economic reasons. And some of them are self-employed in the mechanized leather tanning industry[61].

Mang-Gadudi Community

Mang-Garudi is one of the nomadic castes included in the list of Scheduled Castes in Karnataka state. The Mang-Garudi is traditionally a wandering population as acrobats and mat-weavers. Russell and Hiralal (1916) have described the Mang as Garodia as snake charmers, perhaps taking a clue from the Garudi. However, later studies (census 1963) have not confirmed this but authenticated their traditional occupation of removing the body hair of buffaloes. They are snake-charmers, beggars and jugglers. The Indo-Aryan language, Marathi is their mother tongue. The script used for writing is Devanagari. The same language and script are used for inter group communication.

They are largely unskilled labourers and are not certain about their traditional occupation. Their women and children are also engaged in wage labour. According to the 1991 census, out of their total population, workers account for 33.77 per cent (48.00 per cent males and 19.04 per cent females), of them, 39.31 per cent are engaged in agricultural labourers, 5.57 per cent in cultivation. 7.29 per cent in livestock 3.36 per cent in the household and 7.32 per cent in other-than household industry, 8.10 per cent in trade and commerce and the remaining 29.05 per cent in various other cervices.

Their community council decides intra-group disputes. They are Hindus and besides worshipping Hindu gods and goddesses, they also propitiate family deities. Formal education is favoured only for boys, but they too drop out before completing their secondary education. Girls study only up to the primary level. The literacy rate among them was 16.20 per cent with 25.77 per cent males and 6.28 per cent females[62].

Table–3.1 Distribution of Organisations and Population in Gulbarga District by Caste

Sl. No.	*Caste*	*No. of Organisations*	*Per cent*	*Population*	*Per cent*
1.	Holeya	38	32.20	151109	37.56
2.	Lambani	21	17.80	121842	30.29
3.	Madiga	25	21.19	87755	21.81
4.	Waddar	10	8.47	27893	6.91
5.	Samagar	09	7.63	6114	1.52
6.	Korcha	07	5.93	2893	0.72
7.	Dhor	07	5.93	4094	1.02
8.	Mang-Garudi	01	0.85	612	0.15
	Total	**118**	**100**	**402312**	**100**

It is evident from the Table-3.1 that among the eight scheduled castes communities in Gulbarga district, Holeya community has highest number of organisations (38) constituting 32.20 per cent organisations of functioning. It has a large population (37.56 per cent) and working in a different talukas in Gulbarga. The second widespread organisation represents the Madiga community with 25 branches (21.19 per cent) functioning in different parts of the district. In terms of its population it accounts to 21.81 per cent among the total scheduled castes, the organisational representation of 21.19 per cent supports the fact that the community has organized itself proportionately to fight against the external aggression. Another interesting inference from the table is that the Lambani community which is the second largest scheduled caste population (30.29 per cent) in the district has an organisational strength of only 17.80 per cent. Mang-Garudi community is lowest both in terms of number of Organisations and the population with 0.85 per cent and 0.15 per cent respectively. Among the remaining castes Waddar has an organisational strength of 8.47 per cent with a population of 6.91 per cent followed by Korcha with 5.93 per cent of organisational strength and 0.72 per cent population, Samagar with 7.64 per cent of organisational strength and 1.52 per cent population, and Dhor community with 5.93 per cent of organisational strength and 1.02 per cent population.

Notes and References

1. Gazetteer of India, Karnataka State Gazetteer, Part-II, Government of Karnataka Publications, 1983, p. 212.
2. Gazetteer of India, India, Mysore State, Gulbarga District, Mysore State Gazetteer, Director of printing and Stationary and Publication Division, Government Press Bangalore, 1966, p. 64.
3. The Imperial Gazetteer of India, Vol. 12, p. 75.
4. Sathyan B.N (Eds) 1996: Gazetteer India Mysore State-Gulbarga District, Published by Government of Karnataka, Bangalore, pp. 35-39.
5. Gazetteer of India–Mysore State, Gulbarga District, Government of Karnataka, 1966, Bangalore, pp. 1-15.
6. *Ibid.*, p. XII .
7. Kshirsagar R.K. (1994), *Dalit Movement in India an its Leaders*, M.D. Publications Pvt. Ltd., New Delhi, p. 104.
8. *Ibid.*, p. 106.
9. Saraswathi, (1974), "Minorities in Madras State, Impex India" Delhi, pp. 14, 72-74.
10. Kshirsagar R.K. (1994), *Dalit Movement in India an its Leaders*, M.D. Publications Pvt. Ltd., New Delhi, pp. 88-89.
11. *Ibid.*, pp. 75-76.
12. *Ibid.*, p. 103.
13. *Ibid.*, p. 101.
14. *Ibid.*, p. 91-92.
15. Josheph Mathew (1986), Ideology, Protest and Social Mobility Case Study of Mahars and Pulayas, Inter-India Publications, New Delhi, pp. 109-110.
16. *Ibid.*, pp. 109-110.

17. Kashirsagar (1994), *Dalit Movement in India an its Leaders,* M.D. Publications Pvt. Ltd., New Delhi., pp. 73-74.
18. Kosare (1984), *Vidarbhatil Dalit Chalwalich Itihas*, Gyan Deep Prakashan Nagpur, pp. 115-122.
19. Kshirsagar, *Dalit Movement in India an its Leaders*, M.D. Publications, Pvt. Ltd., New Delhi, p. 92.
20. Venkatswamy P.R., *Ours Struggle for Emancipation*, Vol. I & II Hyaderabad, pp. 18-21.
21. Juergensmeyer (1988), "Religious Rebels in Punjab" *The Social Vision of Untouchables*, Ajanta Publication, Delhi, p. 39.
22. Kharata (1990), "Dr. Babasaheb Ambedkaranchi Patre" Idrayni Sahitya, Shaniwar Pet, Pune, pp. 6-14.
23. Juergensmeyer M. (1988), "Religious Rebels in Punjab" *The Social Vision of Untouchables*, Ajanta Publication, Delhi, pp. 45-56.
24. Kshirsagar (1994), *Dalit Movement in India an its Leaders*, M.D. Publications, Pvt. Ltd., New Delhi, p. 92.
25. Joseph Mathew (1988), "Ideology Protest and Social Mobility", *A case study of Mahars and Pulayas*, Inter-India Publications, New Delhi, p. 110.
26. Kshirsagar (1994), *Dalit Movement in India an its Leaders*, M.D. Publications, Pvt. Ltd., New Delhi, pp. 84-85.
27. Gail Omvedt (1982), *Land Caste and Politics in Indian States*, (ed) Guild Publication, Delhi, pp. 32, 106.
28. Kshirsagar (1994) *Dalit Movement in India an its Leaders*, M.D. Publications, Pvt. Ltd., New Delhi, p. 89.
29. *Ibid.*, p. 95.
30. Peoples Education Society Reports, 1947 Bombay, p. 99.
31. Kshirsagar (1994), *Dalit Movement in India an its Leaders*, M.D. Publications, Pvt. Ltd., New Delhi, pp. 87-88.
32. *Ibid.*, pp. 100-111.
33. *Ibid.*, pp. 85-86.
34. Kharat (1990), "Dr. Ambedkaranchi Patre" Indravani Sahitye, Shanwarpet Pune, pp. 335-338.

35. Jogdand P.G. (1991), *Dalit Movement in Maharashtra*, Kanak Publications, New Delhi, pp. 92-95.

36. Joseph Mathew (1986), *Idology Protest and Social Mobility*, Inter-India Publications, New Delhi, pp. 109-113.

37. Lata Murugkar (1991), *Dalit Panther Movement in Maharashtra*, Popular Prakashan, Bombay, pp. 237-239.

38. Kshirsagar (1994), *Dalit Movement in India an its Leaders*, M.D. Publications, Pvt. Ltd., New Delhi, p. 93.

39. Lata Chandrasekharan (1992), *Social Mobility Amount the Madiga of Karnataka*, Sociological Bulletin 41 I (I & II), March, Sept., p. 123.

40. Shyam Sunder. B. (1987), "They Burn, Dalit Sahitya Academy", Bangalore, pp. 16-18.

41. Jodgand P.G. (1991), *Dalit Panther Movement in Maharashtra*, Kanak Publications, New Delhi, pp. 61-62.

42. D.S.S. (Constitution) Published, Pancham, Kukkarhalli, Mysore, pp. 1-20.

43. KSDSF (Constitution) (1983), Published, DSF State Committee, Coroporation Building Queen's Road, Bangalore, pp. 1-16.

44. Dalit Panther Constitution (1978), Gulbarga Branch.

45. Dalit Shaitya Parished Bylaws (1998), Gulbarga.

46. Karnataka Dalit Sachity Sansad Bylaws (1997), Gulbarga.

47. Jyoti Savitribai Phule Mahila Organisation Bylaws, (1999), Gulbarga.

48. Lamani organisation Bylaws, Gulbarga (1995), Gulbarga, pp. 1-2.

49. Adi-Jambhav organisation Bylaws (1995), Gulbarga, pp. 1-2.

50. Bhovi organisation Bylaws, (1999), Gulbarga, pp. 1-12.

51. Samagar organisation Bylaws Gulbarga (1985), pp. 1-15.

52. Dhor organisation Bylaws, (1995), Gulbarga, pp. 1-15.

53. Korma organisation Bylaws (1995), Gulbarga, pp. 1-15.

54. Mang-Garudis organisation Bylaws (1981), Gulbarga, pp. 1-4
55. Singh, K.S. (1995), "Scheduled Castes", *Anthropological Survey of India*, Oxford University, Press, New Delhi, pp. 600-602.
56. *Ibid.*, pp. 123-125.
57. *Ibid.*, pp. 815-817.
58. *Ibid.*, pp. 259-261.
59. *Ibid.*, pp. 1133-1135.
60. Laxmidevi H. (1993), A Sociological Study of the Korchas of Karnataka in an Urban Setting: A Case Study of Korchas of Raichur. Ph.D. Thesis, Gulbarga University, Gulbarga.
61. Singh K.S. (1995), "Scheduled Castes" *Anthropological Survey of India*, Oxford University Press, New Delhi, pp. 461-463.
62. *Ibid.*, pp. 910-911.

4

Profile of the Respondents

Introduction

An attempt is made in this chapter to analyse the socio-economic characterstics of the respondents. These include the respondent's personal life, their family background, the educational background, political participation and level of awareness, the religious beliefs, and also their association with the organisation.

Growth and development are possible only in a congenial environment. The growths of plant, animal, and human being or for that matter any species needs a proper environment. Similarly for the development of an organisation, or personality of an individual or for the development of an infant into a responsible citizen, the environment around him will be responsible to a larger extent. So for the proper growth or development and sustainability of an organisation suitable environment is needed. The environmental conditions for the development of caste orgnaisations are several in nature. Here an attempt is made to dwelt on some of the environmental conditions favourable for the growth and development of caste and sub caste organisations.

The primary and most important condition for the development of is the community environment. Community environment includes the social composition, nature of community leadership, economic stability and cooperation among the members for sharing the responsibilities of both administrative and organisational activities etc.

Community environment may include individuals of varied interests. Those individuals may be related to each other either by kinship or friendship. They may be of peer groups, or members of the same caste, association of one or the other sort. Further, the community environment includes the relationship between debtors and creditors, seller and buyers, growers and non-growers. It also includes master and servants, patrons and clients, elders and youngsters, males and females and a host of other relationships and inter-dependencies. The community relationship will also include several socio-cultural dimensions and thereby better to call it as social environment. This category also includes the inter-relationship between individual or family with that of the government, market etc., both local and distant or outside the community.

Family Environment

As mentioned above, family environment is the primary factor influencing the caste or sub caste organisation. A suitable atmosphere in the family will enable its leader to devote sufficint time for its all-round development. Though it is very easy to say about the suitable environment or 'atmosphere', it will be equally difficult to describe the contents and pre-requisites of a suitable family environment for the development of caste or sub-caste organisation. Here an attempt is made to capture various dimensions of family environment and their influence on the development or otherwise of caste or sub caste organisations.

It is beyond doubt to accept that, for the development of an individual, the family environment is crucial. A child's future is shaped in the family. A child is socialized in a family so as to be a good citizen as he grows old. It provides an opportunity to learn skills of various sorts depending upon the parents occupations, education etc. Apart from that the children learn the basics of life especially to perform his role in different situations and also during different stages of his life. This means to say that the socialisation process will enable the child to grow into an adult with the knowledge of his or her commitment or expectations of the family, neighbourhood, kith and kin, peers and various inter and intra relationships he has to have in course of his or her life etc., along with the rights and obligations he has to adhere to. All these expectations of an individual also varies with family to family and community to community even though there would be a general expectations of and accepted pattern of role behaviour in different scenarios.

The variations or the deviations from the expected patterns of behaviour of an individual to a great extent depend upon the family environment. First each and every family consists of few individuals with well defined sets of relationships. Based on this, the families are categories into various types. These include nuclear or sub nuclear to joint or extended families. The variations will also be seen in terms of the headship of the family, whether the family or household is headed by male or female member etc. in addition, the number of persons in the family, the sex ratio, educational level, the skills and training in different trades of members of the family will enable an individual in the household to shape his personality. Similarly, the composition of a family or household will determine the success or failure of a family enterprise.

The factors favourable for formation of caste or sub caste organisation, has identified the following traits or features in the composition of the family. Firstly, a large majority of them have reported that the family size should be of medium where sufficient number of working persons in the household is available. Secondly, the household should be headed by a knowledgeable person, with good leadership qualities. Thirdly, the head of the household should be a male number. Finally, there should be a proper combination of male and female persons in the family. Though the types of response vary from person to person, a large majority of them have expressed above factors both during individual discussions and also at group level. The next important component of the family environment suitable for organisational development is the adjustment among the family members. There seem to be unanimity among the respondents that more composition of family or household though a pre-requisite, is not sufficient one, unless there is a proper understanding among the family members.

Finally a large majority of households have reported that the members of the family should be responsible and responsive. The responsibility and responsiveness speaks of the obligations and duties of the members of the family while performing their day to day activities and the members of their family behave responsible and are responsive to the situations.

As mentioned earlier, the family environment is important for the development of caste or sub-caste organisation. In addition to the family environment, environment of the community where the organisations locates is also equally important. In the process of socialisation of a child, the contribution of the community is significant. One cannot think of an individual or a household in isolation.

It is important to note that the community is like a two edged knife. It is true even in case of the socialisation of a child. The community provides both good and evil atmosphere. It is up to the concerned person to choose and pick the type he or she is interested. Based on that, the individual is categorized in the community as good, decent, bad, harmful character. Depending on such qualities he or she is interact with the community.

Of course, there are accepted and expected norms in the community that one has to follow in spite of the fact that the community gives an open access to both good and evil habits. Similarly an organisation will have ample scope for development provided one chooses to positive productive aspects as against destructive ones. In the community environment an organisational leader is expected to extend and build relationships which promote the development of the organisation. For instance, the relationship with kith and kin, his understanding of the local, national and even international relations, links with the government etc. The community environment also includes the interaction with friends and foes, politicians, officials, etc.

Similarly, the contact with several people is essential for the development of any organisation. Unlike other external factors influencing caste or sub-caste organisation, the interdependence between multiple organisations play a dominant role in shaping the future of the organisation.

The Respondents

The analysis of primary data about the demographic characteristics of respondents is presented in the following paragraphs. The data is presented in the in the form of tables followed by the discussions based on the insights derived from these tables.

Table-4.1
Respondents by Sex

Sex	*Frequency*	*Percentage*
Male	140	93.33
Female	10	6.67
Total	**150**	**100.00**

The Table–4.1 reveals the sex wise distribution of respondents where 93.33 per cent are males and the remaining 6.67 per cent are females. It can be inferred that a large number of respondents belong to the dominant sex giving less prominence to the weaker sexes.

Age

The age wise classification of respondents is presented in table 4.2. The table reveals that 40 per cent of the respondents belong to the age group of more than 31 years of age. 33.3 per cent were in the group of 21 to 30 years. The

Table-4.2
Distribution of the Members of the Sample Household by Age

Age	*Frequency*	*Percentage*
15 to 20 years	40	26.67
21 to 30 years	50	33.33
31 years and above	60	40.00
Total	**150**	**100.00**

youngest members of the organisation were in the age group 15 to 20 years constituting 26.67 per cent.

Marital Status

Marital status of a person indicates his or her position in a company. It is generally believed that a married person behaves responsible to run an organisation. In the Table 4.3 the marital status of the respondents are given.

Table–4.3
Distribution of the Members of the Sample Household by Marital Status

Marital Status	*Frequency*	*Percentage*
Married	64	42.67
Unmarried	80	53.33
Widow	4	2.67
Widower	2	1.33
Total	**150**	**100.00**

Table-4.3, out of 150 respondents 42.67 per cent of respondents are married and more than half (53.33 per cent) are unmarried. The remaining (4 per cent) are widowed.

Educational Level

Table-4.4 reveals that a large percentage of respondents are literates. Among the literate, a large percentage have

Table–4.4
Respondents by Educational Level

Education level	*Frequency*	*Percentage*
Illiterate	10	6.67
Primary	10	6.67
High School	25	16.67
College	65	43.33
Post-graduation	15	10.00
Professional Courses	25	16.66
Total	**150**	**100.00**

studied in colleges (43.33 per cent) for their degrees followed by professional course and high schools (16.67 per cent each). There are 10 per cent of respondents who studied up to postgraduate level and those who studied in primary school constitute only 6.67 per cent. There seems to be a very low rate of illiteracy (6.67 per cent) among the respondents.

The low level of education among the scheduled caste population is mainly due to the following factors. Table 4.5 reveals that a large proportion of population could not pursue higher education due to the poverty (40 per cent). Another 20 per cent were not attended the school due to neglect of their parents and 13.33 per cent reported the illiteracy as main cause for not pursuing education.

Table–4.5
Respondents by Reasons for not Pursuing Education

Reasons	*Frequency*	*Percentage*
Poverty	60	40.00
Neglect of parents	30	20.00
Illiteracy of family	20	13.33
Not applicable	40	26.67
Total	**150**	**100.00**

In order to get good education people from the rural areas have to visit the towns and cities for higher education.

Table–4.6
Respondents by Type of Hostel

Type of hostel	*Frequency*	*Percentage*
Government Hostel	10	6.67
Private Hostel	6	4.00
University	5	3.33
Own house	65	43.33
Relatives house	30	20.00
Rented house	25	16.67
Others	9	6.00
Total	**150**	**100.00**

It may not be possible for everyone to make their own arrangements. The government has provided hostel facilities for the Scheduled caste students to support their education. These facilities are available at all taluk, district and state headquarters. In addition to such facilities now extended to the Mandal or Panchayat headquarters are. Table 4.6 reveals that half of the respondents have to depend on outside facility for their lodging and boarding during their studies. Among them 20 per cent stayed in their relation's house as against 6.67 per cent who stayed in the government hostels. A sizeable proportion (16.67 per cent took rented accommodation during their studies. 43.33 per cent have educational institutions very close to their residence and hence stayed in their house. Thus, in spite of the government facilities a large proportion of scheduled caste students depend on non-governmental accommodation and food during their studies.

Table–4.7 reveals that the majority of respondents (53.33 per cent) have studied in government schools and 20 per

Table–4.7
Respondents by Type Educational Institution

Type of Institution	*Frequency*	*Percentage*
Government College	15	10.00
Private	10	6.67
University	5	3.33
Government School	80	53.33
Private School	30	20.00
Not attending	10	6.67
Total	**150**	**100.00**

cent in private schools. About 10 per cent have gone to government colleges as against 6.67 per cent who studied in private college and other institutions. Only 3.33 per cent of respondents have got admission in post graduate course. However, a few (6.67 per cent) have never gone to schools or colleges.

The Family

The analysis of primary data about the demographic characteristics members of the sample households is presented in the following paragraphs. The data is presented in the form of tables followed by the discussions based on the insights derived from these tables.

Population

Table 4.8 gives the sex wise details f the sample household of the respondents. Of the total population of 667 persons 55 per cent are female and 45 per cent are males. The proportion of females and higher than that of the males. The average family size in the village works out to be 4.5 persons per household.

Table–4.8
Respondents of the Sample Households by Sex

Sex	*Frequency*	*Percentage*
Male	301	45.13
Female	366	54.87
Total	**150**	**100.00**

Family Size

Table–4.9 reveals the size of the family of the sample households of the respondents, which shows that a large

Table–4.9
Respondents of the Sample Households by Size of the Family

Family size	*Frequency*	*Percentage*
upto 5 persons	120	80.00
6 to 10 persos	27	18.00
11 to 15 persons	3	2.00
Total	**150**	**100.00**

majority (80 per cent) have only 5 persons per household or family. Of the remaining, 18 per cent of the households have 6 to 10 persons per family or household and only 2 per cent of respondents have a family size of 11 to 15 persons per households.

Age

Age-wise distribution of population of the sample households of the respondents are given in the Table–4.10.

Table–4.10
Members of the Sample Households by Age

Age	*Frequency*	*Percentage*
Upto 10 years	90	13.49
11 to 20 years	125	18.74
21 to 30 years	146	21.89
31 years and above	306	45.88
Total	**667**	**100.00**

It reveals that nearly half (45.88 per cent) of the total population are above 31 years of age. Another 21.89 per cent of the population is between the age group of 21 to 30 years. People between 11 to 20 years constitute 18.74 per cent and the remaining 13.49 per cent of the population are below 10 years of age.

Marital Status

Table 4.11 reveals that more than half of the population (62.51) are married. About 33.89 per cent are unmarried

Table-4.11
Members of the Sample Households by Marital Status

Martial Status	*Frequency*	*Percentage*
Married	417	62.51
Unmarried	226	33.89
Widow	20	3.00
Widower	4	0.60
Total	**667**	**100.00**

and 3.60 per cent are widowed. Though data on age at marriage was not analysed here, the informal discussions with the respondents revealed that they normally prefer 20 years for a boy and 18 years to a girl for getting marriage. Under compelling circumstances (like arranging 3 or 4 marriages together etc.), the age at marriage is lowered to 15 years for a girls and 17 years for a boys.

Educational Status

Parents of the respondents educational level is an indicator to support their children to pursue higher education by providing suitable facilities. However it is not always the case. In the Indian context, education is a luxury for centuries. It was only the higher castes who were eligible to get formal education. People from middle and lower castes were denied or prohibited to study Sanskrit for centuries. Only after the British, who liberalized the education system gave an opportunity to non-Brahmin castes to get educated. However, most of such facilities were available in big towns and cities. It was not possible for rural population to visit towns and pursue education as there were no transport facilities apart from their economic position. It was a distant dream for the rural middle and lower castes to visit a town to pursue higher education.

After independence several facilities are provided to impart education to the general public. Special provision was also made to the scheduled castes by way of free facilities in schools and colleges and also government hostels. In spite of all these, the improvement in the educational levels among the scheduled caste is not encouraging. The reasons attributed are ignorance and literacy of parents, and their socio-economic background, etc.

Table-4.12 reveals that a large percentage of parents of respondents were illiterates. Between father and mother, the illiteracy was high in case of mothers (82 per cent) as compared to the father (66 per cent). Among the literates, most of them have not crossed primary school level where 20 per cent and 11.33 per cent among the respondent's father and mother respectively were reported to have primary level of education. Another 8.66 per cent and 1.33 per cent among the respndent's father and mother respectively has high school education. By virtue of adult education facilities few couples (5.34 per cent each of the father and mother) became functional literates. Though the parents are illiterate they encourage their children to go to schools and colleges with an ambition of seeing well paid jobs.

Table–4.12
Educational Levels of Respondent's Parents

Educational level	*Frequency*		*Percentage*	
	Father	*Mother*	*Father*	*Mother*
Illiterate	99	123	66.00	82.00
Primary	30	17	20.00	11.33
High School	13	2	8.66	1.33
Any other	8	8	5.34	5.34
Total	**150**	**150**	**100.00**	**100.00**

Table–4.13 reveals that about one–third (33.74 per cent) of the members of the respondents households are illiterate. Among the literates 22.48 per cent have studied up to primary level. 19.94 per cent high school and the remaining 19.34 per cent are functional literates.

Table-4.13
Members of the Sample Households by Educational Level

Educational level	*Frequency*	*Percentage*
Illiterate	255	33.74
Primary	150	22.48
High School	133	19.94
Any other	129	19.34
Total	**667**	**100.00**

Type of Family

The categorization of family is done based on the structure of the family. If the family has both the spouses (husband and wife) living along with their unmarried children, the family can be categorized as the nuclear family. If any one of the spouses is dead and other spouse remain unmarried and live with the unmarried children then such a family is referred as the sub-nuclear family. In a joint family there will be more than one generation member living together. If a joint family has only one line of family is called lineal joint family. On the other hand if the joint family has a structure where more than one brother live with their wives and married children along with their parents are termed as collateral joint family. In any of the joint families or even in case of nuclear families if one of its members live separately in another place due to migration or any other reason and keeps his contacts with the family of origin then such a family may be referred as extended family. There is large number of nuclear families among the respondent's household's which is a reflection of growing individualism in the community.

Table-4.14 shows that the share of nuclear families among the sample respondents are 56 per cent. There are

Table-4.14

Type of Family of the Respondents

Type of family	*Frequency*	*Percentage*
Sub-nuclear	6	4.00
Nuclear	84	56.00
Collateral joint	40	26.67
Linear joint	12	8.00
Extended	8	5.33
Total	**150**	**100.00**

few sub-nuclear families (4 per cent) where women took the responsibility of managing the household. More than one-third of the families are joint in nature. For instance 26.67 per cent are collateral joint, 8 per cent are linear joint and the remaining 5.33 per cent are extended family structure>. The change of family type from one to the other (i.e., parent family to the extended one) is a continuous one with the change in the structure of family due to division of family or death of its members, etc.

House Type

Though everybody own or live in a dwelling, there are variations in the number of building owned and the type of

Table-4.15
Type of Ownership of Respondents Residence

Type of ownership of house	*Frequency*	*Percentage*
Inherited	90	60.00
Own construction/purchase	15	10.00
Free	10	6.67
Government assisted	30	20.00
Others	5	3.33
Total	**150**	**100.00**

building. Table–4.15 reveals that nearly 97 per cent of respondents own a building for their living and other purposes. Among them 60 per cent owned a house by inheritance, 20 per cent own by way of government assistance, 10 per cent have constructed the houses on their own, 6.67 per cent have their houses freely and the rest (3.33 per cent) are staying in rented houses.

People live in various types of houses according to their economic status. Table-4.16 reveals that 23.33 per cent of respondents live in huts, which are built by locally available materials with mud walls and thatched root. For walls, unbrunt bricks or raw rocks of unshaped and sized are used along with the mud. The roof is covered with grass along with the bamboo sticks. There are 43.34 per cent of kuccha houses. These houses are built with burnt or unburnt bricks with mud for the walls. The roof is made up of wooden planks or jungle wood with mud cover. With the use of cement and

Table-4.16
Housing Structure of the Respondents

Type of family	*Frequency*	*Percentage*
Hut	35	23.33
Kuccha	65	43.34
Mixed	35	23.33
Pucca	15	10.00
Total	**150**	**100.00**

other materials has drastically changed the house structure. Such an impact is seen in building mixed houses which constitute 23.33 per cent. 10 per cent of households are living in a pucca house built from the external resources. These houses are constructed by using cement and iron extensively.

Social Aspects

Place of residence is an important indicator of social status. Traditionally the rural habitations (villages) are divided into different segments based on castes. Most of the localities are named after the cast which reside in the locality. Till recently, this was the case even in urban centers. The scheduled caste population especially the untouchable segment has a separate location adjacent to the main village or a slum in a town. Excepting in towns and cities, the rural residential segmentation has not changed in spite of several developmental programmes.

In Gulbarga district, Lingayat are in majority group followed by Kuruba and Beda or Walmiki. Among scheduled caste Holeyas, are in majority followed by Lambani and Madiga.

Temple Entry

The untouchable and other lower castes have their own temples. However, they were also devotes of the main village deity. For ages, the untouchables were kept away from entering the temple by imposing religious prohibition. Gradually, temple entry was permitted. However, there was a sort of disguised or invisible force operating in prohibiting the Scheduled Castes to enter the main temple. Even to this day it is in vogue in spite of constitutional safeguards.

In spite of all these, the scenario has changed. The respondents have more or less equally divided and reported that the temple entry is smooth and not conducive. Table-4.17 revels that among those who says the entry was smooth attributed to the factors of organisational efforts (28.67 per cent) followed by social awareness (13.33 per cent) and educational component (6.67 per cent).

Table-4.17
Perception of Respondents by Factors Conductive for Temple Entry for SCs

Conductive factor	*Frequency*	*Percentage*
Social awareness	20	13.33
Educational awareness	10	6.67
Organisational efforts	43	28.67
Not conducive	77	51.33
Total	**150**	**100.00**

Table-4.18 reveals the other factors attributed to the caste feeling (33.33 per cent), lack of social awareness (10 per cent), illiteracy (8 per cent) as main hurdles in the entry to the temples. However every one feels that there are no

Table-4.18
Perception of Respondents by Factors not Conducive for Temple Entry for SCs

Non-conducive factors	*Frequency*	*Percentage*
Lack of social awareness	15	10.00
Caste feeling	50	33.33
Illiteracy	12	8.00
Not applicable	73	48.67
Total	**150**	**100.00**

problems to enter any temple in urban areas as against the rural areas.

Use of Public Well

The concept of public well is fast eroding. The mini water supply schemes, the introduction of bore wells in different localities have to some extent solved the water problems, and the scope for using a common source by different community. The urban water supply schemes never take into account the individuals or households based on caste or religion.

Practice of Untouchability

Though several changes have undergone in the society, still age old practices continue. One such practice is pertaining to Untouchability. Table 4.19 supports the above

Table-4.19
Respondents by Reasons for Practice of Untouchability

Reasons	*Frequency*	*Percentage*
Lack of social awareness	20	13.33
Rigid social system	77	51.33
Illiteracy	30	20.00
Not practicing	23	15.34
Total	**150**	**100.00**

fact where a large majority of respondents (84.66 per cent) confirms the existence of the evil practice. Among them 51.33 per cent attribute it to the rigid social system, 20 per cent to illiteracy and the remaining 13.33 per cent attribute to the lack of social awareness.

However Table-4.20 indicate that there is no practice of Untouchability in the society (15.34 per cent). Social awareness (13.33 per cent) improvement in education (1.33 per cent) and modernizing the life styles (0.67 per cent) are the main factors contributing to the eradication of Untouchability from the society.

Table-4.20
Respondents by Reasons for not Practicing Untouchability

Reasons	*Frequency*	*Percentage*
Social awareness	20	13.33
Education	2	1.33
Modernisation	1	0.67
Practicing	127	84.67
Total	**150**	**100.00**

Traditional Services

Though there are changes in the attitudes of rural upper castes, still certain practice is continuing. One such practice is the non-availability of traditional services like barber, dhobi, priesthood, etc. However, one can find a change in urban and semi-urban areas where these services are available on par with other castes. Here again the type and quality of service varies with the economic position of scheduled caste recipient.

Interaction with people of different sections depends on the needs and opportunities up course, the interaction depends on several factors, like place of residence, work and other meeting grounds. If two persons agree to share their likes and dislikes, joy and sorrow, profit and losses and expect or seek advice, then the two considered as close to each other and friends. The actions of the one person can be affected by the others actions. However such interactions may vary with caste to caste (not always). The attitude of higher caste, towards lower ones must vary.

Table-4.21 reveals that almost all respondents have good relationship with other caste members. 38.66 per cent reported that they have friendship with all castes. Another 26.67 per cent says that they have friends among the lower castes only as agaist 16.67 per cent who have friends among the middle castes. Another 15.34 per cent have friends only from the upper castes, only 2.66 per cent have no friends.

Table-4.21

Relationship of Respondents with other Castes

Castes	*Frequency*	*Percentage*
Upper castes	23	15.34
Middle castes	25	16.67
Lower castes	40	26.67
All castes	58	38.66
Nil	4	2.66
Total	**150**	**100.00**

Among several forms of ill-treatment to the scheduled caste and lower caste people, social boycott is one. The scheduled caste people have to face the wrath of the upper caste population when the castemen claim additional facilities or pressurize the upper caste on any such occasions. The upper casts impose and enforce social boycott on the scheduled caste households or persons if such household or person work against the traditional way of behaviour. If any scheduled caste person violates the generally accepted day to day norms, then such person will be punished. Among several punishments social boycott is one.

Table-4.22

Reasons for Social Boycott

Reasons	*Frequency*	*Percentage*
Temple entry	40	26.67
Hotel entry	30	20.00
Land dispute	20	13.33
Others	10	6.67
No	50	33.33
Total	**150**	**100.00**

Table-4.22 reveals reasons for social boycott. Among other things, the issue of temple entry which was banned to Scheduled Castes and lower castes. If any, downtrodden person goes against the normal practice. 26.67 per cent of the respondents were victimized for entering a temple against the existing practice in the community. Another 20 per cent were socially boycotted for entering a hotel in their village. About 13.33 of respondents were boycotted from the community due to land disputes and 6.67 per cent other reasons.

Table–4.23 reveals that about one third of the total respondents, never experienced by sort of social boycott for

Table-4.23
Reasons for not Practicing Social Boycott

Reasons	*Frequency*	*Percentage*
Social awareness	30	20.00
Education	15	10.00
Both	5	3.33
Not applicable	100	66.67
Total	**150**	**100.00**

any of their actions. The main reason reported was these respondents have high social awareness (20 per cent), good education background (10 per cent) or both (3.33 per cent).

Even though, the bonded labour (zeetha) system was abolished by legislation, in order to secure decent livelihood to the scheduled castes and others who actually follow it, it is still prevalent in the rural area in one or the other form.

Table-4.24 reveals that the bonded labour system is in vogue in the village due to poverty (62 per cent) and illiteracy

Table-4.24
Reasons for Practice of Bonded Labour

Reasons	*Frequency*	*Percentage*
Poverty	93	62.00
Illiteracy	29	19.33
Not applicable	28	18.67
Total	**150**	**100.00**

(19.33 per cent). About 18.67 per cent reported non existence of bonded labour system or practice has given up in the rural community.

Table-4.25 endorse with 9.33 per cent reporting that improvement in economic conditions and education (6.67 per cent) was the important reasons) for not continuing the bonded labour system. About 2.67 per cent reported that the land reforms have facilitated to work independently on their own lands.

Table-4.25
Reasons for Giving Up of Bonded Labour

Reasons	*Frequency*	*Percentage*
Economic improvement	14	9.33
Education	10	6.67
Land reforms	4	2.67
Not applicable	122	81.33
Total	**150**	**100.00**

Economic Aspects

Occupational Structure

Several modes of occupations are essential for the livelihoods of people. Even though such occupations generate income independently, they revolve around main occupation of the household. There is no single occupation for a worker. For example an agriculturist not only perform his agricultural work in addition, it takes care of several other occupations such as petty trade, animal husbandry, managing the household, working for others, public service etc. In spite of all these, one attributes agriculture as one's occupation if he or she holds a piece of land. Livestock, forest lagging, fishing etc., are such occupations, which provide subsidiary income to the individual and hence are not independent enterprise. Instead, they form a part of 'the agriculture' whole.

Unlike the rural population, majority of the urbanites depend on non-land based occupations. Table-4.26 reveals

Table-4.26
Distribution of the Members of the Sample Households by Occupation

Reasons	*Frequency*	*Percentage*
Agriculture only	49	7.35
Agriculture and social work	35	5.25
Agriculture and cooli	135	20.24
Cooli only	63	9.44
Government service	23	3.45
Private service	54	8.10
Self employed	4	0.60
Domestic work	210	30.13
Students	63	9.44
Unemployed	15	2.25
Other	25	3.75
Total	**667**	**100.00**

about 32.84 per cent of the total population of the sample households are engaged in land based occupation mainly agriculture. Among them 7.35 per cent pursue only agriculture as against 5.25 per cent who undertake agriculture with social work or cooli (20.24 per cent). The private sector employment offers work to the extent of 8.10 per cent of the population and the government employment to 3,44 per cent of the total household population. Another 0.67 per cent engaged in self employment and 3.75 in other occupations. A sizable proportion (41.82 per cent) population of the sample households are dependents where 30.13 per cent are domestic workers, 9.44 per cent are students and 2.25 per cent are unemployed youth.

Table-4.27 reveals the mode of occupation of the respondents. Agriculture and related occupations forms main source of employment for 53.33 per cent of respondents. The private sector and government departments provide employment to 8 per cent and 6.67 per cent of respondents

Table-4.27
Respondents by Type of Employment

Reasons	*Frequency*	*Percentage*
Agriculture only	15	10.00
Agriculture and social work	65	43.33
Government service	10	6.67
Private service	12	8.00
Self-employed	4	2.67
Domestic work	5	3.33
Students	25	16.67
Unemployed	6	4.00
Other	8	5.33
Total	**150**	**100.00**

respectively. Another 2.67 per cent of respondents of self employed and 5.33 per cent pursue allied activities. About 24 per cent of respondents are non workers in the sense of official definition of the term as they engage in domestic worker or go to school or unemployed.

Land Ownership Pattern

Land is an important asset not only in terms of livelihood but also in terms of the status. Table 4.28 reveals that a

Table-4.28
Respondents by Ownership of Total Land

Ownership of land	*Frequency*	*Percentage*
Up to 5 acres	55	36.67
5.01 to 10 acres	30	20.00
10.01 to 15 acres	20	13.33
15.01 acres & above	10	6.67
Not applicable	35	23.33
Total	**150**	**100.00**

sizeable proportion of sample households (23.33 per cent) are landless. However, among the land owners 56.67 per cent are small and marginal farmers who own land less than 10 acres and find it very difficult to earn a living from a small piece of land. Another 13.33 per cent are medium and semi-medium farmers owning land between 10 to 15 acres. Only 6.67 per cent own land more than 15 acres.

Table-4.29 reveals that a sizeable proportion of sample households (76.67 per cent) are not having irrigation facility

Table-4.29
Respondents by Ownership of Irrigated Land

Ownership of land	*Frequency*	*Percentage*
Up to 5 acres	20	13.33
5.01 to 10 acres	5	3.33
10.01 to 15 acres	10	6.67
Not applicable	115	76.67
Total	**150**	**100.00**

which includes 23.33 per cent of landless households. However, among the irrigated land owners 16.67 per cent are small and marginal farmers, and another 6.67 per cent are medium and semi-medium landowners with less than 15 acres of irrigated land.

Source of Income

Income is an important indicator of the achievement or performance of the family members in their day to day ventures. This also become an index of the economic status of a family. Further, the level of income determines the ability of an earning member, the manner in which the inputs are used, the supporting activities contributing to the common pool resources of the family and the type of occupations pursued by the family members including their numbers participating in occupations contributing to the family income. The family income comprises of income from main occupation, income from other occupations pursued by family members, and the non-occupational income.

Table-4.30 reveal that 40.67 per cent households have a total income in the group of less than Rs. 5000 per year.

Table-4.30
Households by Annual Income

Income	*Frequency*	*Percentage*
< 5000	61	40.67
5001 to 10000	49	32.67
10001 to 15000	26	17.33
15001 to 20000	14	9.33
> 20000	0	0
Total	**150**	**100.00**

There are 32.67 per cent in the income group of between Rs. 5,001 to Rs. 10,000. Another 17.33 per cent of the households have income between Rs. 10,001 to Rs. 15,000 and only 9.33 per cent of the households have less than Rs. 20,000 per year as their annual income from all sources put together.

Table-4.31
Distribution of the Members of the Sample Households by Sources of Income

Occupation	*Frequency*	*Percentage*
Agriculture Only	49	7.35
Agriculture and social work	35	5.25
Agriculture and Cooli	135	20.24
Cooli only	63	9.44
Government service	23	3.45
Private service	54	8.10
Self employed	4	0.60
Domestic work	201	30.13
Students	63	9.44
Unemployed	15	2.25
Other	25	3.75
Total	**667**	**100.00**

Individual members of the family earn through various occupations and contribute it to the family income. Table-4.31 reveals that most of the earnings of the members was through the joint contribution such as agriculture, animal husbandry, along with non-occupational income such as rent, remittances, gifts, pensions etc. one third (32.84 per cent) share of the income comes from agriculture and other occupations taken up jointly with agriculture. Another 9.44 per cent contribute through their labour either in the agriculture fields or in the off farm sector. The private sector employment contributes to the extent of 8.10 per cent and the government employment contribute about 3.44 per cent of the total household income. Another 0.67 per cent comes from the self employed and 3.75 from other sources like rent, remittance, etc. a sizable proportion (41.82 per cent) population of the sample households are not contributing any thing in tangible terms though they work for the improvement of the household economy in several ways. They include the domestic workers, students and unemployed youth waiting for a better opportunity.

Table-4.32

Respondents by Source of Income

Sources of income	*Frequency*	*Percentage*
Agriculture Only	15	10.00
Agriculture and social work	65	43.33
Government service	10	6.67
Private service	12	8.00
Self employed	4	2.67
Domestic work	5	3.33
Students	25	16.67
Unemployed	6	4.00
Other	8	5.33
Total	**150**	**100.00**

Table-4.32 reveals the source of earnings of the respondents. Though their contribution is included in the table 4.21 as a member of the household, it was felt to deal with their contribution separately as it will through light on their capabilities and responsibilities to both the household and the organistion to which they are the one of the office bearers. Table 4.32 more or less resembles the table 4.31 where the respondents also depend on agriculture and related occupations as main source of income (53.33 per cent). The private sector and government employment contributes to the extent of 8 per cent and 6.67 per cent respectively. Another 2.67 per cent comes from the self employed and 5.33 from other sources like rent, remittance, etc. About 24 per cent of respondents are not contributing any to the household income as they work as domestic workers or the students and unemployed.

Assets

The important asset for an individual or a family is a living house followed by land in the rural community. These are immovable assets. In addition, there are other economic assets which are also not movable like trees, irrigation, wells, etc. these are invariable, grouped under the category of land. Apart from these, there are other assets, which are movable in nature. That is to say, these assets can be transported or carried from place to place, based on the necessity. Such movable assets have either economic or non-economic value or both. It is very difficult to clarify movable assets into these categories as they overlap the three on several counts. For examples, ownership of bullocks and milch animals no doubt, has economic value, but other significance too. The types of bullocks determine the social status of the households and the ownership of a cow will also be of religious significance. The utility of this is difficult to compute.

No doubt, improved economic status will enable persons to acquire new and newer things. Many a times, the utility of an asset becomes insignificant when it is counted from the cultural angle. It is self evident that one must invest in order to make or improve the asset structure. As mode of investment may vary from household to household accordingly the asset structure. Even one intends to make an investment in a venture he or she has to face several problems. Since the respondents belong to socially and economically backward or underprivileged group, making a decent living a luxury and hence the assets are very few and cheep.

Table-4.33
Households by Assets Owned

Assets	*Frequency*	*Percentage*
Immovable		
Land	115	76.67
House	140	93.33
Movable Assets		
Household durables	120	80.00
Ornaments	30	20.00
Livestock	120	80.00
Vehicles-Two wheelers	20	13.33
Vehicles-Four wheelers	4	2.67
Fixed investments	5	3.33
Total	**150**	**100.00**

Table-4.33 reveals that 93.33 per cent and 76.67 per cent of respondents own house and land which are the immovable assets these people own respectively. In addition, 80 per cent each own the livestock like a sheep or a goat a cow etc., and few household durables. Another 20 per cent reported of having some gold ornaments and 3.33 per cent have fixed investment. There are 4 respondents who own four wheelers bought under self-employment for their livelihood.

Expenditure

There is always a tendency for the people to under estimate their income and over estimate their expenditure. Though this may be true at the macro level but variations do found at the micro level. Inspite of low income amng few households, its expenditure on various counts exceeds its income.

Table-4.34

Households by Annual Expenditure

Income	*Frequency*	*Percentage*
< 5000	50	33.33
5001 to 10000	65	43.33
10001 to 15000	28	18.67
15001 to 20000	7	4.67
> 20000	0	0
Total	**150**	**100.00**

Table-4.34 reveals that one-thirds (33.33 per cent) households which spend Rs. 5,000 per household per year. A large majority (43.33 per cent) of household spend between Rs. 5,000 to 10,000 per cent spend Rs. 10,000 to 15,00 per year for the day to day expenses including the occupational expenditure. Only 4.67 per cent of respondents spend Rs. 15,000 to 20,000 per year for the expenditure of their households.

Savings

Ability to save is a complex phenomenon. One may be able to save but never bothered to save. The mode of savings is a cultural aspect. Savings though means household income in excess of household expenditure. Though income is determined by its sources, and fluctuations do occur in the incomes as against one's predictions. But, one cannot go beyond a certain point in the case of spending for the household needs. Again expenditure varies from household to household in spite of uniform in the family size and composition. Inspite of the above, it is difficult to find savings among the Scheduled Caste people. Among schedule caste households savings becomes a luxury as their income and expenditure never meet at any point of time. However, only two persons from among the total respondents reported a savings of about two to three thousands a year.

Indebtedness

Poverty and sufferings are primary ingredients of Indian community especially the depressed communities. Since lower and depressed castes are dominant among the Indian community, their share in the proportion of poverty is also high. Generally poverty is always associated with indebtedness and thereby the Scheduled Caste member is associated with one or the other form of indebtedness from his birth to his death. The main reason are (1) small and marginal holdings of a large proportion of population among Scheduled Caste households which are uneconomical and many a times unproductive as well as counter productive. (2) The general illiteracy also pushed these groups into the clutches of indebtedness (3) Their dependence on others for their livelihood.

Keeping above factors in mind the planners and the administrators have introduced several welfare schemes and programmes to uplift the poor and the Scheduled Castes. Several studies have revealed that most of the money spent on welfare schemes have gone to the middle men or to the implementing agencies rather than the real beneficiary. In spite of all thee, one finds a large gap among the people to avail such benefits and on several occasions not property utilized the intended benefit for the right cause. All these have pushed the depressed castes into a debt trap where one finds it very difficult to over come and cross the vicious ciricle of debt. With this backdrop let us look into the nature of indebtedness and reasons for indebtedness etc.

Table–4.35

Distribtion of Sample Households by Indebtedness

Income	*Frequency*	*Percentage*
< 5000	85	56.67
5001 to 10000	35	23.33
10001 to 15000	16	10.67
15001 to 20000	3	2.00
> 20000	2	1.33
Nil	9	6.00
Total	**150**	**100.00**

In spite of several development schemes to the scheduled caste population, they are unable to come out of the clutches of poverty and indebtedness. Except 9 households (6 per cent) which have reported as not having any outstanding loan of any sort, all other households of the sample are in debt. The proportion of borrowings varies from household to household. For instance table 4.35 reveals that more than half of the households (56.67 per cent) had an outstanding loan of Rs. 5,000/- followed by 23.33 per cent of the households with Rs. 5,000 to Rs. 10,000. Another 10.67 per cent have an outstanding loan of Rs. 10,000 to Rs. 15,000 and the remaining 3.33 per cent have above Rs. 15,000.

Every household had reported that they have borrowed for one or the other purpose. It varies from household to household whether they have really invested in the intended purpose. During the course of general discussions, several people reported that only a few have invested a portion of the loan for the purpose for which it was taken, though not all the borrowings.

Table-4.36 reveals that the second important reason for borrowing was for social obligations like festivals, family rituals etc., (37.3 per cent), followed by general family consumption (36 per cent), House construction and marriage

Table-4.36
Distribution of Sample Households by Purpose of Borrowing

Purpose	*Frequency*	*Percentage*
Domestic use	54	36.00
Social needs	56	37.33
Self employment	2	1.33
House construction of Marriage	30	20.00
Others	8	5.34
Total	**150**	**100.00**

(20 per cent), self employment (1.33 per cent) and followed by other purposes like health, recreation and other emergencies are in the order of preference for spending the loan amount (5.34 per cent). It was also reported during group discussion that the main source of credit is from outside the village, which may be organized financial institutions like banks and chit funds or from labour moneylender. It was reported that the system of interdependency for mutual has became an act of the past. Group also commented that commercial relationship has become the order of the day.

Political

The ways measuring political participation is in terms of people exercising their vote without any fear or pressure. Table 4.37 reveals that 22.67 per cent who vote under pressure, all others exercise their franchise without fear. Among them 53.33 per cent has social awareness, 13.33 per cent has educational development and 10.67 per cent has the political will or awareness.

Table-4.38 reveals those who reported to have undergone stress and strains while voting and reported that it was 16.67 per cent had pressure from the upper caste. Secondly, the

Table-4.37
Reasons for Voting Without Pressure

Reasons	*Frequency*	*Percentage*
Social awareness	80	53.33
Political awareness	16	10.67
Educational development	20	13.33
Not applicable	34	22.67
Total	**150**	**100.00**

educational backwardness was reported by 3.33 per cent and the remaining 2.67 per cent of the sample households have voted under pressure both due to educational backwardness and pressure from the upper caste leaders.

Table-4.38
Reasons for Voting Under Pressure

Reasons	*Frequency*	*Percentage*
Pressure from upper caste	25	16.67
Educational Backwardness	5	3.33
Both	4	2.67
Not applicable	116	77.33
Total	**150**	**100.00**

Those who were actively involved in the political activity, and show greater concern for the development of the community show interest in contenting in the elections to different positions. It is possible in a democratic set up to contest to any position from the local body to that of the president of India. However, mere provision will not be sufficient. Several factors operate even to file one's nominations in an election such being the general case, it would be difficult for the down trodden castes to contest in election as per their wish.

Table-4.39
Respondents Who Contested and Got Elected in the Elections

Mode of elected	*Frequency*	*Percentage*
Unopposed	2	1.33
Cooperation by other castes	16	10.67
Not contested	132	88.00
Total	**150**	**100.00**

Table-4.39 reveals that aobut 12 per cent of the total respondents shown interest in contesting the elections. Out of which 1.33 per cent got elected unanimously whereas 10.67 per cent got elected with the cooperation of other castes.

Table-4.40
Reasons for not Contesting in Elections

Reasons	*Frequency*	*Percentage*
Not interested	90	60.00
Non cooperation of upper castes	12	8.00
Financial problems	30	20.00
Not contested	18	12.00
Total	**150**	**100.00**

Of those, who never contested, table 4.40 reveals that 20 per cent have reported that they were unable to contest in elections due to financial constraints. Another 12 per cent reported that, they were unable to meet the election procedures and 8 per cent have not contested due to non-cooperation from the upper castes. However 60 per cent Table 4.40 were not interested the elections even though they show interest in politics. From the forgoing analysis one can infer that there is a high degree of political awareness among the scheduled caste population. This may be attributed to the organisational efforts supports by the constitutional reservations.

Table-4.41
Membership in Political Parties

Political Parties	*Frequency*	*Percentage*
Congress	70	46.67
Janata Dal (U) & (S)	35	23.33
BJP	5	3.33
BSP	30	20.00
Others	10	6.67
Total	**150**	**100.00**

The question of membership of a political parity is based on several factors in the Indian context. Unless one because the executive member of any of the units, he/she will not hold a formal membership of any political party. However, people will identify themselves with one or the other political party or have alliance or support political parties. Such a support will be based on several criteria including the policies of a political party.

Table-4.41 shows that a large majority of the sample respondents were the members of Congress Party (46.67 per cent) followed by BSP (20 per cent), Janata Dal (S) and (U) (23.33 per cent), BJP (3.33 per cent) and other parties (6.67 per cent).

Table-4.42 reveals the distribution of respondents who contested to the elections to different positions shows that only 3 persons (2 per cent) contested to the assembly elections, 10 persons (6.67 per cent) each contested to Zila parishad and Taluk Panchayat elections. A large number (35) contested to local level village panchayats (23.33 per cent). Only 2 persons (1.33 per cent) contested to other bodies like village cooperative societies, etc.

Table-4.42
Respondents by Contest in Elections

Particulars	*Frequency*	*Percentage*
State Assemble	3	2.00
Zila Parishad	10	6.67
Taluk Panchayat	10	6.67
Village Panchayat	35	23.33
Others	2	1.33
Nil/Not contested	90	60
Total	**150**	**100.00**

Table-4.43 reveals that among the political parties which came to power in Karnataka, 56.67 per cent reported the Congress (I) party has always supports the casue of the Dalits

Table-4.43
Support of Political Parties to Schedules Castes

Political Parties	*Frequency*	*Percentage*
Congrcss (I)	85	56.67
Janata Dal (U) & (S)	25	16.67
BJP	5	3.33
BSP	30	20.00
Others	5	3.33
Total	**150**	**100.00**

and introduced several programmes followed by BSP (20 per cent). Another 16.67 per cent of the respondents attributed that the Janata Dal (U) and (S) which also introduced several measures to uplift the downtrodden. Of the remaining 3.33 per cent projected the BJP as a party which help the scheduled castes. However, another 3.33 per cent reported that the other smaller parties like RPI etc. though not ruled in the state have concern for the scheduled castes.

Religious Aspects

As the fact that man is a social animal is accepted beyond question so also the religion. Social and religion are two faces of the same coin. Whether one accept or not every individual or a society or community is a bundle of belief and rituals. Religious dogmas plays an important role in all spheres of man's life whether economic, political or property dealings etc. irrespective of education, caste, status of the concerned persons.

Fairs and festivals are important component of day to day life of individuals. They form a part of the religious behaviour and also the recreation. The cultural practices beliefs, values, traditions and customs, ritual are all apart of religion. It is also true of the functionaries of the scheduled caste and sub-caste organisation.

Table-4.44
Celebrating Hindu Festivals by Respondents

Reasons	*Frequency*	*Percentage*
Being a Hindu	85	56.67
Custom of family	24	16.00
Force of the elders	15	10.00
Not celebrating	26	17.33
Total	**150**	**100.00**

Table-4.44 reveals that about 83 per cent of respondents celebrate Hindu festivals as against 17 per cent who do not. Among those who celebrate festivals 56.67 per cent says that they celebrate festivals as they belong to Hindu religion followed by 16 per cent as a custom of family. The remaining 10 per cent report that they celebrate the festivals for their elder's sake and force.

Table-4.45 reveal those who are not celebrating or have given up festivals say that they have converted to other religion (10 per cent) and which restrict them or acts against

Table-4.45

Not Celebrating Hindu Festivals by Respondents

Reasons	*Frequency*	*Percentage*
Religious conversion	15	10.00
Social awareness	9	6.00
Both	2	1.33
Not applicable	124	82.67
Total	**150**	**100.00**

the belief of their new religion. Another 6 per cent reported that the social awareness among them paved the way to give up traditional festivals which are based on superstition and blind belief. The rest (1.33 per cent) attributed it to both the reasons.

Table-4.46

Not Offering Sacrifices to God by Respondents

Reasons	*Frequency*	*Percentage*
Religious conversion	26	17.33
Social awareness	60	40.00
Offer sacrifice	64	42.67
Total	**150**	**100.00**

It customary among Hindus to offer sacrifices to certain types of Gods and Goddess. The form of sacrifice varying from caste to caste. The form and intensity of sacrifice is inversely related to caste status. Higher castes abstain from animal sacrifices. The lower and downtrodden castes believe more in animal sacrifice contrary to the above. Table-4.46 reveasl that about 57 per cent of respondents are against to the animal sacrifice during fairs and festivals. The reasons attributed was the religious conversion (17.33 per cent) and social awareness (40 per cent). However, 42.67 per cent report that they believe in and offer animal sacrifice to appease Gods and Goddess not only during fairs and festivals but also at times of personal or family distress.

Table-4.47
Respondents by Celebrations of Festivals, Jayanthis and Religious Ceremonies

Festivals, Jayanthis etc.	*Frequency*	*Percentage*
Festivals		
Dassara	110	73.33
Deepavali	100	66.67
Ugadi	85	56.67
Jayanthis		
Buddha Jayanthi	60	40.00
Ambedkar Jayanthi	90	60.00
Basava Jayanthi	45	30.00
Religious Ceremonies		
Manelli Mahamane	6	4.00
Dharma Deepa	30	20.00
Sathyanarayana Puja	45	30.00
Total	**150**	**100.00**

Table-4.47 reveals that 73.33 per cent of respondents celebrate Dassara festival, 66.67 per cent observe Deepavali festival and 56.67 per cent celebrate Ugadi festival every year. Similarly, considerable number have faith in great leaders and celebrates their birth anniversaries. 60 per cent of respondents celebrate Dr. B.R. Ambedkar's birth anniversary every year. Another 40 per cent celebrate Buddha Jayanthi. Only 30 per cent reported to observe Basava Jayanthi as a holy day.

In addition to the above, certain religious rituals are conducted at the individual household levels based on their needs and convenience. No fixed day common to all for such practices. For example Manelli Mahamane was observed by only 4 per cent of respondents. Another ritual called Dhamma Deepa was observed believe that by celebrating the above rituals they get peace, prosperity and health in the household and to its members.

Festivals and rituals are important occupation when friends and relatives meet and exchange greetings and gifts.

Table-4.48

Respondents by Participating in Upper Caste Religious and Festivals Celebrations

Reasons	*Frequency*	*Percentage*
Personal friendship	25	16.67
Social awareness	65	43.33
No caste feeling	34	22.67
Not attending	26	17.33
Total	**150**	**100.00**

Normally, such good will visits takes place among equal caste and persons. As the improvement in economic status and employment status, many lower castes enjoy the invitations from the upper and dominant castes. Table 4.48 reveals that about 83 per cent of respondents participate in upper caste religious and festivals celebrations. Among them 43.44 per cent opined that there is a general social awareness among the genera public, 22.67 per cent reported that there is a gradual decline of caste feeling among different communities. About 16.67 per cent attributed it to the personal friendship.

Table-4.49

Respondents by not Participating in Upper Caste Religious and Festivals Celebrations

Reasons	*Frequency*	*Percentage*
Caste restrictions	6	4.00
Lack of education	5	3.33
Caste feeling	15	10.00
Not applicable	124	82.67
Total	**150**	**100.00**

Table-4.49 reveals that 17.33 per cent never participate in the upper caste celebrations. The main reasons were caste feelings (10 per cent), caste restrictions (4 per cent) and lack of education (3.33 per cent) are main hurdles to participate.

5

Organisations and Social Change

Introduction

Since the Scheduled Castes themselves are the victims of several the atrocities of the higher castes, it will be note worthy to see how the various process of development of the organisations meant for their welfare and the ways and means adopted to meet the day to day challenges from the upper caste dominant society. In this chapter an attempt is also made to see how the scheduled castes organized themselves to fight against socio-religious disabilities, atrocities, caste-based discrimination and the economic exploitations, educational privileges and political power, etc. It also aims at understanding the nature and characteristic of these organisations and how the organisations contributed to bring about significant socio-economic and political changes among the scheduled caste and communities particularly in Gulbarga district.

It is generally believed that the caste plays dominant role in shaping the destinies of a person. In the Indian context, caste is indispensable. A person is born in one or the other caste. Society normally recognizes every person as belonging to and or the other caste. Persons born to inter-caste married couples are looked down and get treatment lower than the lower and scheduled castes. Such being the social recognition to a caste, it is very difficult to disown the caste tag by any member of the community.

Just like social hierarchy is associate to the caste system, so also with the occupations, ownership of assets, education, employment etc. it is undisputed and foregone conclusion that there exists a direct relationship between the addition to caste, kinship has a vital role to play in the development of their fellow beings. For instance, the kinship network's (caste organisation) contribution to uplift a paupered entrepreneur among Marwari community is a best example. This type of help is not new to the people in a community. Such help is not freely available to each and everybody in the community. The assistance from the kinsmen depends on several factors. They include, firstly, the relationship between the kith and kin. Secondly, the efforts of the person in the past to tied over such calamities. Thirdly, the personal behaviour and character of the person concerned. Foruthly, the person should have *Atma Gauravam* (Self-respect), such that the assistance should be returned in due course with gratitude. Fifthly, there should be good will relationship between the kith and kin. And finally, the person providing support should have a good economic base and high degree of leadership qualities.

Role of social institutions in reformation is well-documented. As mentioned above, though all scheduled castes are grouped under one category, they are not homogeneous groups. They differ in several ways. The prominent differences are the ritual status of the respective caste groups and the mode of interactions with the rest of the community. Over the years the above scenario has undergone gradual change in the lives of the people. In spite of all the changes one can find a number of factors which contribute to a distinct identity of a caste, one such distinct identity is the formation of caste organisations to protect the interests of its members. Thus, within the broader canvas of scheduled castes, there are several caste and/or sub caste organisations.

Several factors contribute to the development of an organisation. The encouragement from the fellow caste's men is necessary to have a firm foundation and for further development of caste or sub caste organisation. It is the network of kinship or relationship, which provides social, moral, physical and economic support for its development. In addition, external factors also play a major role in shaping the growth of an organisation. These external factors include links with political leadership, access to information, the personally traits of the leader like health, education, capabilities, etc play a dominant role in process of development of an organisation. In addition, the social and ecological factors, the economic factors are also important in deciding the forward and backward linkages for the development. The economic factors include occupational structure, assets structure, etc. It is common knowledge that the impact of an organisation for which it was intended will depend on how strong the organisation penetrate its roots and establish itself to withstand the strong forces working in the society. Since the scheduled castes themselves are the victims of several the atrocities of the higher castes, it will be note worthy to see the various process of development of the organisation meant for their welfare and the ways and means adopted to meet the day to day challenges from the upper caste dominant society. In addition an attempt is also made to see how the organisation contributed to bring the changes and improvement among the Scheduled Castes particularly in Gulbarga district.

In order to protect their interests and also fight against the atrocities of the upper castes, the scheduled castes unite together and formed an organisation. The scheduled caste communities are organizing themselves to fight against socio-religious disabilities atrocities, caste-based discrimination and the economic exploitations. They agitate for their legitimate right in economic opportunities, educational privileges and political power. Wide spread collective mobilization, centred around such interests, has led to the formation of social organisations with defined ideology and leadership, which have brought about significant socio-economic and political changes among the scheduled caste communities. By forming caste organisations, a process of social, economic, religious, educational and political awakening has been created among the scheduled castes, not only in Gulbarga district but also in the country as well.

NATURE OF ORGANISATIONS

Organisations of Scheduled Castes in Gulbarga

Dalit Sangharasha Samiti (DSS)

The nineteen-seventies were a turbulent time in India that spawned many social movements. B. Krishnappa and other dalit youths initially joined the *Samaj Wadi Ujal Sabha* (SWUS), Socialist Party Wing in 1972. this began supposedly as a general anti-caste movement, but it soon became clear that it was directed against Brahmins only. After many anti-Brahmin agitations, there was a split between Brahmins and shudras in this loose anit-caste federation.

Influenced by the literature of Lohia and Ambedkar, the dalit members of this shurda movement felt their main enemy was Brahmanical values and thinking, rather than the Brahmins *per se.* An ideological versus practical argument ensued. The shudra youth activists argued that Brahmins were the cause of untouchability, and that their dominance needed to be wiped out to improve the lot of the untouchables, yet, after land reforms most Brahmins vacated their landlord fields and migrated to the cities. The shudras themselves had become the dominant landed castes, Vokkaligas in south Karnataka and Lingayats in the north, and therefore the immediate oppressors. One year prior to the Emergency a rift occurred. The Dalit Sangharsha Samiti was formed in 1974. The young Dalit Panther movement[1]. This new social movement was aimed at both the caste system and the dalits' unique economic situation: they argued that social and economic equality must be fought for by dalits solely under their own leadership.

In 1978 the DSS took to the rural areas and agitations began. They focused primarily on what could be called "boundary crossing" politics: social taboos were broken when DSS activities in the company of dalit villagers drew water from the common wells, entered previously forbidden hotels and temples, and walked down streets reserved for upper caste people. They also staged land grab movements. Although Ambedkar's 'three commandments' were to 'educate, organise, and agitate' most of the early DSS activities were agitations. Other contemporary movements in India, such as West Bengal's Marxist and Naxalbari uprisings, had provided the DSS with a severe, possibly simplistic, and secular model for protest, one specifically rejected by Ambedkar. Krishnappa in one of the protest marches of the DSS said that, 'whether or not we dialogue with the upper castes we will be pacified [that is, repressed]. So, let us attack first'. As a consequence of these agitations, the atrocities on dalits also became common and the nineteen-eighties were full of burning in Karantaka[2].

The DSS has formed committees at several levels: state, divisional, district, block, taluk and village. Each of these has a core team of about fifteen and is represented by three functionaries: a Convener, an Organizing Convener and a Treasurer. Each committee ideally sets out its own constitution, in complement with the state level. The DSS has matured into the nineteen-nineties and has now spread across the state. Factions have also formed, some say more so between the leaders than among the cadres. The entire membership numbers into the thousands. Two main reasons are given for division in the DSS.

First, there are differences in opinion over alignment with formal political parties. A second source of contention is 'whether to take a hermeneutical and somewhat eclectic approach, or a strictly exclusive reading, of Ambedkar'. Here, factional lines tend to be drawn between educated and less-educated dalits; the latter are more likely to treat Ambedkar with the reverence as a guru.

Through the DSS, the direction for dalit struggle has filtered from the top to the bottom: from educated urban to illiterate rural, from top leadership down through the cadres and finally to the mass. Educated dalits, like Krishnappa, acknowledge that bottom-up flow of information would be ideal: however, since the rural people in Karnataka are illiterate, most activities believe villagers cannot understand their own exploitation. Further, activists stress it is difficult for villagers to organise resistance on their own behalf. DSS members realize increasingly, however, that education and organisation must coincide with agitation.

Owing to the personal differences of the leaders and to some extent the caste differentials, the DSS was split into several groups in Karnataka. At present there are three DSS organisations functioning in almost all the talukas of Gulbarga district viz., (i) Karantaka State Dalit Sangharsha Samithi led by Sagar [KSDSS (sagar)], (ii) Dalit Sangharsha Samithi led by Mavalli and Jayanna group [DSS (M&J)] and (iii) Dalit Sangharsha Samithi led by Murthy group [DSS (M)].

The scheduled castes of the state are in the lowest strata. They are Holeyas, Madiga, Dhor, Samagar, Bhovi, Lambani, Kormas Mang-Garudi are the members of the DSS. There are several Scheduled Caste Organisations in Gulbarga which put forth its efforts to bring social change, social awareness, and political consciousness among the scheduled castes. These organisations have passed through several stages witnessing both positive and negative developments not only in the growth of the organisations but also in their efforts to bring the intended change in the district, the present analysis is confined to only to eight organisations namely Holeya, Lambani, Madiga, Waddar, Samagar, Korcha, Dhor and Mang-Garudi.

In order to understand various dimensions of the Scheduled Caste organisations, a structured questionnaire was canvassed to the members of eight caste organisations and also to a few other respondents belonging to different organisations of the Scheduled Castes as a whole in Gulbarga district. The Table 4.1 (see Chapter 4) reveals that 118 (78.67 per cent) respondents were from 8 sub-caste organisations and the reaming 32 (21.33 per cent) were from the other branches of state level scheduled organisations located in Gulbarga district.

Table-5.1
Scheduled Caste Organisations in Gulbarga District

Sl. No.		*Caste Percentage*	*No. of Organisations*
1.	Holeya	38	25.33
2.	Lambani	21	14.00
3.	Madiga	25	16.67
4.	Bhovi	10	6.67
5.	Samagar	09	6.00
6.	Korcha	07	4.67
7.	Dhor	07	4.67
8.	Mang Garudi	01	0.67
9.	KSDSS (S)	10	6.67
10.	KSDSF (S)	10	6.67
11.	DSS (M&J)	7	4.67
12.	DSF (M&J)	4	2.67
13.	DSS (M)	1	0.67
	Total	**150**	**100.00**

Table-5.1 reveals that among the caste organisations 38 (25.33 per cent) have affiliated to the Holeya organisation followed by 25 (16.67 per cent) from Madiga caste organisation, 21 (14 per cent) from Lambani, 10 (6.67 per cent) from Waddar or Bhovi, 9 (6 per cent) from Samagar, 7 (4.67 per cent) each from Korcha and Dhor organisations. Only one (0.67 per cent) was from Mang-Garudi caste organisation. The remaining 32 were representing the main scheduled caste organisations in Karnataka which includes 10 (6.67 per cent) each from KSDSS (S) and KSDSF (S), 7 (4.67 per cent) from DSS (M&J), 4 (2.67 per cent) from DSF (M&J) and one (0.67 per cent) from DSS from each taluk.

Table-5.2
Respondents Position in the Organisation

Reasons	*Frequency*	*Percentage*
President	116	77.3
Vice-President	10	6.7
Secretary	10	6.7
Treasurer	0	0
Executive Member	14	9.3
Total	**150**	**100.00**

Table-5.2 gives the details of the positions held by the office bearers of the organisations. The composition of respondents consists of about 77.33 per cent of the presidents of organisations followed by 9.33 per cent of executive member and 6.67 per cent each of vice-president and the secretaries of the organisations.

Table-5.3
Motivation for Membership in the Organisation

Reasons	*Frequency*	*Percentage*
Own	30	20.00
Ideology of B.R. Ambedkar	60	40.00
Dalit Panther	35	23.33
Forced by Elders	20	13.33
Others	5	3.33
Total	**150**	**100.00**

There may be several factors which motivated the respondents to become members of scheduled caste organisations. However, Table 5.3 reveals the important motivating factors. Majority (40 per cent) of respondents becomes members influenced by the ideology of Dr. B.R. Ambedkar followed by Dalit Panther's ideology (23.33 per cent). Another 20 per cent became members on their own to serve their community and 13.33 per cent became members due to the pressures and persuasions from other members. The remaining 3.33 per cent became members with/or their own reasons.

Table-5.4
Objectives of the Organisations

Objectives	*Frequency*	*Percentage*
Economic	30	20.00
Political	45	30.00
Social	65	43.33
Other	10	6.67
Total	**150**	**100.00**

Table-5.4 reveals that majority of respondents (43.44 per cent) are of the view that the scheduled caste organisations were formed with an objective of attaining social quality in the community. Another 30 per cent are of the opinion that those organisations were formed to enter the politics so as to achieve the above objectives. 20 per cent of respondents believe that these organisations were established with an objective to improve the economic conditions of the scheduled castes and 3.33 per cent have no definite idea of the objective for which the organisations were formed.

Table-5.5
Mode of Resource Mobilization for the Organisation

Mode	*Frequency*	*Percentage*
Community Members	48	32.00
Caste elders	32	21.33
Govt. Servants	30	20.00
Political Leaders	30	20.00
Others	10	6.67
Total	**150**	**100.00**

For any organisations, financial resources are important to meet the day to day expenses. Table-5.5 reveals that one-half of the respondents say the majority contribution comes from community measures (32 per cent) and caste elders (21.33 per cent). Another 20 per cent each say that the political leaders and the government servants contribute to the organistion. 6.67 per cent of respondents believe that the organisation has also got other sources of revenue for meeting the needed finances.

Table-5.6

Mode of Support to the Organisation

Mode	*Frequency*	*Percentage*
Financially	48	32.00
Politically	42	28.00
Morally	55	36.67
Other	2	3.33
Total	**150**	**100.00**

Table-5.6 reveals that apart from the outside sources nearly one-third (32 per cent) of respondents also contribute to the functioning of the organisation. Among the rest, 36.67 per cent of respondents gave their moral support, 28 per cent supports the organisation politically and 3.33 per cent contribute in other ways. Thus all respondents contribute to the success of the organisation in one or the other way.

Table-5.7

Frequency	*Frequency*	*Percentage*
Daily	20	13.33
Weekly	30	20.00
Once in fortnight	35	23.33
Monthly	55	36.67
Occasionally	10	6.67
Total	**150**	**100.00**

In order to discuss the organisational issues and problems along with the issues conceiving the public, the office bearers of the organisation has to meet at regular intervals. Table-5.7 reveals that only a few people (13.33 per cent) meet daily. 20 per cent of respondents said that they assemble at the organisations office at least once in a week Table 5.7. Another 23.33 per cent reported that the office bearers meet once in a fortnight and a majority (36.67 per cent) said that they meet once in a month. The rest (6.67 per cent) reported their meeting occasionally. This shows that the members have constant touch with the organisation either or through other members.

Table-5.8
Mode of Communication from People

Mode of communication	*Frequency*	*Percentage*
Personal visits	30	20.00
Community people	60	40.00
Office bearers	50	33.33
Other means	10	6.67
Total	**150**	**100.00**

One of the main objectives of the organisation is to solve the problem of the people at community level. In order to achieve the objective, there should be a good communication links with the general community to know the daily happenings in the district. Table 5.8 reveals that majority (40 per cent) of respondents reported that community will send the message to the organisation to seek its interventions. In addition, 33.33 per cent reported that the office bearers manage to get the message and another 20 per cent of respondents reported that they will make personal visit to different parts of the district based on media information or to collect first hand information about the incidents or for general enquiry of the welfare of the people. Only 6.67 per cent say that the media and source of information.

Table-5.9
Mode of Communication to People

Mode	*Frequency*	*Percentage*
Handbills	54	36.00
Posters	46	30.67
Newspaper	12	8.00
Volunteer	38	25.33
Total	**150**	**100.00**

As mentioned above, it is necessary to have a good communication with the community. All decisions taken at the organisational level should reach the grassroots level activists and general people. In order to achieve this, the organisation has several mechanisms to ensure good communication with people far away from the information to the activists will be sent through the handbills. Another 30.67 per cent report the use of posters. 25.33 per cent of respondents say that the volunteers personally carry the message and deliver through small group meeting or informally. Only 8 per cent report the message will pass on to the general public through the media i.e. newspapers.

Table-5.10
Purpose of Respondent's Visits to the Organisational Headquarters

Reasons	*Frequency*	*Percentage*
Leaders of the Organisation	70	46.67
Caste leaders	45	30.00
Party leaders	30	20.00
Others	5	3.33
Total	**150**	**100.00**

Though the above type of communication may be relevant and effective it takes long time to reach the right people. In order to take quick decisions the members of the organisations have to visit the District headquarters or State headquarters. Table-5.10 reveals that 46.67 per cent of respondents visit the headquarters to meet the organisational leaders. Another 30 per cent make their visit to meet the caste leaders. Some of them also visit the headquarters to meet the party leaders (20 per cent) and others (3.33 per cent)

Table-5.11
Distribution of Respondents by Preference for Solving the Problems

Particulars	*Ranking*
Atrocity	3
Untouchability	1
Social boycott	2
Other problems	4
Total	**150**

Though there are several problems faced by the scheduled caste in Karnataka as well as in Gulbarga, the respondents have prioritized several problems as shown in the Table-5.11 which need to be addressed. Among them, the practice of Untouchability emerges on top which has to be addressed on priority followed by the issues related to social boycott, atrocities on caste people especially on women, and other related problems.

Table-5.12
Organisations Links with Political Parties

Reasons	*Frequency*	*Percentage*
Congress (I)	16	10.66
BSP	20	13.33
RPI	1	0.67
Others	40	26.67
Nil	73	48.67
Total	**150**	**100.00**

The organisations both at the state level as well as the district level were formed keeping certain issues on priority list. Table-5.12 reveals that more than half of the respondents reported that it will be useful if the caste organisations have tie up with one or the other political parties for speedy redressal of cases if any. Among them 13.33 per cent preferred BSP party followed by congress party (10.66 per cent). 0.67 per cent expressed their desire to have links with RPI and the rest (26.67 per cent) have no preference for a particular party. However 48.67 per cent were against any type of political affiliations.

Table-5.13
Against Organisation Links with Political Parties

Reasons	*Frequency*	*Percentage*
Social organisation	45	30.00
Cultural organisation	28	18.67
Not applicable	77	51.33
Total	**150**	**100.00**

Table-5.13 reveals that among those who opposed to have any links with political parties, 30 per cent expressed that these organisations were primarily established as social organisations and hence not a right decision to have links with the political parties. Another 18.67 per cent opposed as they felt these organisations were established for the cultural purposes.

Table-5.14
Merits of Organisations Links with Political Leaders

Particulars	*Frequency*	*Percentage*
Better links with Government	70	46.67
Strengthening the organisation	30	20.00
Both	25	16.67
We feeling	22	14.66
Nill	3	2.00
Total	**150**	**100.00**

Though the caste organisations were came into existence apolitically, majority of the members expressed the view that the political links will enhance the capacity of the organisation in several ways. Table 5.14 highlights merits of such linkages where 46.67 per cent of respondents reported that it bridges the gap between the decision makers in the government and the general public. Further, 20 per cent opined that such a type of linkage will strengthen the organisation's capacity both in terms of financial stability and ability to bargain for the deprived sections of population. Another 16.67 per cent subscribe to the above two views. 14.66 per cent felt that such a type of affiliation will create a sense of we feeling or feeling of belongingness among the members of different castes affiliated to an organisation. Only 2 per cent expressed reservation against any usefulness with such political links.

Table-5.15
Demerits of Organisations Links with Political Leaders

Particulars	*Frequency*	*Percentage*
Groupism and leads to divisions	61	40.67
Use to serve political ends	39	26.00
Destroy Activism	27	18.00
Keep safe Distance	18	12.00
Nil	5	3.33
Total	**150**	**100.00**

However few members expressed concern about the negative impacts of linking the caste organisation with the political parties as is evident from the Table-5.15. 40.67 per cent of respondents opined that it will lead to factionalism among the members of the organisation and leads to groupism and division of organisation based on political partly affiliations Table-5.15, another 26 per cent felt the politicians may misuse the organisation for their political ends. 18 per cent foresee the links may destroy the basic nature or essence of activism among the members and thereby the basic objective of reforming the community will remain as a dream.

Only 12 per cent suggested keeping the politicians at a safe distance and utilising their services whenever situations demands.

Achievements of Scheduled Caste Organisations

Contributions of macro-level SC organisations

In this section the contributions of the State level organisation which have their units in the Gulbarga district are analysed. The discussion pertains to the efforts of five organisations viz: KSDSS(S), KSDSF(S), DSS(M&J), DSF (M&J) and DSS (M).

Though Gulbarga District has a population of 610641 persons belonging to the Scheduled Caste, all of them are not the registered members of the organisations. However, they are emotionally attached to one or the other organisations. Many of them participate in several activities undertaken by these organisations. As mentioned earlier the organisations in the district have at least three district identities based on the nature of the location, affiliation to the leadership and caste affiliations. Table 5.16 below shows the extent to which different organisations, representing all Scheduled Castes irrespective of membership structure, have responded and solved the problems of the affected population in different talukas of the district.

The Table-5.16 reveals that K.S.D.S.S. (Sagar) organisation is effectively functioning in all ten talukas of Gulbarga district. Out of 390 problems in Shahapur taluk, Sagar organisation has resolved 51.28 per cent. These problems were related to the community and general problems like harassment by upper castes, practice of untouchability, atrocities, land disputes, temple entry, hotel entry and social boycott, etc. Similar problems were solved in other talukas. About 47.61 per cent of the reported problems were solved in Chitapur, 46.51 per cent in Chincholi, 46.05 per cent in Surpur, 41.38 per cent in Afzalpur, 40 per cent in Yadgir, 35.70 per cent in Aland, 28 per cent in Jewargi and 23.81 per cent in Gulbarga. Since the problems in Gulbarga taluk were addressed by several organisations by sharing informally as they were located in

Table-5.16

Organisations and Problems Solved by Taluk

Organisation	Taluka-wise Problems Resolved											
	Gul	*Ala*	*Afa*	*Jaw*	*Sha*	*Sur*	*Chit*	*Sed*	*Chin*	*Yad*	*Total*	*%*
KSDSS (S)	300 (30.00)	200 (45.45)	120 (54.54)	100 (33.33)	200 (54.05)	350 (47.30)	300 (52.63)	240 (46.60)	200 (48.78)	200 (51.14)	2210	44.97
KSDSF (S)	200 (20.00)	100 (22.73)	100 (45.45)	100 (33.33)	170 (45.95)	200 (27.02)	150 (26.32)	100 (19.42)	100 (24.31)	150 (42.66)	1370	27.88
DSSM (M & J)	200 (20.00)	80 (18.18)	—	100 (33.33)	—	150 (20.28)	120 (21.05)	75 (14.56)	80 (19.52)	—	805	16.38
DSF (M & J)	100 (10.00)	60 (13.64)	—	—	—	40 (15.40)	—	100 (19.42)	30 (7.31)	—	330	6.71
DSS (M)	200 (20.00)	—	—	—	—	—	—	—	—	—	200	4.06
	1000	**440**	**220**	**300**	**370**	**740**	**570**	**515**	**410**	**350**	**4915**	**100**

Gulbarga and hence each organisation has addressed a few cases.

K.S.D.S.F. (Sagar), is a sub organisation of KSDSS (Sagar). It resolved various problems of scheduled caste students in all ten talukas. The problems were related to issues like hostels, fees, room rent, scholarship, etc. taluk wise anaylsis shows that it has resolved more problems in Shahapur (43.59 per cent) followed by Afzalpur (34.49 per cent), Jewargi (28.58 per cent), Surpur (26.31 per cent), Chitapur (23.80 per cent), Chincholi (23.26 per cent), Yadgir (30 per cent), Aland (17.86 per cent) and 15.87 per cent in Gulbarga city.

DSS (M&J) is functioning only in seven talukas and not in the entire district of Gulbarga. The above table clearly indicates that the organisation has addressed about 28.58 per cent of scheduled castes problems and resolved them successfully in Jewargi taluk. Similarly, 19.4 per cent in Chitapur, 19.73 per cent in Surpur, 15.18 per cent in Gulbarga, 1860 per cent in Chincholi, 14.29 per cent in Aland and 11.81 per cent of problems in Sedam were resolved.

DSF (M&J) is a sub organisation of DSS (M&J) which primarily concentrate to address the problems of dalit students in Gulbarga district. It speareds its activities to five talukas in Gulbarga district. It was able to solve 7.93 per cent of the student problems in Gulbarga city and taluk. Further in Aland 10.7 per cent, in Surpur 5.26 per cent, in Sedam 15.74 per cent and Chincholi 6.97 per cent of the student's problems were resolved.

DSS (M) is an organisation which primarily concentrate to address the problems of dalit especially Dalit women particularly Devadasis and child and bonded labours. Its activities pertain to Gulbarga. It was able to solve 20 per cent of the problems in Gulbarga city and taluk.

Contributions of Micro-level SC Organisations

In this section the contributions of the district level sub-caste organisations which are analysed. The discussion pertains to the efforts of eight organisations viz: Holeya, Lambani, Mandiga, Bhovi Samagar Dhor, Korcha and Mang Garudi.

HOLEYA COMMUITY ORGANISATION

Table-5.17
Achievements of Holeya Community Organisations in Gulbarga District

Sl. No.	Taluk	DPI	SSD	SS Dal	KDSP	KDSS	KJSPMO	Total	Per cent
1.	Gulbarga	120	100	100	60	50	100	530	24.70
2.	Aland	70	80	20		40		210	9.76
3.	Afzalpur	50			50			120	4.66
4.	Jewargi	50		40	30			200	5.59
5.	Shahapur		100	20	80			125	9.32
6.	Surpur	20	50	30	25			175	5.83
7.	Sedam	40	40	35	40			285	8.16
8.	Chitapur	90	60	25	70	40		200	13.29
9.	Yadgir	100	80		20			200	9.32
10.	Chincholi	70	80		30	20		200	9.32
	Total	630	590	270	405	150	100	2145	
	Percen-tage	29.37	27.50	12.59	18.88	6.99	4.66		100.00

Table-5.17 reveals that the Holeya organisations have resolved 2145 cases in Gulbarga district. Out of which nearly one quarter (24.70 per cent) pertains to Gulbarga taluk, followed by Chitapur taluk (13.29 per cent). Of the remaining 9.32 per cent each in Alnad, Shapur, Yadgir and Chincholi the organisation's share in solving the cases is 9.32 per cent. Similarly, the organisation addressed the problems successfully to the extent of 8.16 per cent in Sedam, 5.83 per cent in Surpur, 5.59 per cent in and 4.66 per cent in Afzalpur.

Among the constituent organisations, it is the DPI which has solved 29.37 per cent of the total cases received in Gulbarga district by the sub caste organisations. SSD closely follow the DPI by resolving 27.50 per cent of the cases in the district. The share of or the contribution of KSDP is to the extent of 18.88 per cent followed by SS Dal with 12.59 per cent and RDSS with 6.99 per cent and KJSPMO with 4.66 per cent.

If one looks at the achievements of individual sub organisations within the Holeya caste the following picture emerges (Table 5.3). the distribution of cases resolved in each taluk by these organisations reveal that DPI emerged as the most successful organisation in Afzalpur (50 per cent), Chincholi (50 per cent) and Jewargi (41.67 per cent) talukas contribution to resolve 40 to 50 per cent of the cases. In other talukas like Yadgir (35 per cent), Chitapur (34 per cent), Aland (33 per cent) and Sedam (31.5 per cent) these organisations have contributed to resolve to the extent of 31 to 55 per cent of the total cases. Its pressure is felt in Gulbarga taluk to the extent of solving 22.64 per cent of cases as against in Surpur (16 per cent). In Shapur the DDI organisation has no branch.

The next important Holeya caste organisation in Gulbarga is the SSD which is working in 8 talukas. It has contributed to resolve 40 to 50 per cent of cases in Shapur, Surpur, Chincholi, and Yadgir. In Alnad it has resolved 38 per cent of cases and in Chitapur and Sedam 24 and 21 per cent respectively. It is more powerful in Shapur as compared to the Sedam taluk.

SS Dal, another Holeya organisation serving Scheduled Caste population in general and Holeya community in particular in seven talukas and contributed to resolve 270 cases of atrocities on scheduled castes. The taluk wise contribution of in Jewargi taluk by attending to one-third of the total cases reported in the taluk. Next, the organisation is prominently seen is Surpur where 24 per cent of the total cases of the taluk are attended followed by Chitapur with 20 per cent and Gulbarga with 18.8 per cent. In the remaining three talukas its contribution varies from 8 per cent to 10 per cent.

KDSP is also in important Holeya caste organisation in the district working in all talukas excepting Aland. It has resolved 405 cases far in the district. Among the talukas it shares 50 per cent of the cases reported in Afzalpur taluk with DPI organisation followed by 40 per cent in Shapur. Its presence is moderately found in talukas like Jewargi, Surupur, Chitapur and Sedam where it contributed to an extent of resolving 20 to 25 per cent of cases. Among the remaining talukas its contribution ranges from 10 to 15 per cent.

KDSS is a small organisation of Holeya community working in four talukas in Gulbarga distrct. Though it is small, its presence is very much evident in Aland taluk where it contributes to resolve 19.5 per cent of the cases reported in the taluk followed by Sedam taluk with 14 per cent. In the remaining talukas, the organisation has resolved 10 per cent of the cases in Yadgir and 9.4 per cent in Gulbarga.

KJSPMO is functioning in Gulbarga taluk only contributing its share in resolving 19 per cent of the total cases reported in the taluk. It contributes to an extent of resolving 4.67 per cent of the total cases of the district.

Both in terms of population and number of organisations, the Holeya caste is dominant caste group among different castes of the scheduled castes in Gulbarga district. In terms of organising protests, creating awareness among the public and to address the problems pertain to the scheduled castes in general and the Holeya caste in particular the Holeya caste organisations together form a major contributing force in the district.

Table-5.18
Achievements of Lambani Community Organisations in Gulbarga District

Sl. No.	*Taluk*	*RSSD*	*NBHO*	*BO*	*Total*	*Per cent*
1.	Gulbarga	20		35	55	5.5
2.	Aland	150		30	180	18.0
3.	Afzalpur		20		20	2.0
4.	Jewargi	50	30	50	130	13.0
5.	Shahapur	50	15	50	115	11.5
6.	Surpur	40		60	100	10.0
7.	Sedam	30		120	150	15.0
8.	Chitapur	20		30	50	5.0
9.	Yadgir	80		40	120	12.0
10.	Chincholi	60		20	80	8.0
	Total	500	65	435	1000	
	Percentage	50.00	6.50	43.15	100.00	

Table 5.18 shows that of the total cases addressed by the Lambani organisation, 50 per cent were resolved by RSSD in Gulbarga District. Of the remaining 43.15 per cent were resolved by BO and 6.5 per cent by the NBHO. Taluk wise analysis shows that except the NBHO which has concentrated only in three talukas, the other two have covered all the talukas excepting Afzalpur taluk. The distribution of cases resolved by these organisations across the talukas show that Aland tops with the distribution of solving 18 per cent of the problems by these organisations followed by Sedam with 15 per cent, Jewargi with 13 per cent, Yadgir with 12 per cent, Shapur with 11.5 per cent and Surpur with 10 per cent. In the remaining talukas, the importance of these organisations are to the extent of 5 to 8 per cent and the lowest reported in Afzalpur where only one organisation—NBHO—is working with an average of 2 per cent cases resolved to the total cases addressed by all these organisations in the district.

Table-5.18 reveals that there are three Lambani community organisations working in Gulbaraga district. Among them Rashtriya Banjara Seva Dal (RBSD) is functioning only in Shahapur and Gulbarga city. In Shahapur taluk it has resolved 43.48 per cent of the cases and in Gulbarga it resolved 36.37 per cent of the reported problems. This organisation had tried to resolve their community problems such as family, marriage dowry, divorce, land disputes, property disputes etc.

National Banjara Horata Organisation (NBHO) is another organisation of Lambani community in Gulbarga district. This organisation is working only in three talukas. Table 5.18 shows that through the organisational efforts, it had tried to solve number of problems of Lambani community in these talukas, i.e. 100 per cent in Afzalpur and Jewargi talukas and 13.51 per cent in Shahapur taluk.

Banjara Organisation (BO) is the third important Lambni organisation in Gulbarga district. It is effectively functioning in seven talukas, except Aland, Afzalpur and Jewargi. This organisation tried its level best to reduce the Lambani community problems. It is noteworthy to find the organisation has solved all problems related to the community in several talukas especially in Chitapur, Sedam, Chincholi, Yadgir and Surpur talukas. In Gulbarga taluk it has solved 63.63 per cent and in Shahapur 43.46 per cent.

MADIGA COMMUNITY ORGANISATIONS

Table-5.19 reveals that the Madiga caste organisation has addressed about 3570 cases in the district out of which

Table-5.19
Achievements of Madiga Community Organisations in Gulbarga District

Sl. No.	*Taluk*	*AJ*	*MRHS*	*MS*	*MRHSD*	*JYO*	*Total*	*Per cent*
1.	Gulbarga	200			210		410	11.48
2.	Aland	200	150	100			450	12.60
3.	Afzalpur	150	100				250	7.00
4.	Jewargi	150	200		150		500	14.00
5.	Shahapur	300	100				400	11.20
6.	Surpur	200	150				350	9.80
7.	Sedam	100	150			110	350	9.80
8.	Chitapur	120	200	50		30	400	11.20
9.	Yadgir	120					120	3.36
10.	Chincholi	250		40		40	330	9.34
	Total	1790	1050	190	360	180	3570	
	Percentage	50.14	29.41	5.32	10.09	5.04	100.00	

the AJ organisation emerges as most successful organisation contributing to resolve 50.14 per cent of the total complaints received by this caste organisation. The next is the MRHS organisation solving 29.41 per cent of the total cases. The remaining three organisations MRH&D (10.09 per cent), MS (5.32 per cent) and JY (5.04 per cent) together contributed to resolve the reaming 20 per cent of cases.

Taluk wise analysis of cases resolved by these organisations shows more or less uniform pattern across the talukas (Table 5.19). Excepting Afzalpur taluk (7 per cent) and the Yadgir taluk (3.36 per cent), in all other talukas the total cases reported as well as the cases resolved were in the range of 9 to 14 per cent and Yadgir taluk with 3.36 per cent.

Table-5.19 indicates that there are five Madiga community organisations functioning in Gulbarga district. They include Adi Jambava which is effectively working in ten talukas to fight against community problems like harassment by upper caste, practice of Untouchability, temple entry, land disputes, social boycott etc. the organisation has solved several cases which include 80 per cent in Jewargi taluk, 75.76 per cent in Yadgir, 75 per cent in Shahapur, 57.14 per cent in Surupur and 4.44 per cent in Aland effectively.

MRHS is another organisation of Madiga community which is functioning in Six talukas. It has resolved various problems like, student'scheduled caste hostels, education fees, room rent, reservation in government service, etc. Taluk wise statistics shows that highest problem were tackled in Sedam taluk (50 per cent) followed by Surpur (42.86 per cent). Chitapur (41.67 per cent), Aland where in, 40.00 per cent in Jewargi, 40.00 per cent in Aland and 22.22 per cent in Shahapur respectively.

Matanga Organisation is effectively working in Aland only and resolved their community problems to the extent of 22.22 per cent through the organisational efforts.

MRHDS: Madiga Dondor is another organisation which is functioning only in two talukas namely Gulbarga city and Aland. This organisation has facilitated to resolve 51.21 per cent of problems in Gulbarga and 22.22 per cent in Aland.

Jagjiwan Ram Youth Organisation is work in Chitapur and Yadgir only. Is also settled various problems of Madiga students and also their community problems. The organisation has resolved 42.31 per cent of problems in Chitapur and 30.80 per cent of problems in Yadgir taluk.

BHOVI COMMUNITY

In line with the general trend of forming cast based organisation in Gulbarga district, Bhove or Waddar community has also formed organisation in all talukas of Gulbarga district. So far these organisations have addressed 614 problems concerning the caste successfully.

Table-5.20
Achievements of Bhovi Community Organisations in Gulbarga District

Sl. No.	Taluk	Frequency	Per cent
1.	Gulbarga	100	16.29
2.	Aland	135	21.99
3.	Afzalpur	55	8.99
4.	Jewargi	40	6.53
5.	Shahapur	14	2.29
6.	Surpur	50	8.17
7.	Sedam	30	4.90
8.	Chitapur	40	6.53
9.	Yadgir	100	16.29
10.	Chincholi	50	8.17
	Total	**614**	**100.00**

Table 5.20 shows that Bhovi community organisation had addressed and resolved more number of problems in Aland taluk (135) followed by Gulbarga (100) and Yadgir (100) talukas. In the remaining talukas here were about 5 to 8 per cent of problems reported concerning their community, which were addressed successfully. Less number of problems was reported in Shahapur taluk constituting 2.29 per cent only. It is clear that the Bhovi community organisations are functioning in entire Gulbarga district. Most of their problems are concerned with the disputes among the community members, land disputes, marriage and dowry, problems of housing plots, house, etc, in addition to the general problems concerning the Scheduled caste as a whole.

Samagara Community

Like other Caste organisations, the Samagar Caste organisation war established to serve their interest. It has the branches in all talukas of Gulbarga district excepting Chincholi taluk. So far the organisation has received about 370 cases pertaining to community and general problems. The taluk level organisations have addressed all these problems successfully.

Table-5.21
Achievements of Samagar Community Organisations in Gulbarga District

Sl. No.	*Taluk*	*Frequency*	*Per cent*
1.	Gulbarga	80	26.62
2.	Aland	20	5.40
3.	Afzalpur	10	2.70
4.	Jewargi	10	2.70
5.	Shahapur	20	5.40
6.	Surpur	80	26.62
7.	Sedam	40	10.81
8.	Chitapur	30	8.10
9.	Yadgir	80	26.62
10.	Chincholi	-	-
	Total	**370**	**100.00**

Table-5.21 indicates that highest number of problems were resolved in talukas of Gulbarga, Surpur and Yadgir (26.62 per cent each) followed by Sedam 10.81 per cent and Chitapur 8.10 per cent. In Aland and Shahapur talukas, the caste organisation was able to solve 5.10 per cent each of the community's problems. Jewargi falls in last place where only 2.70 per cent of community problems were reported and resolved by the organisation.

Korcha Community

Table-5.22 gives a clear picture about korma community organisations in Gulbarga district. The organisation mainly

Table-5.22
Achievements of Korcha Community Organisations in Gulbarga District

Sl. No.	*Taluk*	*Frequency*	*Per cent*
1.	Gulbarga	60	23.53
2.	Aland	50	19.61
3.	Afzalpur	35	13.72
4.	Jewargi	-	-
5.	Shahapur	-	-
6.	Surpur	10	3.92
7.	Sedam	30	11.71
8.	Chitapur	30	11.71
9.	Yadgir	-	-
10.	Chincholi	40	15.68
	Total	**225**	**100.00**

focused its attention to solve such problems as pertained to the family, marriage, education, land disputes etc. It has its branch organisations in seven talukas. The absence of organisation in Chincholi, Jewargi and Shahapur is evident from the table. A total of 255 cases were reported from the community members from all over the district and the concerned organisations at the taluk level where the cases were reported were resolved smoothly. Organisation in Gulbarga city had resolved 23.53 per cent of various types of problems followed by Aland with 19.61 per cent, Chincholi with 15.68 per cent and Afzalpur with 13.72 per cent successfully. Another 11.71 per cent each of problems were solved in Chitapur and Sedam talukas. Only 3.92 per cent of problems were addressed in Surpur taluk.

Dhor Community

As mentioned earlier Dhor community is one of the smallest community in the district. In order to safeguard the interests of its members, the caste elders formed an organisation in Gulbarga city and latter spread over to another six talukas in the district.

Table-5.23
Achievements of Dhor Community Organisations in Gulbarga District

Sl. No.	*Taluk*	*Frequency*	*Per cent*
1.	Gulbarga	40	29.63
2.	Aland	10	7.40
3.	Afzalpur	-	-
4.	Jewargi	10	7.40
5.	Shahapur	-	-
6.	Surpur	5	3.70
7.	Sedam	15	11.11
8.	Chitapur	25	18.52
9.	Yadgir	-	-
10.	Chincholi	30	22.22
	Total	**135**	**100.00**

Table-5.23 reveals that the organisation so far received only 135 cases from the whole district which were solved by the concerned taluk level organisations. Of the seven talukas, Gulbarga has highest problems (29.63 per cent) which were resolved buy the organisation followed by Chincholi (22.22 per cent) and Chitapur (18.52 per cent). Among the remaining talukas 11.11 per cent of problems were in Sedam and 7.40 per cent each were in Aland and Jewargi which were addressed by the organisation. Only 3.70 per cent problems were reported and resolved in Shahapur taluk.

Mang Garudi Community

Of all the caste groups of scheduled castes in Gulbarga district, the Mang Garudi community has very less population and are most backward ones. Due to their backwardness and lack of proper education, the caste was unable to establish its organisations in different talukas of the district. Since it is a beginning for the community to come together on matters related to their community at the organisation's office in Gulbarga the community is hopeful of percolating into different alukas slowly. Sine four years of its origin, the organisation has received 100 complaints pertaining to the community problems like internal conflicts, etc. which were solved amicably.

Perception of Respondents

Though the organisation acts as a catalyst in resolving major problems encountered by the scheduled caste population, it also suggests settling such disputes amicably using the local resources.

Table-5.24

Mode of Settlement of Caste Disputes

Mode	*Frequency*	*Percentage*
Caste elders	65	43.34
Caste Panchayat	35	23.33
Police	20	13.33
Others	30	20.00
Total	**150**	**100.00**

Table-5.24 reveals that 43.34 per cent of respondents prefer the caste elders to intervene and settle disputes among the caste people and also with outsiders. Another 23.33 per cent extend the argument that the caste Panchayat should take initiative to solve such problems. While 13.33 per cent prefer the police action and the rest (20 per cent) prefer other modes of resolving such disputes.

Table-5.25

Types of Problems Resolved

Particulars	*Frequency*	*Percentage*
Atrocity cases	70	46.67
Social boycott	40	26.67
Land disputes	10	6.67
Caste conflicts	27	18.00
Nil/No problems	3	2.00
Total	**150**	**100.00**

It is interesting to see from the Table 5.25 that nearly 98 per cent of the respondents agreed that the caste organisations have involved fully in addressing the day to day issues pertaining to the problems faced by the members of the Scheduled Castes in the district. Nearly half of respondents (46.67 per cent) reported that they were involved in dealing with cases pertaining to atrocities on women followed by 26.67 per cent who resolved cases related to Social boycott. Another 18 per cent reported the Caste conflicts and land disputes by 6.68 per cent. All these problems were resolved by these organisations. In the absence of which, such problems continued to be unresolved.

Table-5.26

Campaign Against Social Problems

Particulars	*Frequency*	*Percentage*
Untouchability	75	50.00
Social boycott	30	20.00
Harassment	30	20.00
Not involved	15	10.00
Total	**150**	**100.00**

Members of these caste organisations involved in educating the general public on various issues related to illtreatment to the caste. Such campaigns not only empower the scheduled caste population, but also create a sense of responsibility and responsiveness to the problems of scheduled caste by the non scheduled caste population.

Table-5.26 reveals that 50 per cent of the members involved in campaigning to create awareness among the people about the problems of untouchability. Another 20 per cent each campaigned against social boycott and harassment to scheduled caste members. Only 10 per cent of the members of caste organisations have not participated in any of the campaigns.

Table-5.27
Type of Atrocities Against Scheduled Castes

Particulars	*Frequency*	*Percentage*
Caste conflicts	350	55.12
Temple entry	150	23.62
Hotel entry	50	7.87
Land dispute	60	9.45
Others	25	3.94
Total	**635**	**100.00**

Table-5.27 endorse the respondents claim that about 635 atrocities cases have reported. Among them more than half (55.12 per cent) relates to caste conflicts followed by restrictions imposed by higher castes against the scheduled caste for the entry to the temple in the village (23.62 per cent). Another 9.45 per cent cases related to land disputes and 7.87 per cent related to restrictions imposed against entry to the hotel. Only 3.94 per cent have one or the other types of cases reported to the organisation.

The education, economic, improvement and awareness among the scheduled caste population has resulted in more and more atrocities. This is mainly the intolerant nature of the higher and dominant caste population who expect the scheduled caste to be their slaves for ever.

Table-5.28
Reasons for Increase in Atrocities

Reasons	*Frequency*	*Percentage*
Consciousness	50	33.33
Self respect	35	23.33
Economic improvement	30	20.00
Higher position	25	16.67
Others	10	3.33
Total	**150**	**100.00**

Table-5.28 reveals that one-third of respondents (33.33 per cent) opined that the increasing consciousness among the caste population followed by self respect (23.33 per cent), economic improvement (20 per cent), higher position (16.67 per cent) and others (3.33 per cent) are responsible for increase in the cases of atrocities against the Scheduled Castes.

Table-5.29
Measures for Reducing Atrocities

Reasons	*Frequency*	*Percentage*
Educating people	50	33.33
Strictly following the rules	42	28.00
Strength of unity	35	23.33
Pressure on government	18	12.00
Others	5	3.33
Total	**150**	**100.00**

In order to reduce the atrocities on scheduled caste people, the respondents suggested several measures. Table-5.29 reveals that one-third of respondents (33.33 per cent) suggested that the general public should be educated such that they learn to treat their beings as humans. Similarly 28 per cent suggest to enforce the exiting rules strictly and punish the offender so that other will learn from such examples and 12 per cent suggests to bring pressure on the government to act properly and protect the interest of the scheduled caste population. About 23.33 per cent suggest that the community should get unite and show the unity among the members of the caste such that it will acts as a control mechanism to arrest the increasing atrocities on scheduled caste population.

Table-5.30

Measures for the Improvement of Community

Reasons	*Frequency*	*Percentage*
Education	55	36.67
Provide employment	40	26.67
Economic conditions	20	13.33
Political power	30	20.00
Other	5	3.33
Total	**150**	**100.00**

In addition to empowering the community, the organisations take several measures for the improvement of the community. Table-5.30 reveals that 36.67 per cent of the respondents reported that the organisation work for the educational improvement of the community. Another 26.67 per cent mention that it will facilitate to increase the employment opportunities for the unemployed youth of the community. While political empowerment was reported by 20 per cent of the respondents another 13.33 per cent reports that the organisations work for the improvement of the socio-economic condition of scheduled caste population. The remaining 3.33 per cent says that the organisation take several other measures which will have a bearing on the development of the community.

Table-5.31
Burning Problems of the Community in Order of Preference

Reasons	*Frequency*	*Percentage*
Untochability	60	40.00
Customary duties	40	26.67
Land disputes	30	20.00
Bonded labour	20	13.33
Total	**150**	**100.00**

The respondents identified and rated the burning problems faced by the scheduled caste population. Table-5.31 shows that 40 per cent of respondents reported that Untouchability as a major problem faced by the community. The next burning issue was reported by 36.67 per cent who highlighted the pressures to serve the dominant castes with the customary duties. Further litigation and land disputes (20 per cent) and continuation of bonded labour system (13.33 per cent), though not in its original form are the other problems faced by the Scheduled Caste population.

Organisational Efforts and Social Change

Though Caste organisations have helped to solve several problems related to the respective castes, it will be interesting to know how such efforts have really changed the lives of these people and the role played by these organisations. It will also be worth to learn the negative aspects of these organisations.

In the context of the present study author used the term social change, means economic, political, social, education, religious and cultural changes have taken place in the life of scheduled castes and communities through the impact of their caste based organisations.

There are five major schools of thinkers who had interpreted in the causes of social change. According to St. Augustine (354-430 A.D.) History is only an unfolding of a divine plan. According to August Comte (1798-1857), L.T. Hobhouse (1864-1029), Max Weber (1864-1920)[3] and Emile

Durkheim (1958-1917) the religion or culture is important in shaping social structure. Herbert Spencer (1820-1903) believed that an evolution in the society is bound to take place in the course of time. According to H.T. Buckle (1821-1862)[4] a change may take place in the society because of geographical factors including climate, food, soil, and other aspects. According to Karl Marx (1818-1888)[5] the mode of production determines the social structure. He thought that the social structure is but the by-product of the economic structure. It is not the 'intellect' or 'idea' but the pattern of economic production and distribution which shape the structure of a given society.

Thus, it means that there are two extreme views in this respect, one giving importance to personal factors like reason, morality, ability and one's notion of right or wrong: an other giving importance to impersonal factors like divinity, environment and economic condition.

In the view of Dr. B.R. Ambedkar both the personal as well as impersonal factors are important in bringing about social change. However, he thought that the personal factors in this respect. He said very categorically that, it is "quite wrong in holding the impersonal forces are everything and that man is no factor in the making of history". The fact that the impersonal forces are determining factor cannot be denied. But one must also admit that the effect of impersonal forces depends on man. Man therefore, is a factor whether impersonal or social, if they are the first, are not the last things[6].

Table-5.32
Need for an Organisation

Reasons	*Frequency*	*Percentage*
Improve caste people	40	26.67
Unity	70	46.67
Both	15	10.00
Not required	25	16.66
Total	**150**	**100.00**

Table-5.32 reveals that a large majority of respondents (93.34 per cent) expressed their desire to have an organisation which will facilitate for the improvement of caste members. Among them 46.67 per cent felt the need for an organisation in order to bring unity among different castes followed by 26.67 per cent for the improvement of general population and 10 per cent for both the improvement and unity among the members. On the contrary, about 17 per cent expressed their reservation against the need for Caste organisation.

Table-5.33
No Need for an Organisation

Reasons	*Frequency*	*Percentage*
Disunity	20	13.33
Caste organisations will progress	5	3.33
Not required	125	83.34
Total	**150**	**100.00**

Table-5.33 reveals the main reasons against the formation of an organisation. Among them 13.33 per cent feared that it will lead to the disunity among the members and 3.33 per cent felt that such organisation will not progress.

Table-5.34
Increase in Awareness Among Scheduled Caste

Particulars	*Frequency*	*Percentage*
Education	60	40.00
Unity	40	26.67
Modernisation	20	13.33
Nill	30	20.00
Total	**150**	**100.00**

Table-5.34 reveals that 40 per cent of members reported that the organisation have played positive role in educating the general public about the need to treat the scheduled caste population with due respect. Similarly, 26.67 per cent of respondents felt that these organisations have enabled its members along with the other depressed community to fight unitedly against atrocities and any such torchers inflicted upon scheduled caste population. Another 13.33 per cent of respondents high lighted the significance of caste organisation which has facilitated its members to modernize their way of thinking, behaviour and the way of life which in itself protect them. The remaining 20 per cent says that the organisations have not created awareness among the people.

Table-5.35

Lack of Awareness Among Scheduled Castes

Particulars	*Frequency*	*Percentage*
Lack of education	20	13.33
Superstition	10	6.67
Nil	120	80.00
Total	**150**	**100.00**

On the contrary to the above proposition table-5.35 reveals that the caste organisations have not changed the lives of the scheduled caste population as majority of them lack formal education and are illiterate (13.33 per cent). 6.67 per cent of respondents reported that they are living with superstitions and as such these organisations are unable to create mass awareness among the Scheduled Castes.

Table-5.36

Elders Support for Organisations

Particulars	*Frequency*	*Percentage*
Full support	60	40.00
Partial support	30	20.00
Both	10	6.67
Nil	50	33.33
Total	**150**	**100.00**

In order to be a successful organisation, the support from all related corners is a necessary. So also for the caste organisations of the Scheduled Castes. Table-5.36 reveals that three fourth of the respondents reported that the elders from all the downtrodden castes have extended their support. Among them, 40 per cent have supported the organisational efforts fully. Another 20 per cent reported to have extended only a partial support. Another 6.67 per cent of the respondents felt that the organisation is functioning with a moral support from the concerned caste.

Table-5.37
Elders Non-support for Organisations

Particulars	*Frequency*	*Percentage*
Not supported	30	20.00
Lack of interaction	10	6.67
Negligence	10	6.67
Nil	100	66.66
Total	**150**	**100.00**

Table-5.37 reveal that about 20 per cent of the respondents reported that the organisations are not working on the support and advice of the caste elders. The other reasons were lack of proper interaction (6.67 per cent) and due to negligence (6.67 per cent).

Table-5.38
Members Meet of Special Occasions

Reasons	*Frequency*	*Percentage*
Ambedkar Jayanthi	70	46.67
Budha Poornima	30	20.00
Jagajeevan Ram Jayanthi	20	13.33
Others	30	20.00
Total	**150**	**100.00**

Table-5.38 reveals that since several respondents became members on the basis of the ideology and influence of great leaders and hence it is imperative for them to celebrate their birth or/and death anniversaries. Table 4.38 reveals that 46.67 per cent of respondents celebrate Dr. B.R. Ambedkar's Jayanthi, followed by 20 per cent who celebrate Buddha Poornima in hnour of Bhddha's Nirvana and 13.33 per cent celebrate Jagajeevan Ram Jayanthi. The rest (20 per cent) celebrates or participate in these celebrations.

Table-5.39

Change in the Status of Scheduled Castes

Particulars	*Frequency*	*Percentage*
Education	60	40.00
Modernisation	25	16.67
Westernization	5	3.33
Nil	60	40.00
Total	**150**	**100.00**

Table-5.39 reveals that 40 per cent of respondents are of the opinion that the change could be brought among scheduled castes by improving their educational status 22.66 per cent felt that change chould be brought by providing a suitable employment. Another 20 per cent suggested modernising the life styles of the scheduled caste population and 13.33 per cent propose to wsternize their culture so that the higher caste will accept them though not immediately but in due course. In this direction another 4 per cent have no idea as to what can bring changes in the status of scheduled caste per cent population.

Table-5.40

No Change in the Status of Scheduled Castes

Particulars	*Frequency*	*Percentage*
God fear	20	13.33
Superstitution	15	10.00
Rigidity of Hinduism	25	16.67
Not applicable	60	20.00
Total	**150**	**100.00**

Here suggestions will not translate themselves into actual practice. It is the community which should have the jeal to transfer. Table-5.40 reveals the various factors affecting the change of status. About 16.67 per cent attribute it to the rigidity and Hinduism followed by God fearing nature of scheduled caste population (13.33 per cent) and superstitions (10 per cent). However 20 per cent of respondents are positive in the sense they don't agree on the argue and say status will improve in due course.

Notes and References

1. Jogdand P.G. (1991), "Dalit Panther Movement in Maharashtra" Kanak Publications, New Delhi, p. 90.
2. Gokhale (1990), *Janakala Mela*, A Souvenir Published by DSS, Bangalore, pp. 51-52.
3. Dronberger IISC (1971), *The Political thought of Max Weber*, Meredith Corporation, New York, p. 55.
4. H.T. Buckle (1964), Development of Social Thought.
5. Sabine G.H. (1961), *History of Political Theory*, Oxford Publishing Company, Calcutta, p. 21.
6. Ambedkar. B.R. (1991), *What Congress and Gandhi have done to the Untouchables?* Vol. 9, Government of Maharashtra, Bombay.

6

Elites and Organisations

Introduction

This chapter introduces the opinion of the caste elites on the status of the scheduled caste organisations working in Gulbarga district. The views of these elites pertain to not only the positive side of the organisations but also to their negative impacts, in addition their suggestion for the improvement of these organisations is also dealt here.

The history of any society needs to be reviewed and reassessed in its real perspective. The shining deeds of the actors in the history would serve as a beacon to their fellow caste men. If the role played by such actors is ignored, their dedication to the cause would go into oblivion and the society would lose its guiding spirits in finding the future path. In order to have a holistic picture of the organisations, it is proposed to know the perceptions of the elites among the scheduled castes, with special emphasis on the role of organisation and leaders individually and collectively for the brining social changes among their communities.

In the following paragraphs an attempt is made to review important works on the concept of elite and its relevance in the context of the Scheduled Castes. In a review like this the prime task would be to thrash out significant theoretical issues which could be ought to bear upon the empirical fact for the purpose of validation of existing knowledge which in turn provides relevance and meaning for the findings of the present scientific inquiry. In the present research investigation, the author has selected only the social, political administrative and intellectual elites for the study.

Scheduled Castes Elites

In the present study, the term 'elites' means senior people or influential persons among the Scheduled Caste and communities. Gaetano Mosca (1939) has narrated that in all societies, there are two classes of people where one class that rule and another class that is ruled. The ruling class is always a minority but performs all political functions, monopolises power and enjoys all the advantages. While the second category–the ruled, is though more numerous, they are directed and controlled by the first. The minority is the ruling class and attaches great deal of importance to the political formula by which it is able to perpetuate in power and control the society[1].

Operationally, the elite are those who use intellect and rational judgment while participating in the decision making process and occupy some position of trust and responsibility. Vilfred Pareto (1963) contributing to the theory of elite said that in every society there are people who possess in a marked degree, the qualities of intelligence, character, skill, capacity of whatever kind[2].

Bottomore (1966) analysed five types of elites who control or influence the society: They include the revolutionary intellectuals, the nationalist political leaders, the military officers, the government officials and the businessmen. It becomes clear from the above that the elite generally belong to the following categories. They are political elite, administrative elite, intellectual elite, business elite, elite of special skill (like artists, film stars, religious heads and military elite[3].

Individuals in every society are stratified into various groups and such groups are reckoned as castes in some societies and classes in others. From each of such groups, one can see that few individuals may be preeminent in a particular field and enjoy good status. Due to such preeminence, the individuals may gain the recognition in various fields like political, administrative, educational, jurisprudence, medical, engineering, religious etc. these individuals or group of individuals constitute the elite in the society[4].

In every activity and every corresponding sphere of social life, there is elite. In fact, this is the sense in which Pareto had used this term. There is however, an important factor that differentiated these various elites, apart from their different skills and talents; some of them have more social weight than others because their activities have greater social significance. It is these elites–variously referred to ruling elite, the top influentials, or the power elite which arouse particular interest because they are the prime movers and models for the entire society.

In every differentiated society, there are patterns of belief and values, shared means of communication, major social institutions, and leading individuals or groups concerned with the maintenance and development of the society and its culture. These leading elements, by focusing attention and coordinating action, help to keep the society in working order, so that it is able to mange recurrent crises in collective life. The varied and differentiated groups of elites can be classified in terms of their strategic functions. They are: goal attainment, adaptation, integration and pattern maintenance. Goal attainment refers to the setting and realization of collective goals, adaptation refers to the use and the development of effective means of achieving these goals, integration involves the maintenance of appropriate moral consensus and social cohesion within the system, and finally, pattern maintenance and tension management involve the morals of the system's units, individuals groups and organisations.

Among the above four types of strategic elites one can identify a large number of elites. They include the political elite (under the category of elites of goal attainment), the economic, military, diplomatic and scientific elites (elites of adaptation), elites exercising moral authority-religious leaders, philosophers, educators, and social workers (elites of integration) and elites that keep the society knit together emotionally and psychologically, consisting of such celebrities as outstanding artists, writers, theatre and film stars, and top figures in sports and recreation (pattern maintenance elites). Societies, however, differ in the way they corporate these functions into living institutions. In few societies, usually at simpler states of development one agent assumes responsibility for all four system functions whereas in others, several specialized agents emerge[5].

The provision of special privileges to the scheduled castes has created opportunities in various fields like political, educational and administrative. In order words several opportunities have been provided to this section of the society to improve their position and attain the status as equivalent to the rest of the community in the society if not the higher status. Since this section of the population were traditionally meant to live for serving the upper castes and on no occasions were they to use their intellect in serving themselves since there were no organized efforts. Thus, the emergence of caste organisations has provided an opportunity for the first time to the organisation's leaders to enter into the inner wheels of power and authority. In this study it is proposed to explore how the scheduled caste leaders are emerged as a force to bring changes in the overall status or livelihoods of the scheduled caste population in various fields like social, economic, political, administrative, intellectual and other professional areas in Karnataka state in general and Gulbarga district in particular.

Caste organisations also play an important part in enhancing the status of the caste. Through this, they seek to resolve their corporate status dissonance. Some of them may even desire to project their distinct and separate ethnic identity so that they may claim advantages for the community and also act as pressure group. In Gulbarga city and district there are Branches of state level scheduled caste organisations and eight major scheduled castes organisations formed in Gulbarga district, to uplift their brethrens and the communities.

However, whatever the views expressed as elites leaders of their own community will slowly percolate into the larger masses of people. May be the study of the elite gives us a picture of the shape of things to come for the entire scheduled castes in Gulbarga and district. Being educated and thereby comparatively more enlightened than the rest of the community, they are better equipped to perceive social change and also to take better advantage of the various concessions and ameliorative measures taken by government for them. They are also better able to articulate their feelings and formulate their views, aspirations, demands or grievances. But it is strange to find most of these senior elites have not associated themselves actively with the organisational activities.

Opinions of Scheduled Castes Elites towards Caste Organisations

Views of a cross section of elites were collected on various dimensions of the organisations working in Gulbarga district. The main purposes of eliciting the views of the elite are many fold it will throw light on the existing scenario of different organisations their past history, policies and programmes. The mode of operation, the pit falls and corrective measures required for strengthening the organisations. A simple questioner was conversed to have their views on the history of these organisations their objectives, mode of working, nature of its leaders, reasons for success and failures, corrective measures needed for the improvement organisations, etc. In addition, a free, frank and open discussion was also held with them to get other insights. Such a detailed discussion was very useful as it was an eye opener to the author on several aspects which were not covered or not possible to cover with a structured questionnaire. A simple of 40 persons from different walks of life was selected.

Table-6.1
Sample of Elites by Caste

Particulars	*Frequency*	*Percentage*
Holeya	13	32.50
Madiga	10	25.00
Lambani	7	17.50
Waddar	3	7.50
Korcha	2	5.00
Dhor	2	5.00
Samagar	2	5.00
Mang Garudi	1	2.50
Total	**40**	**100.00**

Table-6.1 reveals that of the total elite respondents majority (32.50 per cent) are from the Holeya caste followed by Madiga 25 per cent, Lambani with 17.50 per cent, Waddar 7.50 per cent, The Korcha, Dhor and Samagar with 5 per cent each. Only 2.50 per cent of respondents are from Mang Garudi caste.

Table-6.2
Elites by Profession

Particulars	*Frequency*	*Percentage*
Political leaders	10	25.00
Caste leaders	9	22.50
Social workers	8	20.00
Government officials	6	15.00
Teachers	4	10.00
Lawyers	3	7.50
Total	**40**	**100.00**

In terms of their professional background, the elites are from different walks of life who command respect not only from their caste and from the other Scheduled Castes but also from other non scheduled castes in the society. Table-6.2 highlights that one-fourth (25 per cent) of the sample elites respondents are the local political leaders. Of the remaining 22.50 per cent are the Caste leaders or headmen, 20 per cent are the Social workers, 15 per cent are the Government officials, 10 per cent are Teachers and 7.50 per cent are the practicing Lawyers.

Glorifying past is a common in all spheres of life so also in the case of the organisations of the past. Almost all respondents were of the opinion that the organisations established during the life time of Dr. B.R. Ambedkar were committed to the principles and objectives for which they were established or formed.

Table-6.3

Nature of Organisations of the Days of Dr. B.R. Ambedkar

Particulars	*Frequency*	*Percentage*
With committed followers	11	27.50
Self protective	12	30.00
People follow the leader	17	42.50
Total	**40**	**100.00**

Table-6.3 depicts the views of the elites about the nature of the organisations formed during the life time of Dr. B.R. Ambedkar. A large majority (42.50 per cent) are of the opinion that the followers of the organisations of the past were following the leaders without questioning. Nearly one-third (30 per cent) of respondents mentioned that the members were self protective and the rest (27.50 per cent) opined that the members of the past organisations had a commitment.

Table-6.4

Motivation for Membership in the Organisation

Reasons	*Frequency*	*Percentage*
Bring socio-economic change	17	42.50
Bring awareness	11	27.50
Bring unity	3	7.50
Volunteers persuasion	9	22.50
Total	**40**	**100.00**

The elite expect that the quality of members in the organisation should be high as it will enhance the strength of an organisation to fight against the evil practices prevailed in the community. Table-6.4 revels that about 42.50 per cent of elite respondents reorted that the various organisations enrolled the members mainly to bring socio economic changes in the society. Another 27.50 per cent joined the organisation with a hope to bring social awareness among the masses. Another 22.50 per cent of people joined the caste organisations due to the persuasions of the volunteers and the activists of the organisations. The remaining 7.5 per cent joined the organisation to bring unity among different sections of people in the society.

Table-6.5

Reasons for Non-membership in the Organisation

Particulars	*Frequency*	*Percentage*
Personality clashes	1	2.50
Disrespect to others	3	7.50
Ideological difference	1	2.50
Other	4	10.00
Not applicable	31	77.50
Total	**40**	**100.00**

However there are people who never become members of any organisation. Table-6.5 highlights various reasons for not enrolling themselves as members of the caste organisations. 7.5 per cent of the respondents were of the opinion that the leaders of organisations show disrespect to others. Another 2.50 per cent each reported that the personality clashes and ideological difference as main reasons for not becoming members. About 10 per cent respondents gave other reasons like lack of time, money, distance etc. as main factors for non membership in the organisation.

Table-6.6
Difference in Managing the Organisation due to Generation Gap

Particulars	*Frequency*	*Percentage*
Youths do not take suggestions	3	7.50
Lack understanding	26	65.00
Less prominence to elders	8	20.00
Youths work for common goal with understanding	3	7.50
Total	**40**	**100.00**

The elite were of the opinion that there is a wide gap between the older generation and the younger generation in managing the affairs of the caste organisations or the state level organisation. Table-6.6 supports the view and also endorses it with specific reasons for the same. A large majority (65 per cent) of respondents reported that the younger generation lack proper understanding of the problems. They give little importance to the elders and do not take the elders suggestions (20 per cent). Only 7.5 per cent reported that many young work for the common cases with a better understanding of problems.

Table-6.7
Mode of Functioning of Office Bearers

Particulars	*Frequency*	*Percentage*
Work as per aims and objectives	14	35.00
As per directions of the leaders	5	12.50
Own decision	3	7.50
No	18	45.00
Total	**40**	**100.00**

For an organisation to be result oriented it should have a committed workforce or people who work with devotion. Table 6.7 reveals that, it was about 35 per cent of respondents who reported that the office bearers work as per the aims and objectives of the organisations. Another 12.50 per cent of elites reported that the office bearers are working as per the directions of the leaders. About 7.50 per cent respondents has reported that the functionaries and office bearers take independent decision with bothering to the views of others members. On the contrary, 45 per cent expressed that these functionaries will never bother thc welfare of the people and do not work as per the guidelines of the organisations.

Table-6.8
Reasons for Office Bearers not Functioning as per Aims and Objectives of the Organisations

Reasons	*Frequency*	*Percentage*
Not aware of aims and objectives	2	5.00
Acting on the directions of the leaders	4	10.00
Own decision	10	25.00
Other scheduled caste influence	2	5.00
Work as per guidelines	22	55.00
Total	**40**	**100.00**

A proper understanding of the objectives and the aims for which an organisation is built is essential for all the members including the functionaries. Table 6.8 reveals that about 25 per cent of the respondents through know the rules and regulation but take their own decision without bothering about the organisations objectives. Another 10 per cent of the respondent reveals that the functionaries and the other members work as per the leader's decision. About 5 per cent expressed the view that the organisation's functionaries and the members have no proper knowledge or understanding of the rules and regulation of the organisations. And work accordingly another 5 per cent reported that in spite of knowing the rules, they work as influenced by others. More than half (55 per cent) of the respondents reported that the members of the office bearers of the organisations have the knowledge of aims and objectives for which the caste and sub-caste organisations were formed and work accordingly.

Table-6.9
Opinion about the Leaders of the Organisations

Particulars	*Frequency*	*Percentage*
Broad minded leaders	4	10.00
Social commitment	10	25.00
Selfish leaders	25	62.50
Other	1	2.50
Total	**40**	**100.00**

The composition of the ruling group is a reflection of the outcome of the organisation. If the organisation is run by committed and selfless leaders, such an organisation thrives better and achieve its aims and objectives. Table-6.9 depicts a glory or dismal picture of the composition of caste and sub-caste organisations in terms of the qualities of the leaders. About 62.50 per cent of respondents were of the opinion that the leaders of caste and sub-caste organisations were selfish. However the rest have social commitment (25 per cent) with broad mindedness (10 per cent) and has other good qualities (2.50 per cent).

Table-6.10
Opinion about the Office Bearers of the Organisation

Particulars	*Frequency*	*Percentage*
Full time workers	16	40.00
Part time workers	6	15.00
Honest and Dedicated workers	8	20.00
Non-responsive	10	25.00
Total	**40**	**100.00**

Contrary to the above, the office bearer of these organisations seems to be move committed to the cause in spite of their ignorance of the aims and objectives of the organisation as compared to the leaders. Table 6.10 reveals that three fourth (75 per cent) of the office bearers are dedicated to the cause as against one fourth (25 per cent) who seems to be non responsive to the issues. Among those who are very responsive a majority (40 per cent) work full time for the cause of the down trodden as against 15 per cent who work as and when they find leisure. The remaining 20 per cent are honest and dedicated workers who sacrifice their energies for the development of Scheduled Castes.

Table-6.11
Use of Office by the Office Bearers of the Organisation

Particulars	*Frequency*	*Percentage*
Using properly	29	72.50
Using as a force to show strength	2	5.00
Misusing for personal gains	9	22.50
Total	**40**	**100.00**

Table 6.11 shows that in pursuing the cause, nearly three fourth (72.5 per cent) of the elites reported that the soffice bearers are using their office properly. Another 5 per cent were of the opinion that the office bearers use their office as a force to show their strength. The remaining 22.5 per cent expressed their dissatisfaction against the office bearers because they misusage their office for the personal gains.

Table-6.12

Ability of the Organisation to Protect the Community

Particulars	*Frequency*	*Percentage*
Community interest	20	50.00
General interest	3	7.50
Individual interest	9	22.50
Not protecting	8	20.00
Total	**40**	**100.00**

Under the divergent interest of the leaders and the office bearers, it is interesting to know how far the organisation really protects the interest of the community. Table 6.12 reveals that more than three fourth of the elites were of the view that these organisations were able to protect the interests of the community. Among them, 50 per cent reported that the organisations were able to protect the community's interest as against 7.5 per cent who reported that these organisations look after the general interest. Nearly one fourth (22.50 per cent) felt that the organisations are able to satisfy the individual interests. However, 20 per cent were of the opinion that these organisations were not able to provide any protection to the community.

Table-6.13
Inability of the Organisation to Protect the Community

Particulars	*Frequency*	*Percentage*
Negative attitude about community interest	4	10.00
Negative attitude about general interest	2	5.00
Negative attitude about individual interest	2	5.00
Not applicable	32	80.00
Total	**40**	**100.00**

Table-6.13 endorses the existence of few deficiencies in the organisation to protect the community. The main reasons seem to be negative attitude of the leaders of the organisation about the community interest as reported by 10 per cent of elites. Another 5 per cent each say lack of general interest and the individual interest.

Table-6.14
Leader's Knowledge about the Organisation's Objectives

Particulars	*Frequency*	*Percentage*
To eliminate social evils	13	32.50
Improve socio-economic conditions	16	40.00
Acquire political powers	5	12.50
Create educational awareness	4	10.00
Others	2	5.00
Total	**40**	**100.00**

Every organisation has a goal to achieve. Such goals vary with the type of organisations. The organisational leaders contribute for the welfare of the society and work for the welfare of the people. Since these organisations were established to serve the downtrodden population of the society, the leaders have to support such organisations. In order to support any organisation's efforts, the leaders have to understand the objectives of such organisations.

Table-6.14 reveals that 40 per cents of respondents are of the opinion that the leaders knew the fact that the caste organisations in Gulbarga District were established to improve the economic conditions of Scheduled Caste population. These organisations also strive to eliminate social evils in society (32.50 per cent). About, 12.5 per cent of respondents were of their opinion that the leaders are aware that these organisations were established with an objective for acquiring political power in the district as well as in the State and the country. Another 10 per cent felt that the organisation's main objective was to create awareness among people and educate them to be the better citizens of the country. Only 5 per cent of elites have not specified the objectives of the organisations.

As mentioned earlier, the elites and the elders of the community are the important source of providing guidance and advice during emergencies. Though many of the elders are not the members of the organisations but their involvement in support of the organisations is noteworthy.

Table-6.15
Organisations Seeking Elite's Advice

Particulars	*Frequency*	*Percentage*
Social boycott	10	25.00
Atrocities	22	55.00
No	8	20.00
Total	**40**	**100.00**

Table-6.15 reveals that more than half (55 per cent) of the organisations seek the advice of the elites to take suitable preventive measures regarding atrocities on the scheduled caste population. Another 25 per cent reported that the organisations seek the advice of the elders in order to curtail the problem of social boycott. However, 20 per cent of the elites reported that the organisations never seek their advice.

Table-6.16
Organisations not Seeking Elite's Advice

Particulars	*Frequency*	*Percentage*
Lack of cooperation	2	5.00
Misunderstanding	3	7.50
Neglecting seniors	3	7.50
Not applicable	32	80.00
Total	**40**	**100.00**

Table-6.16 highlights the reasons for the passive attitude of functionaries towards the elites. 5 per cent of elites reported that lack of cooperation in the organisation. The remaining 7.50 per cent each reports that the misunderstanding and neglecting the senior citizens are the main reasons for not seeking the elite's advice.

Table-6.17
Nature of Working of Organisations

Particulars	*Frequency*	*Percentage*
Fighting for real causes	25	62.50
For getting social justice	4	10.00
Fighting for power within organisation	10	25.00
Others	1	2.50
Total	**40**	**100.00**

One of the ways by which an organisation can be evaluated is the way one is functioning. Table 6.17 reveals that the organisations were working towards fulfilling the real causes (62.50 per cent), and securing social justice (10 per cent). In fighting among the members within the organisation in order to gain power was reported by 2.5 per cent of the respondent. Only 2.5 per cent expressed that these organisations also engage themselves in other activities.

Table-6.18
Mode of Solving the Problems

Particulars	*Frequency*	*Percentage*
By comprise	26	65.00
By police force	9	22.50
By government intervention	5	12.50
Total	**40**	**100.00**

In order to achieve the objectives, the organisations have chosen several methods. Table 6.18 reveals that a large percentage of respondents (65 per cent) reported that the organisations settle the issues and problems through compromise. Another 22.50 per cent reports that the issues will be settled with the intervention of the police and the rest (12.50 per cent) expressed the view that the problems have to be solved through the government's intervention by pressuring it to enact or bring suitable policy legislations for the protection and welfare of the Scheduled Castes.

Table-6.19
Elites Perception of the Organisation

Particulars	*Frequency*	*Percentage*
As social organisation	16	40.00
As politial organisation	14	35.00
As self-protecting organisation	9	22.50
Others	1	2.50
Total	**40**	**100.00**

It was generally believed that the caste organisations are meant for fighting against the upper caste and dominant groups in the community. Contrary to the above view the Table-6.19 reveals that 40 per cent of elite respondents consider the caste organisations function like a social organisation followed by 35 per cent who labeled them as political organisations. Another 22.50 per cent were subscribing to the general view where the organisations act as a self protecting institution. Only 2.50 per cent reports it differently.

Table-6.20
Expectations from the Office Bearers of the Organisation

Particulars	*Frequency*	*Percentage*
Greater need for mutual understanding	12	30.00
Possessing self respect	20	50.00
Selflessness qualities	8	20.00
Total	**40**	**100.00**

It is quite natural for people to expect the functionaries of any organisations to conduct themselves in a disciplined way. The elite group (respondents) appreciates the way the office bearers behave with the people. It is evident from the Table 6.20 that half of the respondents (50 per cent) view the office bearers work with self respect and another 20 per cent reports that the office bearers posses selfless qualities, which are essential qualifications for a social worker). Nearly one-third (30 per cent) of the respondents expect the office bearers to work with a greater concern and by mutual understanding of the circumstances while dealing with people.

Table-6.21
Elite's Views on Organisations Functions

Particulars	*Frequency*	*Percentage*
Unable to resolve real problems	7	17.50
Create misunderstanding among the members	10	25.00
Create awareness the members	21	52.50
Others	2	5.00
Total	**40**	**100.00**

The functioning of the caste organisations are many fold. Table 6.21 reveals various dimensions of the issues or problems where the organisations have to tackle with care. Majority of respondents (52.50 per cent) were of the opinion that the organisations strive to create awareness among the members of the Scheduled Castes to fight for their rights. More than one third of the respondents criticise the organisations for not addressing the real problems. Among them 25 per cent report that the organisations are creating misunderstanding among members by not giving clear picture of the problem and 17.50 per cent opined that the organisations fail to solve the real problems faced by the Scheduled Castes. Only 5 per cent have no opinion about the problems faced in functioning of the organisations.

Table-6.22
Organisations Attachment with the Political Parties

Particulars	*Frequency*	*Percentage*
To get politicians support	11	27.50
To enter politics	8	20.00
To get power (man bring change)	8	20.00
Not attached	13	32.50
Total	**40**	**100.00**

In a democratic society the politics plays an important role in decision making. The politics and programmes of the government are influenced by the political parties. Table 6.22 reveals that about two-thirds of the elite respondents expressed their supports the organisations to have a formal link with political parties. Among them 27.50 per cent reported that the existing organisations in Gulbarga have links with the political parties in order to get their support to solve the problem or to initiate developmental activities for the community etc. another 20 per cent each reported to enter into politics and to get power in order to bring structural changes in the society. However nearly one third (32.50 per cent) of respondents reported that the caste and sub-caste organisations have not attached to any political parties.

Table-6.23
Organisations Non-attachment with the Political Parties

Particulars	*Frequency*	*Percentage*
It is a social organisation	5	12.50
It is a caste organisation	6	15.00
It is an independent organisation	2	5.00
Other	27	67.50
Total	**40**	**100.00**

Table-6.23 gives the reasons against the organisations allying with the political parties, 15 per cent of respondents believe that these organisations are based on the caste and alignment with political parties may lead to division within the caste for political ends or dividing caste on political party basis. Such a move will not help to solve the caste problem as it ends up with disunity and factionalism in the organisation. Similar views were endorsed by another 12.50 of respondents who opined that these are social organisations. The rest (5 per cent) were of thc opinion that these organisations are independent and any external interventions will create problems for the very existence of the organisations.

Table–6.24
Factors Responsible for Rise Caste Organisations

Particulars	*Frequency*	*Percentage*
Divide and rule policy of the upper castes	11	27.50
Selfish interest of leaders	23	57.50
To show of strength of leaders	5	12.50
Others	1	2.50
Total	**40**	**100.00**

Increase or multification of organisations is a positive sign of development provided the multiplication takes place vertically. If such mortification takes a horizontal shape, parallel organisation mob up based on protest and conflates among the leaders on several grounds. One can see the growth of scheduled caste organisations in Gulbarga district both horizontally and vertically based on the lines of the state level development.

Table 6.24 reveal the opinions of elites for divisions and sub divisions of organisations in the district. 27.50 per cent of respondents say that it was the policy of upper castes who wanted to rule the lower and scheduled caste population by dividing them into smaller units. The role of internal factors such as selfish interest of the leaders (57.50 per cent) and to show the strength of a disappointed leader (12.50 per cent) are more responsible for the divisions within the caste and sub-caste organisations. Only 2.50 per cent reported that these organisations split due to various other reasons like personal difference among the leaders or ideological difference etc.

Table–6.25
Dimensions of Organisation Performance

Particulars	*Frequency*	*Percentage*
Bring we-feeling	23	57.50
Knowing each other	4	10.00
Discuss their problems	1	2.50
Creating superior and inferior feeling	8	20.00
Conflict of power	2	5.00
Abuse each other	2	5.00
Total	**40**	**100.00**

Table-6.25 reflects the opinion of the elites on the organisation's capabilities to influence the people. Majority of elites (57.50 per cent) were of the view that these caste organisations have brought a sense of we-feeling among the followers irrespective divisions among them. Another 10 per cent reported that these organisations have created a platform for the people of both within the caste and across the castes to know each other. Only 2.5 per cent felt that these organisations were instrumental in providing a space for the people or members to discuss their various problems and look for solutions. On the contrary 30 per cent of the respondents have highlighted the negative direction of these organisations. Among them 20 per cent opined that these organisations have created divisions among castes based on superior and inferior feelings and the remaining 5 per cent each reported conflict of power and abusing each others respectively.

Table-6.26
Performance of Organisations

Particulars	*Frequency*	*Percentage*
KSDDS(S)	23	57.50
DSS (M&J)	8	20.00
DSS (M)	1	2.50
MRHS	4	10.00
Lambani	1	2.50
Others	3	7.50
Total	**40**	**100.00**

Though there are several organisations working for the welfare of Scheduled Castes in Gulbarga district, only a few are functioning properly. It is evident from the Table-6.26 that a large majority of elites (57.50 per cent) expressed their satisfaction of the KSDSS(S) organisation and appreciate the efforts of its leaders and functionaries for their dedicated and selfless service to the downtrodden community. Next to KSDSS(S) organisation, the elites commended the functionaries of DSS (M&J) organisation, which got the appreciation of 20 per cent of respondents who observe these organisations closely. Among the rest of the organisations, 10 per cent of elite respondents rated the MRHS organisation as one of the good organisations working effectively followed by DSS (M) and Lambani (2.50 per cent each). The rest (7.50 per cent) related a few other miscellaneous organisations in the district working for the deprived population.

Table-6.27

Proposal to merge different caste organisations

Particulars	*Frequency*	*Percentage*
Through committed leaders	9	22.50
Learn to give respect to others	8	20.00
Protect sub-caste interest	1	2.50
Involve leader from religious, caste elders, politicians, youth organisations	2	5.00
Not possible	20	50.00
Total	**40**	**100.00**

In the wider interest of the downtrodden castes and communities elites suggested that the various organisations should came together and work unitedly. Trough the elites wish to unite these organisations, their opinion is divided on the issue of possibility of merger equally. Table-6.27 reveals that 22.50 per cent of the elites favour for a possible to merge different subgroups as the leaders are committed. 20 per cent opined that the functionaries of the organisations have learned to respect each other and hence it will be convenient for a merger. Another 5 per cent felt that the merger will possible by involving the leaders from religious institutions, caste elders, politicians and youth organisations. The remaining 2 per cent felt that by protecting caste interests, the unity and merger among different groups of caste organisations is possible.

Table-6.28
Proposal Against the Merger of Different Caste Organisations

Particulars	*Frequency*	*Percentage*
Lack of committed leaders	9	22.50
Increase of selfish nature	3	7.50
Vote bank of political leaders	8	20.00
Total	**40**	**100.00**

Table-6.28 reveals that half of elite respondents feel that there is no possibility of merger of different caste organisations. 22.50 per cent of elites felt that the merger was a difficult task due to lack of committed leaders. 7.50 per cent were of the opinion that these leaders were highly selfish in nature. Further, 20 per cent of respondents pointed out increased political concern of the leaders to have their own vote banks come in the way of merging different caste organisations in the district for a common cause.

Notes and References

1. Gaetano Mosca (1939), *The Ruling Class*, McGraw-Hill, New York, p. 49.
2. Vilfredo Pareto (1963), *The Mind and Society*, The theory of general Society, Rower Publishers, New York, pp. 516-519.
3. Bottomore. T.B. (1956), *Elite and Society*, Middle Sexs, Penguin.
4. Y.B. Abbayasulu (1978), *Scheduled Caste Elite*, Booklinks Corporation Narayana Guda, Hyderabad, p. 17.
5. S. Akinchan (1995), *Caste and Class and Politics*, Emerging Horizons of Political Sociology, Gyan Publishing House, New Delhi, p. 247.

7

Conclusion

Summary of Findings

The statement of the problem of the present study entitled "Organisations of Scheduled Castes and Social Change", covers various dimensions of Scheduled Caste crganisations. The organisations were evolved due to historical reasons. Before going for further analysis of the problem it will be relevant to understand the social structure of Indian society, more prominently, the caste system in India. Here an attempt is made to apply the structural and functional theoretical frame work for the study of organisations of scheduled castes in Gulbarga. And at the same time institutional framework as conceived by Parsons has been also taken into consideration in the presentation of the data about scheduled castes communities and their organisations.

It is generally believed that the caste plays a dominant role in shaping the destinies of a person. In the Indian context, caste in indispensable. A person is born in one or the other caste. Society normally recognizes a persons belonging to some caste. Such being the social recognition to a case, it is very difficult to disown the caste tag by any member of the community.

Indian society is heterogeneous, wherein people belonging to various castes and communities reside. The people of Indian society are divided on the basis of castes.

Caste system is based on Varna system where the Brhamins are at the top of the hierarchy, followed by Vysyas, Kshatriyas and Sudras. In the traditional setup a person in the society pay and get respect based on one's caste. At the top of the hierarchy are the Brahmins who enjoy all privileges and the bottom of the hierarchy are the Scheduled Castes who were denied the basics of life and are the untouchables in the society living in a condition beyond reporting. Those people who were outside the Varna system were known as Avarnas or Antajas or Panchamas or Chandalas. They are external in the sense that they were required to stay outside the village settlement. The concept of pollution attached to them and they were treated as untouchable castes. Those people belonging to the last Varna namely the Sudra and Avarnas include many caste groups which have suffered social and economic inequality since the ages.

To identify the 'Depressed Classes' the term 'Untouchables' was first used by the Maharaja of Baroda before the Depressed Classes Mission of Bombay in 1909. these castes were systematically listed in the 1931 census of India. These untouchable castes in India were officially defined as depressed castes in 1932.

The then British officials used the term 'Scheduled Castes' in 1932 and finally, in 1935 as recommended by thc Simon Commission, the term 'Scheduled Castes' was adapted by the British Government as a substitute to all other words hitherto used for identifying the 'Untocuhables'. The term 'Harijan' meaning' Children of God' was first Used by Narasingh Metha, a Gujarati saint poet in the 19th century and popularized by Gandhiji to refer to the people of untouchable castes in India. The constituent assembly used the word scheduled castes, while drafting the constitution. Scheduled caste means such castes, race or tribes parts of groups within such castes, race or tribe or tribe as are deemed under Article 341 to be the scheduled castes for the purpose of the constitution of India.

Scheduled castes are backward socially, economically, politically, educationally, and culturally. Therefore, the constitution gives special protection of them. Under Article

46 of the constitution, it is the responsibility of the state' to promote with special care the educational and economic interests or the weaker sections of the people, and the scheduled castes and scheduled tribes in particular and to protect them from social injustice and all forms of exploitation.

Scheduled caste is part and parcel of Indian society. It is further divided into non scheduled caste Hindus and scheduled castes Hindus. For nearly two thousand years the practice Untouchability had been rooted in the social and religious life of the country. In terms of residence, housing, health condition, social economic, education political awareness too backward and poor. In most villages, they to suffer residential segregation and in towns also it is difficult for even well-to-do members of the scheduled cased to get a house in decent residential locality. On account of their poverty and unhygienic living conditions, they suffer from malnutrition, physical disabilities and diseases such as tuberculosis, leprosy, malria, venereal diseases, etc., in large numbers. Scheduled castes were in minority all over the India, especially in villages. Caste Hindus, therefore, found it easy not only to exploit them but also to harass their women folk.

Although constitutional guarantees are seen as an ideal opportunity to achieve caste mobility, the extent and nature of such mobility varies from one ex-untouchable caste to another. Castes with low in their social status are also those which are economically poor and vulnerable.

In order to bring these untouchables into the main stream society, several reformists like Raja Ram Mohan Roy, Jothi Rao Phule, Mahatma Gandhi, Narayana Guru, Dr. B.R. Ambedkar and others, the governments both the British and the Independent India have brought several policy and welfare measures especially the Constitutional privilege and many voluntary organisations strive for overall development of Scheduled Castes. In spite of all these measures for over a century, there is not much improvement in several spheres of Scheduled Castes especially in the social and religious aspects.

For several decades the general mass among the Scheduled castes were unble to protest against the illtreatment and other forms of harassment. It was only after Dr. B.R. Ambedkar intervention, the momentum of protest to ascertain their rights took a formal shape. The inspiration from the national leaders to unite and fight has led to the formation of several organisations among the Scheduled Castes. These organisations aim to fight against inequality, discrimination, social boycott, inhuman treatment and deprivation. These organisations violently agitate for their legitimate share in economic opportunity, educational privileges and political power. Widespread collective mobilisation centered on such interests, has led to the rise of several Scheduled Caste and sub-caste organisations in all states of India including Karnataka State.

Just like social hierarchy is associate to the caste system, so also with the occupations, ownership of assets, education, employment etc. It is undisputed and foregone conclusion to say that there is a direct relationship between the ritual status of caste and the economic development or social development.

Study of organisations is not a new phenomenon. There are scholarly several studies focusing on various dimensions of organisations. Organisations emerge due to various factors. Organisations can be classified based on the purpose for which they are established like social, cultural, literary, voluntary, political, protest, religious and reformation organisations, caste organisations, trade union organisations, etc. it is very difficult to trace the origin of these organisations because it emerge with the history of the primitive man. The process of its development is seen along with the development of human civilization itself. Today we find an organisation at the bottom of small community to that of an international level. Every organisation has a specific purpose or objective for the improvement or protection of the interests of its members.

The process of international organisation had its origins in the nineteenth century, largely in Europe. Industrial development, improvement in transportation and communication, urbanization, trade and commerce, education and advancement of science and technology etc. laid foundation for several types of organisations. The first to emerge were the International Telegraphic Union (1865), Universal Postal Union (1874) etc.

The major characteristics of these organisations are: International in nature, show the supranational characters, mainly deal with issues related to war, collective security, fight against racial discrimination, to protect the human rights, poverty alleviation and fight against gender discrimination, etc.

In the Indian context, the formation of organisation can traced to pre-historic and Vedic period. However the reflection of the development of Organisations at the International level during Nineteenth and twentieth centuries is also witnessed in the Indian context.

After the Independence in addition to the existing ones several new organisations were emerged keeping their interest in mind. Even the older organisations have modified their objectives to suite to the Independent Indian Context. The fruits of Independence have not percolated to all sections of the society equally. The ruling class which was numerically insignificant started cornering all benefits. It took several years to the general mass to realize the magnitude of the problem. Gradually protests started at various levels with both organized and unorganized. At the organized level the important were the Trade Union Organisations, Peasant organisation, Caste and community Organisations, Student organisations, Backward Class and Minority Organisations, etc. In addition, the country is witnessing a strongly organized protest movement for the rights of the downtrodden and neglected lot. These include People's War Groups in Andhra, Nexalbar Organisation in West Bengal, Mahoits in Bihar, Tamil Elam and Dravida Kazagam in Tamil Nadu, Dalit Panthers in Maharastra, Bodo and Kuki Organisations in Assam and Nagaland, Bheem Sena in Karantaka, Maharastra, Andhra and West Bengal.

Though there are variations across different organisations, all are to some extent cater to the welfare of the community in general and the members of the organisations in particular. In the present context this study address on the protest Organisations which emerged to fight against age old evil practice of caste system in India especially among the Hindu social order. Further, these organisations also evolved to secure social justice, equality and fraternity to the oppressed and depressed castes and class in the society.

Discrimination' is a part of human life. Discrimination is found in all societies, however they are developed. The nature of discrimination varies from society to society. Karnataka is the premier state in India where the question of inequality and resultant backwardness of communities or caste groups came to be addressed trough protective discrimination.

Post-independent India has been a witness to many developmental measures for the welfare of the ex-untouchables. These have been in the form of administrative, political and legal concessions. Popularly known as the policy of reservations, they have been an important constitutional means of attacking inequality between castes. The inhuman practice of Untouchability was also abolished through Art. 17 of the constitution. Creation of new institutions like the Social Welfare Department, National Commission for Scheduled Castes and Scheduled Tribes and the policy of reservations has succeeded in integrating low caste people into institutions at a higher level. Thus change is thrust both from above and with people's participation from below with the reviving of the Panchayat institutions.

Formation of scheduled caste and sub caste organisation in Karantaka/Gulbarga is an attempt to mobilize the masses, through their castes men, to fight against exploitation of all sorts prevailing within the caste system. An attempt in made by the scheduled castes to improve their political bargaining power, to elevate their collective status and to enable members of caste to raise the upward mobility of the group. In Gulbarga district major scheduled castes like Holeya, Madiga, Lambani, Bhovi, Samagar, Dhor, Korcha and Mang-Garudi have formed their own caste organisations and a few state level Scheduled

Caste organisations like KSDSS (S), KSDSF (S), DSS (M&J), DSF (M&J) and DSS (M) are also functioning in the district.

The caste organisations have attempted to bring some structural and cultural changes even among the Scheduled Castes and to some extent they have facilitated to narrow down the social distance between the castes among the scheduled castes by coming together and living an association life.

Though many sociologists and social anthropologists have studied different castes and communities, no study has attempted to analyse the significance of sub-caste organisations. The review of literature has shown the following gaps: 1. There seems to be wide gap between the theory and the ground level scenario; 2. The role of caste leaders and their contribution was restricted to the State or national level neglecting the district and more importantly the grassroots level leaders; 3. The role of multiple organisations at the district level and the interface between these organisations with the state level organisation; 4. Implications of factionalism on the development of the community; 5. The linkages or the networking of organisations and their positive and negative implications on the community.

The study has to a large extent fulfill the above research gap through critically examine, understand and determine the nature and type of changes that have taken place in all spheres and are continually taking place among these castes in Gulbarga district through the organisations. The study has also examined the socio-economic conditions, political education awareness among these castes. Each sub-caste has tried to establish its own organisation. Sub-caste based organisations are emerging in the present context are on a rise.

Gulbarga District is chosen for the study just not because of the familiarity of the district but also owing to the specific reasons. They include: 1) In Karnataka state Gulbarga district has higher concentration of scheduled castes, 2) Scheduled castes of Gulbarga are influenced by Dr. B.R. Ambedkar's ideology and philosophy, Sri B. Shyam

Sunder's revolutionary thoughts and Jyothibha Phule's principles and 3) Gulbarga district has more number of scheduled castes organisations representing various castes and sub-castes within the broader canvas of the 'Scheduled Castes'.

There are about 101 castes and sub-caste which are listed under scheduled caste category in the Karnataka State. For the present purpose the author has selected the state level scheduled caste organisations DSS and its sub groups which have their units any where in Gulbarga district. In addition eight sub-castes of scheduled castes in Gulbarga district were selected. They are Holeya, Lambani, Madiga, Bhovi, Samagar, Korcha, Dhor and Mang Garudi. On an average each taluk in the district has thirteen scheduled castes organisations which were functioning at the time of the commencement of the study. In order to understand these organisations the author has chosen one executive member from each organisation for an in depth investigation. Thus 118 respondents were selected from the 10 talukas of the district. In addition 32 persons representing the State level organisations located in Gulbarga district were randomly chosen taking the total sample size to 150. In addition, 40 key informants, who are the 'Scheduled Caste Elites', were chosen to have information on not only the functioning of the Scheduled Caste and sub-caste organisations but also the holistic picture of the problems of the organisations, issues of leadership, inter and intra organisational relations, the corrective measures required to strengthen these organisations for effective functioning etc.

Since the approach is holistic in nature, the scheduled castes organisations has been studied in terms of its various dimensions such as nature organisation and its functioning, objectives, achievements and failures, its links with the other institutions like the social, economic, religious and political etc. In order to substantiate the primary data, an effort is also made to collect secondary data from various sources. The main source of information available from Gazetteers, Census reports, Articles in Journals and community studies was collected and suitably documented. Primary data was collected by using two types of interview schedules-one for the organisational functionaries and the other for caste elites.

An in-depth analysis of the physical, Historical Demographic and social background of the Gulbarga district reveal that the total geographical area of Gulbarga district is 16224 sq. km. Amongst the 27 districts of Karnataka state, Gulbarga happens to be the second largest and ranks next to Bijapur. According to the 1991 census, the total population of Gulbarga district is 2,582,169 persons and since there are ten talukas in the district the average population of a taluk comes to 258,217 persons. It terms of population size, Gulbarga ranks first and Chitapur follows as a second, while Afzalpur occupies the bottom most, i.e., the tenth place. The population of Gulbarga taluk alone which is 523,481 accounts for 20.29 per cent of the total population of the district where as the population of Chitapur taluk (309,481) constitutes 11.99 per cent. The other taluks Surpur, Yadgir and Aland which are fairly large in geographical area and have above average population. Surpur is in fact the second largest taluk. The population of these three talukas form 31.62 per cent of the total population of the district. The remaining 36.10 per cent of the population of the district is shared by five talukas including Jewargi, the taluk with the largest area. It terms of population size, Jewargi holds the eight place while Sedam and Afzalpur hold the ninth and the tenth places respectively. The population of these three talukas constitutes 7.32 per cent, 6.32 per cent and 5.84 per cent respectively of the district total.

Organisational structure of scheduled caste organisations has a distinct identity based on location, sub caste, and the alliance to a leader. Accordingly there are several organisations with common objectives functioning at several levels like State, District, taluk and the village, At times there will be two or three factions of the same organisation working at a place.

Among the eight scheduled castes or communities in Gulbarga district, Holeya community has highest number of organisations (38) constituting 32.20 per cent organisations functioning in different talukas in Gulbarga. The second widespread organisation represents the Madiga community with 25 branches (21.19 per cent) functioning in all parts of the district. In terms of its membership which accounts to 21.63 per cent among the total scheduled castes, the organisational representation of 21.19 per cent supports the fact that the community has organised itself proportionately to fight against the external aggression. The Lambani community has a strength of second largest scheduled caste population (23.29 per cent) in the district has an organisational strength of only 17.80 per cent. Mang Garudi community is lowest in number of organisations and the membership with 0.85 per cent and 1.16 per cent respectively.

Though several changes have undergone in the society, still age old practices continue. Among several forms of ill-treatment, the Untouchability is one and the social boycott is the other which are attributed to the rigid social system, lack of social awareness etc. The scheduled caste people have to face the wrath of the upper caste population when the castes men claim additional facilities or pressurise the upper caste on any such occasions. The upper casts impose and enforce social boycott on the scheduled caste households or persons if such household or person go against the traditional way of behaviour like the issue of temple entry, entering a hotel in their village etc. Since the respondents belong to socially and economically backward or underprivileged group, making a decent living becomes a luxury.

The sample households have a total population of 667 persons of which 366 (55 per cent) are females and 301 (45 per cent) are males. The average family size in the village is 4.5 persons per household. There are large number of nuclear families among the respondent's households, which is a reflection of growing individualism in the community.

Age wise distribution of population of the sample households reveals that nearly half (46 per cent) of the total population are above 31 years of age. Another 22 per cent of the population is between the age group of 21 to 30 years. People between 11 to 20 years constitute 19 per cent and the remaining 14 per cent of the population are below 10 years of age.

More than half of the population in the village is married. About 34 per cent are unmarried and 4 per cent are widowed. The normal age of marriage for boys is 20 years and for girls 18 years. However under compelling circumstances the age at marriage is lowered to 15 years for a girls and 17 years for a boys.

A large percentage of respondents are literates. Among them majority have studied up to degree course (43.33 per cent) followed by professional course and high schools (16.67 per cent each). There are 10 per cent of respondents studied in post graduate colleges and those who studied in primary school and illiterates are 6.67 per cent each.

The literacy level among the parents of the respondents shows an opposite trend where a large percentage were illiterates. Between father and mother, the illiteracy was high in case of mothers (82 per cent) as compared to the fathers (66 per cent). Among the literates most of them have not crossed primary school level and only a few has high school education.

When one looks at the total literacy level of the households of the respondents, the picture is not very optimistic as about one-third of the members of the respondents households are illiterate. Among the literates 22.5 per cent have studied up to primary level. 20 per cent high school and the remaining 19 per cent are functional literates.

The low level of education among the scheduled castes population is mainly due to the following factors: A large proportion of population could not pursue higher education due to the poverty (40 per cent). Another 20 per cent were not attended the school due to neglect of their parents and 13.33 per cent reported the illiteracy and their socio-economic background, etc as main cause for not pursuing education.

After independence several facilities are provided to impart education to the general public. Special provision was also made to the scheduled castes by way of free facilities in schools and colleges and also in government hostels. In spite of all these, the improvement in the educational levels among the scheduled caste is not encouraging. In order to get good education and hostel facilities people from the rural areas have to go to the towns and cities for higher education. It may not be possible for everyone to make there own arrangements. Nearly half of the respondents have to depend on outside facility for their lodging and boarding during their studies like the government hostels (14 per cent) and in the rented accommodation (16.67 per cent). Thus, in spite of the government facilities a large proportion of scheduled caste students depend on non-governmental accommodation and food during their studies.

The ways measuring political participation is in terms of people exercising their vote without any fear or pressure. 22.67 per cent who vote under pressure, all others exercise their franchise without fear. Social awareness, educational development and the political will or awareness are some of the factors for political participation of large percentage of SC population. Among those who reported to have undergone stress and strains while voting and reported that it was both due to pressure from the upper caste and their educational backwardness.

The distribution of respondents who contested to the elections to different positions reveals that it is a small proportion as compared to their population in the district. It was only 3 persons (2 per cent) contested to the assembly elections, 10 persons each contested to Zila Parishad and Taluk Panchayat 37 contested to local level village panchayats and to other bodies like village cooperative societies, etc.

In spite of several housing schemes, the housing needs of the scheduled castes are not met. Still nearly three-fourths of SC population lives in huts (23. 33 per cent) and of Kuccha houses (43.34 per cent). Among the remaining 22.33 per cent and 10 per cent live in mixed houses and pucca house respectively.

Though land was allotted to landless especially to the Scheduled Castes, it was not possible for the government to make them landed. It was reported that 23 per cent are landless and a large majority (57 per cent) among the land owners are small and marginal farmers. Only 20 per cent of the Scheduled Caste population own land more than 10 acres.

House and land are the important immovable assets for majority of the Scheduled Caste people. In addition, small ruminants like sheep and goat or a cow or a pair of bullocks along with few househol durables are other forms of movable assets these people own.

About 25 per cent of the total population of the sample households is engaged in productive employment like wage labourers (19 per cent), agriculture mainly or in association with other occupations (4 per cent) and a very few persons in private or government jobs (2 per cent). Nearly Three-fourths of the population are non-workers who include school going children and women engaged in domestic work. The household annual income for three-fourth of the households has less than Rs. 10,000 per year. The rest have an annual income of between Rs. 10,001 to Rs. 20,000. the expenditure pattern of the households more or less resembles the income pattern leaving no scope for any savings.

Every household had reported that they have borrowed for one or the other purpose. Important reason for borrowing was for social obligations like festivals, family rituals etc., followed by domestic consumption, marriage, health, recreation and other emergencies. The source of credit was from banks, private chit funds or from moneylenders or as advance for their labour from the landlords.

Among those who celebrate festivals say that they celebrate festivals as they belong to Hindu religion (57 per cent) followed by custom of family (16 per cent) and for their elder's sake and force (10 per cent). They celebrate Dassara, Deepavali and Ugadi festivals every year. Similarly, celebrations of the birth anniversaries of Dr. B.R. Ambedkar, Buddha, Basava are conducted both on community and household levels.

In addition to the above, certain religious rituals like Manelli Mahamane, Dhamma Deepa, and Sathyanarayana Pooja are also conducted at the individual household levels based on their needs and convenience to get peace, prosperity and health in the household and to its members.

The lower and downtrodden castes believe more in animal sacrifice. But, contrary to the above it was revealed that about 57 per cent of respondents are against to the animal sacrifice during fairs and festivals. The reasons attributed was the religious conversion and social awareness. About 20 per cent of respondents have coverted to Buddhism under the influence of Dr. B.R. Ambedkar and his teachings and ideals but only half of them are reporting. In the changed circumstance there is a great intermix of people during fairs and festivals especially the participation of the scheduled caste members in upper caste religious and festivals celebrations.

Several factors contributions to the development of an organisation which include the encouragement from the fellow castes men, the network of kinship or relationship, the external factors like links with political leadership, access to information, the leader capabilities, etc. Majority of respondents (43.44 per cent) are of the view that the scheduled caste organisations were formed with an objective to attain/bring social equality in the community followed by entering the politics (30 per cent), to improve the economic conditions (20 per cent). The ideology of Dr. B.R. Ambedkar was the important motivating factor followed by Dalit Panther's ideology for the people to become members of the scheduled caste organisations. Another few became members on their own to serve their community and also due to the pressures and persuasions from other members. In order to discuss the organisational issues and problems along with the issues conceiving the public, the office bearers of the organisation use to meet at regular intervals.

Though there are several problems faced by the scheduled caste in Karnataka as wel as in Gulbarga, the respondents have prioritized several problems which need to be addressed. Among them, the practice of Untouchability emerges on top which has to be addressed on priority followed by the issues related to several boycott, atrocities on the caste people especially on women, land disputes and other related problems.

The respondents have claim that about 635 actrocities cases have reported. Among them more than half (55.12 per cent) relates to caste conflicts followed by restricing imposed by higher castes against the scheduled caste entry to the temple in the village (23.62 per cent). Another 9.45 per cent cases related to land disputes and 7.87 per cent related to restrictions imposed against entry to the hotel. Only 3.94 per cent of other types of cases were reported to the organisation.

KSDSS (Sagar) and its sub organisation KSDSF (Sagar) is functioning in all the ten talukas and the organisation has addressed about 3580 cases constituting 73 per cent of the total scheduled castes problems reported in the district. DSS (M&J) and its sub organisation DSF (M&J) is functioning only in seven talukas and the organisation has addressed about 1135 cases constituting 23 per cent of the total scheduled castes problems and DSS (M) is an organisation which primarily concentrate to address the problems of Dalit especially Dalit women particularly Devadasis and child and bonded labours. It was able to solve 200 cases constituting 4 per cent of the total problems in Gulbarga district.

The Madiga caste organisation addressed about 3570 cases and the Holeya organisations have solved 2145 cases in Gulbarga district. Though the organisation acts as a catalyst in resolving major problems encountered by the scheduled caste population, it also suggests to settle such disputes amicably using local resources like mediation of caste leaders and caste Panchayat to intervene and settle disputes among the caste people and also with outsiders. Only few preferred for the police action and other modes of resolving such disputes.

It is interesting to see that 98 per cent of the respondents agree that the caste organisations have involved fully in addressing the day to day issues pertaining to the problems faced by the members of the Scheduled Castes in the district. Nearly half of respondents (46.67 per cent) reported that they were involved in dealing with cases pertaining to atrocities on women followed by Social boycott (26.67 per cent), caste conflicts (18 per cent) and land disputes (6.67 per cent). All these problems were resolved by these organisations. In the absence of which, such problems continued to be unresolved.

In order to reduce the atrocities on scheduled caste people, the respondents suggested several measures. One-third of respondents suggested that the general public should be educated such that they learn to treat their fellow beings as humans. Similarly 28 per cent suggest enforcing the existing rules strictly and punishing the offender so that other will learn from such examples and also bring pressure on the government to act proper and protect the interest of the scheduled caste population (12 per cent). About 23.33 per cent suggest to the community to get unite and show of the caste unity will itself acts as a control mechanism to arrest the increasing atrocities on scheduled caste population.

In addition to empowering the community, the organisations take several measures for the improvement of the community like the educational improvement of the community (36.67 per cent), facilitate to increase the employment opportunities for the unemployed youth of the community (26.67 per cent). While political empowerment was reported by 20 per cent of the respondents another 13.33 per cent reports that the organisation works for the improvement of economic condition of scheduled caste population. The remaining 3.33 per cent says that the organisation take several other measures which will have a bearing on the development of the community.

Though Caste and sub-caste organisations have helped to solve several problems related to the respective castes, it will be interesting to know how such efforts have really changed the lives of these people and role played by these organisations. It will also be worth to learn the negative aspects of these organisations.

A large majority of respondents (93.34 per cent) expressed their desire to have an organisation which will facilitate for the improvement of caste members (26.67 per cent) unity among different castes (46.67 per cent) and both the improvement and unity among the members. On the contrary, about 17 per cent expressed their reservation against the need for caste or sub-caste organisations. The main reason reported was that 13.33 per cent among them feared that there will be disunity among the members and 3.33 per cent felt that such organisation will not progress.

Caste and sub caste organisations also play an important part in enhancing the status of the caste. The respondents are the opinion that the change could be brought among scheduled castes by improving their educational status (40 per cent) providing suitable employment (22.66 per cent). Another 20 per cent suggested modernizing the life styles of the scheduled caste population and 13.33 per cent propose to westernize their culture so that the higher caste will accept them though not immediately but in due course. In this direction another 4 per cent have no idea as to what can bring changes in the status of scheduled caste population.

The elites and the leders of the community are the important source of providing guidance and advice during emergencies. Though many of the elders are not the members of the organisations but their involvement in support of the organisations is noteworthy. More than half (55 per cent) of the organisations seek the advice of the elites to take suitable preventive measures regarding atrocities on the Scheduled Caste population. Another 25 per cent reported that the organisations seek the advice of the elders in order to curtail the problem of social boycott.

The elite expect that the quality of members in the organisation should be high as it will enhance the strength of an organisation to fight against the evil practices prevailed in the community. Table 3.4 reveals that about 42.50 per cent of elite respondents reported that the various organisations enrolled the members mainly to bring socio economic changes in the society. Another 27.50 per cent joined the organisation with a hope to bring social awareness among the masses people were interested in joining caste organisation to bring awareness. Only 7.5 per cent joined the organisation to bring unity among different people in the organisation.

The elite were of the opinion that there is a wide gap between the elder generation and the younger generation in managing the affairs of the caste and sub caste or the state level organisation.

For an organisation to be result oriented it should have a committed workforce or people who work with devotion. It was about 35 per cent of respondents who reported that the office bearers work as per the aims and objectives of the organisations.

The composition of the ruling group is a reflection of the outcome of the organisation. If the organisation is run by committed and selfess leaders, such an organisation thrives better and achieve its aims and objectives. Table-3.9 depicts a glory or dismal picture of the composition of caste and sub caste organisations in terms of the qualities of the leaders. About 62.5 per cent of respondents were of the opinion that the leaders of caste and sub caste organisations were selfish. However the rest have social commitment (25 per cent) with broad mindedness (10 per cent) and has other good qualities (5 per cent). As far as the nature of the office bearers are concerned, about three fourth (75 per cent) of the office bearers are dedicated to the cause. In pursuing the cause nearly three fourth (72.5 per cent) of the elites reported that the office bearers are using their office properly.

Under the divergent interest of the leaders and the office bearers, it is interesting to know how far the organisation really protects the interest of the community. It was reveled that more than three fourth of the elites were of the view that these organisations were able to protect the interests of the community.

In order to achieve the objectives, the organisations have chosen several methods. A large percentage of respondents (65 per cent) reported that the organisations settle the issues through compromise. Another 22.50 per cent reports that the issues will be settled with the intervention of the police and the rest (12.50 per cent) expressed the view that the problems have to be solved through the government's intervention by pressuring it to enact or bring suitable policy legislations for the protection and welfare of the Scheduled Castes.

It was generally believed that the caste and sub caste organisations are meant for fighting against the upper caste and dominant groups in the community. Contrary to the above view 40 per cent of elite respondents consider the caste and sub-caste organisations function like a social organisation followed by 35 per cent who labeled them as political organisations. Another 22.50 per cent were subscribing to the general view where the organisations act as a self protecting institution. Only 2.50 per cent reports it differently.

It is evident that half of the respondents (50 per cent) view the office bearers work with self respect and another 20 per cent reports that the office bearers posses selfless qualities, which are essential qualifications for a social worker. Nearly one-third (30 per cent) of the respondents expect the office bearers to work with a greater concern and by mutual understanding of the circumstances while dealing with people.

In a democratic society the politics play an important role in decision making. The policies and programmes of the government are influenced by the political parties, keeping this in view, two-thirds of the elite respondents expressed their supports the organisations to have a formal link with political parties.

Increase or multiflication of organisations is positive sign of development provided the multiplication takes place vertically. If such mulitiflication takes a horizontal shape, parallel organisation mop up based on protest and conflate among the leaders on several grounds. One can see the growth of scheduled caste and sub-caste organisations in Gulbarga district both horizontally and vertically based on the lines of the state level development. The opinions of elites for divisions and sub divisions of organisations in the district reveal that 27.50 per cent of respondents say that it was the policy of upper castes who wanted to rule the lower and and scheduled caste population by dividing them into smaller units. The role internal factors such as selfish interest of the leaders (57.50 per cent) and to show the strength of a disappointed leader (12.50 per cent) are more responsible for the divisions within the caste and sub-caste organisations. Only 2.50 per cent reported that these organisations split due to various other reasons like personal difference among the leaders or ideological differences etc.

The opinion of the elites on the organisation's capabilities of influence the people shows that a majority of them (57.50 per cent) were of the view that these caste and sub caste organisations have brought a sense of we feeling among the followers irrespective divisions among them. Another 10 per cent reported that these organisations have created a platform for the people of both within the caste and across the castes to know each other. Only 2.5 per cent felt that these organisations were instrumental in providing a space for the people or members to discuss their various problems and look for solutions. On the contrary 30 per cent of the respondents have highlighted the negative direction/rule of the organisations. Among them 20 per cent opined that these organisations have created divisions among castes based on superior and inferior feelings and the remaining 5 per cent each reported conflict of power and abusing each other respectively.

Though there are several organisations working for the welfare of Scheduled Castes in Gulbarga district, only a few are functioning properly. A large majority of elites (57.50 per cent) expressed their satisfaction of the functioning of KSDSS (S) organisation and appreciate the efforts of its leaders and functionaries for their dedicated and selfless service to the downtrodden community. Next to KSDSS (S) organisation, the elites commended the functionaries of DSS (M&J) organisation, which got the appreciation of 20 per cent of respondents who observe these organisations closely. Among the rest of the organisations, 10 per cent of elite respondents rated the MRHS organisation as one of the good organisations working effectively followed by DSS (M) and Lambani (2.50 per cent each). The rest (7.50 per cent) rated a few other miscellaneous organisations in the district working for the deprived population.

In the wider interest of the downtrodden castes and communities elites suggested that the various organisations should came together and work unitedly. Through the elites wish to unite these organisations, their opinion is divided on the issue of possibility of merger. One half of elites feel that it is possible to merge different subgroups as the leaders are committed (22.50 per cent) and learn to respect each other (20 per cent). The merger will be possible by involving the leaders from religious institutions, caste elders, politicians sub-caste interests, the unity and merger among different groups of caste and sub-caste organisations is possible. However another half of elites respondents feel that there is no possibility of merger of different sub-groups as the leaders lack commitment (22.50 per cent) and highly selfish in nature (7.50 per cent). Further, 20 per cent of respondents pointed out increased political concern of the leaders to have their own vote banks.

Suggested Measures

Keeping in view of the facts emerging out of the present study, consideration of the following few measures will go a long way in the upliftment of the Scheduled Caste population in the state.

1. It is advisable that the Government of India should formulate uniform guidelines to support the all forms of SC organisations, so that they can afford to work for the improvement of SC population. Government of India should make it mandatory on all states to follow such guidelines.
2. In accordance with the guidelines provided by the Government of India, every state government should further evolve additional policies beneficial to the SC people keeping in view the socio-cultural, economic and environmental needs of the downtrodden population.
3. It is not sufficient to frame policy guidelines. Such guidelines should be put into action by dedicated staff.
4. A bench mark survey of the socio-cultural economic, environmental aspects of the SC population should be undertaken. This will help the authorities to understand the problem and also identify the priorities for the formulation of micro level planning for the development of Scheduled Castes.

5. Provision of alternative land or other assets for the Scheduled Castes should be made as far as possible in their own village. This can be made possible (i) through the allotment of government lands, lands belonging to the local bodies, forests, etc,; (ii) in case, such lands are not available, government should create land pools in each village by compulsorily acquiring a portion of land from the big landlords (large and medium sized farmers).
6. When the government is unable to provide alternative land, the Scheduled Caste people should be encouraged to buy a minimum extent of land of their choice (in the open market) through allocation of special funds.
7. Compensation to the victims of atrocities should be paid immediately. The other benefits like ex-gratia money, subsidy for income generating activities etc., should be fixed and paid to the affected people on priority.
8. While providing housing sites, the present mode of allotment of a free site to each adult member be followed. The provision of allotment of free sites should be extended to all the male members and also female members (especially unmarried, widowed, separated, divorced, Devadasi etc.) in the family. Such site should be provided along with other castes in the village community rather than providing them exclusively.
9. Maintaining a minimum level of living through a suitable alternative employment schemes are to be offered to the Scheduled Caste people: (i) identification of jobs suitable for the SC people keeping in view the people's skills; (ii) if such jobs demand further additional skills, such skills should be imported through short term intensive training to them; (iii) people who are willing to pursue self-employment schemes on their own should be encouraged by providing necessary infrastructural facilities including finances generously.

10. In order to lessen the burden on the people to update the land records, officials of the concerned departments should conduct camps at the village level and update all documents and settle the disputes if any by involving and taking them into confidence.
11. Government's welfare schemes like Integrated Rural Development Programme, Jawahar Rojagar Yojana, old pension, Bhagyajothi lighting scheme, Rural housing scheme, social forestry, skill and entrepreneurial development training scheme etc., should be implemented in an integrated way on priority basis as a package.
12. Concurrent evaluation studies involving people and the NGOs will go a long way in the welfare of Scheduled Castes in a proper perspective.
13. There is a need for the establishment of people's committees to check the atrocities on the backward and the downtrodden communities and to look after the community needs its security etc.

Implications for the Community

1. The socio-cultural identity of the community should be maintained. This oculd be achieve by strict enforcement of constitutional safeguards to the welfare of Scheduled Castes.
2. The community should take the responsibility or involve itself in the process of implementation of the polices.
3. The community should avoid exploitation of its members by the corrupt officials and middlemen by providing and assisting people the needed help through an organised association of their own.
4. The community should enforce social control and see that the Scheduled Caste community people should not fall prey to the evils of urbanisation, gambling etc., which not only spoil their family but also spread to the community.

5. The community should facilitate formation of co-opertives and help the individuals to improve their economic conditions. In this respect community lift irrigation, dairy development, mini-indsutries, co-operative fishing etc., in accordance with the local culture and available skills should be undertaken in the community.

Implications for the Household

The impact of the organisations is primarily on the family first and then on its individual members. In order to minimise the adverse impact and get benefit, people should make use of the positive aspects of the policies, by which people can maintain their living conditions and even improve them. If they fail to do so their conditions gradually deteriorate. Keeping these aspects in mind, the following guidelines which are only indicative in nature are suggested:

1. In the event of harassment and atrocities, the family or household should prepare to protest by the help of local organisation instead of waiting for the government support.
2. All persons in the family should know both the negative aspects and the positive aspects of thc role of organisations.
3. The family should plan for its living taking into account the total asset structure, provisions available in the government and other such benefits.
4. The members of the family should take alternative jobs possible for them in addition to the traditional ones.
5. Expenditure on non-productive items should be curtailed at least for few years or until the family gets regular income.
6. Dependency on government programmes for day to day living (subsistence) should be avoided. The family should concentrate on asset acquisition, construction of house, land development etc., along with regular earnings for the family needs.

7. The increase in the number of school going children among all castes in an indication for future demand for non-secular jobs.
8. The role of women will change as their earnings become a major source of income.
9. Increase in the number of female children going to school is a desirable change, which would improve the status of women by reducing the incidence of Devadasi and child marriage.

Implications for Further Research

The study of caste and sub-caste organisations is an important aspect in the growing knowledge of social science. At present, only a few studies are available on the topic. Keeping in view of the above considerations, it is felt that there is scope for further research in the following aspects:

1. There is no comprehensive study that covers all aspects of caste and sub-caste organisations in India or at least in any one of the states. Further, establishment of organisations leads to empowerment of people and claims and counter claims for higher status not only among the SC sub groups but also between the Scheduled Castes and non-Scheduled Castes. In this respect also there is no study which covers the entire country or any state. There is a need for initiating such studies.
2. It is true that the government provides constitutional safeguards. But, such measures have not been uniformly percolated among all communities within the state or among the states. Hence, there is a need for preparing a comparehisive plan to be followed in the future. In this direction, an inventory of the various policies of different state governments should be compiled for preparing uniform guidelines to be followed by all states. Further, every state should formulate its own policies keeping in view of the socio-cultural inventory of the Scheduled Caste people.

3. In order to formulate comprehensive development policy guidelines, a few micro-level studies are essential wherein large measure address to the problem of Scheduled Castes keeping with the existing guidelines as a reference frame in each state.
4. The role of organisation, their inter action with other agencies, other parallel organisation and the community in addressing the burning problems in the community has to be studied to arrive at a better understanding of the means of solving the problems along with the management of the organisation.

Glossary

1. DSS - Dalit Sangharsha Samiti
2. KSDSS - Karnataka State Dalit Sangharsha Samiti (S) Sagar group
3. KSDSF - Karnataka State Dalit Student Federation (S) Sagar group
4. DSS (M&J)- Dalit Sangharsah Samiti Mavalli and Jayanna Group
5. DSF (M&J)- Dalit Student Federation Mavalli and Jayanna Group
6. DSS (M) - Dalit Sangharsah Samiti Murthy Group
7. SSD - Samata Sainik Dal
8. SSD - Shoshita Seva Dal
9. DPI - Dalit Panther of India
10. KDSP - Karnataka Dalit Sahitya Pariwshad
11. KDSS - Karnataka Dalit Sahitya Sansand
12. KJSPMO - Kranti-Jyothi Savitribai Phule Mahila Organisation
13. AJO - Adi Jambav Organisation
14. MRHS - Madiga Reservation Horata Samiti
15. JRO - Jagajivan Ram Organisation
16. MO - Matang Organisation

17. RBSD - Rastria Banjara Seva Dal
18. NBHS - National Banjara Horata Organisation
19. BO - Banjara Organisation
20. SC - Schedule Caste
21. MRHSD - Madiga Reservation Horata Samiti Dandor

Interview Schedule
Personal Information

Part–I

1. Name of the Respondent : ....
2. Place of Birth : ....
3. Age : ....
4. Sex : (1) Male (2) Female
5. Marital Status
   (1) Married
   (2) Unmarried
   (3) Any other
6. Educational Qualification
   (1) S.S.L.C.
   (2) Graduation
   (3) Post-graduation
   (4) Professional Course
   (5) Any other
7. Are you pursuing your studies now?
   (1) Yes (2) No

(a) If yes, mention the class and name of the college
   (1) Government College :
   (2) Private Colleges :
   (3) University :
   (4) Any others :

(b) If No, mention to the reasons.

(1) Poverty

(2) Negligence by parents

(3) Illiteracy family

8. Do you stay in a hostels?

(1) Yes (2) No

(a) If yes, mention the name of the hostels

(1) Government hostels

(2) Private hostels

(3) University hostels

(4) Any others

(b) If No, where do you stay?

(1) Own house

(2) Rented house

(3) Relative house

9. Where you are employee?

(1) Yes (2) No

(a) If yes, state the office

(1) Government Office

(2) Private

(3) Any others

(b) If No, mention the reasons,

(1) Social worker

(2) Unemployed

10. Family Composition

Sl. No.	*Name*	*Relations With Respondent*	*Age*	*Sex*	*Marital Status*	*Education*	*Occupation*	*Income*
1								
2								
3								
4								
5								

Social Aspects

11. Which caste constituted majority population?

    (1) Lingayats

    (2) Kurubas

    (3) Reddies

    (4) Any other

12. Which caste constituted minority population?

    (1) Scheduled castes

    (2) Scheduled tribes

    (3) Christians

    (4) Muslims

    (5) Any other

13. Mention the name of the dominant caste in your taluka/ district

    (1) Lingayats

    (2) Kurubas

    (3) Scheduled castes

    (4) Scheduled tribes

14. Whether scheduled castes are allowed to enter into temples of upper castes?

    (1) Yes (2) No

(a) If Yes, state the reasons.

    (1) Social awareness

    (2) Educational awareness

    (3) Orgnisational efforts

(b) If No, state the reasons

    (1) Illiteracy

    (2) Lack of social awareness

    (3) Caste felling

15. From where you bring drinking water?

    (1) Public well

    (2) Public Tube Well

    (3) Caste Feeling

    (4) Handpump

16. Whether the practice of untouchability is in practice?

    (1) Yes (2) No

(a) If Yes, state the reasons.

    (1) Lack of education

    (2) Lack of social awareness

    (3) Rigid social system

(b) If No, mention the reasons.

    (1) Education

    (2) Modernisation

    (3) Social awareness

17. Whether the following service are made available to scheduled castes?

    (1) Barber

    (2) Dhobi

    (3) Any other

18. Do you enjoy equal status on par with member of other castes at?

    (1) Community festival

    (2) Marriage with non Harijans

    (3) Worship in temples

    (4) Any other

19. Do you have friendship with the members of other castes?

    (1) Yes (2) No

(a) If Yes, state the name of the castes

    (1) Upper castes

(2) Middle caste

(3) Lower castes

(4) All castes.

(b) If No, sate the reasons

(1) Social equality

(2) Lack of education

(3) Caste feeling

20. State the nature of relationship with the members of other

(1) Assisting each other at the time of financial crisis

(2) Participating in the marriages of other caste

(3) Helping each other during communal clashes

(4) Any other

21. Have you faced social boycott by the upper castes?

(1) Yes (2) No

(a) If Yes, state the incidents

(1) Temple entry

(2) Hotel entry

(3) Land disputes

(4) Any others

(b) If No, state the reasons

(1) Social awareness

(2) Education

(3) Both

22. In your taluka/district the system of Bondage/Jeeta is still in practice?

(1) Yes (2) No

(a) If yes, state the reasons

(1) Economic problems (poverty)

(2) Lack of education

(b) If No, state the reasons

(1) Economically improved

(2) Educationally forwarded

(3) Land reforms

Economic Aspects

23. What was the traditional occupation of your family?

(1) Agriculture

(2) Business

(3) Lobour

(4) Any other

24. Whether your family members own land?

(1) Yes (2) No

(a) If Yes, mention the acres

(i) Irrigated land	(ii) Dry land in acres
(1) 1–5	(1) 1–5
(2) 6–10	(2) 6–10
(3) 11–15	(3) 11–15
(4) 16 and above	(4) 16 and above

25. Yearly income of the respondent

(1) Less than Rs. 2000

(2) 2001 3000

(3) 3001 4000

(4) 4001 and above

26. Material possession of the respondents

Mobile property	Immobile property
(1) Scooter	(1) Land
(2) Jeep	(2) Plots
(3) Car	(3) House
(4) Any other	(4) Any other

Political Aspects

27. Have you exercised franchise of the following

    (1) MP Election

    (2) MLA Election

    (3) ZP Election

    (4) TP Election

    (5) Any other

28. Whether you are *allowed* by upper castes to exercise franchise freely and frankly?

    (1) Yes (2) No

(a) If Yes, state the reasons

    (1) Social awareness

    (2) Educational awareness

    (3) Political awareness

(b) If No, state the reasons

    (1) Pressure of Upper castes

    (2) Educational backwardness

    (3) Both

29. Are you a member of political party of the following?

    (1) Congress I

    (2) Janata Dal (U) & (S)

    (3) BSP

    (4) BJP

    (5) Any other

30. Have you contested in any of the following election?

    (1) Parliament Election

    (2) Assembly Election

    (3) ZP Election

    (4) Taluka Panchayat Election

    (5) Any other

31. Have you got elected?

(1) Yes (2) No

(a) If Yes, state the reasons

(1) Unopposed

(2) Cooperation by other castes

(b) If No, state the reasons

(1) Not interested

(2) Financial problems

(3) Non-cooperation of upper castes

32. According to you, which political party protect the interest of the scheduled castes

(1) Congress I

(2) Janata Dal (U) & (S)

(3) BSP

(4) BJP

(5) Any other

Religious aspects

33. Mention the name of your family deity?

(1)

(2)

(3)

34. Do you celebrate the Hindu festivals?

(1) Yes (2) No

(a) If Yes, state the reasons

(1) Being Hindu

(2) Custom of family

(3) Elder forces

(b) If No, state the reasons

(1) Religious conversions

(2) Social awareness

(3) Both

35. Do your family members offer sacrifices to Go and Godesses?

(1) Yes (2) No

(a) If Yes, state the animals to be a sacrificed

(1) Hen

(2) Sheep or Goat

(3) All

(b) If No, state the reasons

(1) Social awareness

(2) Religious conversion

36. Which festivals do you observe?

(1) Dasara

(2) Deepavalli

(3) Ugadi

(4) Any other

37. Do you celebrate Jayanti of following?

(1) Buddha Jayanti

(2) Ambedkar Jayanti

(3) Basava Jayanti

(4) Any other

38. Are you conducting religious activities in your house?

(1) Mannelli Mahamane

(2) Dhamma Deepa

(3) Satyanarana Puja

(4) Any other

39. Have you embraced Buddhism?

(1) Yes (2) No

40. Are you freely participating in upper castes religious

(1) Yes (2) No

(a) If Yes, state the reasons

(1) Social awareness

(2) Personal friendship

(3) No caste feeling

(b) If No, state the reasons

(1) Caste restrictions

(2) Lack of education

(3) Caste feeling

Part–II
GENERAL INFORMATION

1. Name of the Oganisation: ....
2. Address of the Organisation (Office) ....
3. Year of formation: ....
4. Nature of the Organisation

   (1) Registered

   (2) Non-Registered
5. Mention the Registered number, Date and Year: ....
6. What is the total strength of your organisation: ....
7. Whether, your organisation is scheduled caste organisation or sub-caste organisation?

   (1) Scheduled caste organisation

   (2) Sub-caste organisation

(a) If scheduled caste organisation, whether all the members of sub-caste are members of the organisation

(1) Yes (2) No

(b) If Yes, mention the sub-caste

(1) Scheduled castes

(2) Sub-castes

(c) If No, indicate the sub-castes

(1) Holeya

(2) Madiga

(3) Lambani

(4) Bhovi

(5) Korcha

(6) Dhor

(7) Samagar

(8) Mang Garudi

8. State the status/position of the prepondent?

(1) President

(2) Vice-President

(3) Secretary

(4) Treasurer

(5) Executive Member

9. Who motivated you to became the members of the organisation

(1) By own will and wish

(2) Influcned by the ideologies of Dr. B.R. Ambedkar

(3) Influenced by the Dalit Panther

(4) Forced by the elders

(5) Any other

10. What are the reasons for formation of the caste organisation:

(1) To protect the community interest

(2) To create awareness among the community members

(3) To minimize the grievances

(4) Any other

11. State the objectives of your organisation?

(1) Economic objectives

(2) Political objectives

(3) Social objectives

(4) Any other

12. Do you think that caste organisations are essential?

    (1) Yes (2) No

(a) If Yes, state the necessities

    (1) Unity

    (2) Improve caste people

    (3) Both

(b) If No, state the reasons

    (1) Disunity

    (2) Caste organisation will not progress

13. How do you mobilize the resources?

    (1) Through community members

    (2) Through caste leaders

    (3) Through government servants

    (4) Through political leaders

    (5) Any other

14. Whether your organisation is attached to any political party?

    (1) Through financially

    (2) Through politically

    (3) Through moral support

    (4) Any other

15. Whether your organisation is attached to any political party?

    (1) Yes (2) No

(a) If Yes, mention the name of the party

    (1) Congress (I)

    (2) B.S.P.

    (3) R.P.I.

    (4) Others

(b) If No, state the reasons

(1) Social organisation

(2) Cultural organisation (Dalit lit.)

16. How often the office bears meet?

(1) Daily

(2) Weekly

(3) Once in fortnight

(4) Monthly

(5) Occasionally

17. What are the means to collect information on the conditions of the life and activities of your caste fellows living at other places?

(1) Own visits

(2) Community people

(3) Office bearers

(4) Any other

18. How do you manage to send massage at qross root level organisation

(1) By Hand bills

(2) By posters

(3) By newspapers

(4) Any other volunteers

19. Why and when do you make the trips to the town, district and state headquarters?

(1) To meet organisation leaders

(2) To meet caste leaders.

(3) To meet party leaders.

(4) Any other

20. What are the problems being undertaken into consideration?

(1) Atrocities

(2) Untouchability

(3) Social boycott

(4) Any other

21. How do you settle caste disputes?

(1) By members of caste elders

(2) Caste Panchayats

(3) By the assistance of police

(4) By members of other castes

22. Have you resolved the problems of your caste people?

(1) Yes (2) No

(a) If Yes, mention the problems resolved

(1) Atrocity Cases

(2) Social boycott

(3) Land disputes

(4) Conflict

(b) If No, state the reasons

(1) No problems

23. State the means adopted to resolve the disputes?

(1) By compromise

(2) By court

(3) Any other

24. What are the nature of the problems that community people generally bring to your notice?

(1) Harassment by the upper castes

(2) Refused to perform of customary duties

(3) Use of cremation and burial grounds

(4) Social boycott

(5) Any other

25. Mention the method of protest for justice?

(1) Public meeting

(2) Picketing

(3) Hunger strike

(4) Holding peaceful march

(5) Any other

26. Have you ever tried to initiate or implement some of these?

    (1) Yes (2) No

(a) If Yes, what kind of problems did you faced

(1) Untouchanility

(2) Social boycott

(3) Harassment

(b) If No, mention the reasons

(1) Never faced my problems

27. On what occasions all the members of the scheduled caste and sub-caste meet each other?

    (1) Ambedkar Jayanti

    (2) Buddha Purnima

    (3) Jagjivan Ram Jayanti

    (4) Any other

28. What measures would you suggest to improve the over all conditions of your community?

    (1) To provide proper education

    (2) To get jobs

    (3) To improve economic conditions

    (4) To capture the political powers

    (5) Any other

29. State the burning problems in order of preference?

    (1) Practice of untouchability

    (2) Force to undertake customary duties

    (3) Practice of Jeeta system

    (4) Land disputes

30. Do you think that, atrocities on scheduled castes have increased

    (1) Increased

    (2) Decreased

31. If increased do you have static's

    (1) Yes (2) No

(a) If Yes, give statistics

    (1) Caste conflicts

    (2) Temple and Hotel entry

    (3) Land disputes

    (4) Other

32. State the factors responsible for atrocities?

    (1) Increasing consciousness among scheduled castes

    (2) Developing concept of self-respect in scheduled castes

    (3) Improved economic conditions of scheduled castes

    (4) Occupying higher position of scheduled castes

33. Measures undertaken by caste organisation to decrease atrocities.

    (1) By educating people

    (2) By rules and regulations

    (3) By showing strength of unity

    (4) By putting pressure on government on various levels

34. Do you think that, political leaders of your community extended financial help to protect the interest of organisation?

    (1) Yes (2) No

(a) If Yes, state the reasons

    (1) We-feeling

    (2) Strengthening organisations

(b) If No, state the reasons

    (1) No contact

(2) Distance

(3) Both

35. According to you who is the devoted leader?

(1) Late B. Basavalingappa

(2) T.N. Narishamurthy

(3) Mallikarjun Kharge

(4) Any other

36. It is generally said that having acquired certain status, scheduled castes elites maintain distance from their own community

(1) Agree

(2) Disagree

(3) Not to say

(4) Any other ____________________

37. Do you feel that there is a change in the status of your caste people?

(1) Yes (2) No

38 (a) If there is a change what are the reasons?

(1) Education

(2) Modernisation

(3) Westernisation

(4) Any other

(b) If No, what are the reasons?

(1) God fear

(2) Superstitions

(3) Rigidity of Hinduism

(4) Any other

39. Do you think that awareness is increasing among scheduled castes?

(1) Yes (2) No

39 (a) If Yes, mention the reasons

(1) Education

(2) Modernisation

(b) If No, state the reasons

(1) Lack of education

(2) Superstitions

40. Whether elder member support to your activities?

(1) Yes (2) No

(a) If Yes, state the reasons

(1) Cooperation by elders

(2) Partially supported

(3) Both

(b) If No, state the reasons

(1) Not supported

(2) Lack of interaction

(3) Negligence

Part–III
OPINION OF THE ELITE OF SCHEDULED CASTES

(1) Name of Respondent: ....

(2) Educational Qualification: ....

(3) Profession/Occupation: ....

(4) Caste: .... Sub-caste: ....

(5) Sex: (1) Male (2) Female

(6) Place of Birth: .... Age: ....

(7) Address: ....

(8) State the nature of organisation during the days of Dr. B.R. Ambedkar

(a) Organisation by Committed followers

(b) Self protective organisation

(c) People follow one leader

(d) Any other

(9) Are you active member of organisation?

(a) Yes (b) No

(a) If Yes, state the reasons

(a) Try to bring socio-economic change

(b) Try to bring educational and political awareness

(c) Try to bring oneness feeling

(d) Any other

(b) If No, state the reasons

(a) Personality clashes

(b) Dis respect to others

(c) Ideological differences

(d) Any other

10. Do you feel that, there is a generation gap in the function of old and present organisations?

(a) Yes (b) No

(a) If Yes, mention the reasons

(a) Never take any suggestions

(b) Lack of proper understanding

(c) Less importance to seniors

(d) Any other

(b) If No, mention the reasons

(a) Proper understanding

(b) Due respect of youth

(c) Work for common goal

(d) Any other

11. Do you think that, office bearers of organisation are, working according to aims and objectives?

(a) Yes (b) No

(a) If Yes, state the reasons

(a) According to aims and objectives of organisation

(b) According to direction of leaders

(c) According to situation

(d) Any other

(b) If No, state the reasons

(a) Not aware of aims and objectives or organisation

(b) Acting on the direction of the leaders

(c) According to own decision

(d) Any other

12. What is you opinion about present leaders of organisation

(a) Broad minded leaders

(b) Social commitment leaders

(c) Selfish leaders

(d) Any other

13. What is you reaction towards work nature of office bearers organisation at present?

(a) Full time workers

(b) Part time workers

(c) Honest workers

(d) Dedicated workers

(e) Any other

14. How office bearers are using organisation?

(a) Using properly

(b) Misusing for personal gains

(c) Using as a force to show strength

15. Whether organisations are protecting the interest of the community members at present?

(a) Yes (b) No

(a) If Yes, mention the reasons

(a) Community interest

(b) General interests

(c) Individual interests

(d) Any other

(b) If No, mention the reasons

(a) Negative attitude about community interests

(b) Negative attitude towards general interests

(c) Negative attitude towards individual interests

(d) Any other

16. What are the main objectives of the organisations?

(a) Eliminate social evils

(b) Improve socio-economic conditions

(c) Acquire political powers

(d) Educational awareness

(e) Any other

17. Whether office bearers of the organisations seek advise from you

(a) Yes (b) No

(a) If Yes, state the areas

(a) Social boycott

(b) Atrocities

(c) Land disputes

(d) Any other

(b) If No, state the reasons

(a) Lack of cooperation

(b) Misunderstanding

(c) Neglecting seniors

(d) Any other

18. How they are working at present?
    (a) Fighting for real causes
    (b) For getting social justice
    (c) Fighting for power within organisation
    (d) Any other
19. How they are trying to resolve the problems?
    (a) Through compromise
    (b) Through the police
    (c) Through the involvement of government
    (d) Any other
20. How they are using organisations at present?
    (a) As social orgnisation
    (b) As political organisation
    (c) As self protecting organisation
    (d) Any other
21. What do you expect from the office bearers of organisations?
    (a) Greater need of mutual understanding
    (b) Possessing self respect
    (c) Selflessness qualities
    (d) Any other
22. What is your opinion regarding functioning of organistions at present?
    (a) Unable to resolve the real problems
    (b) Creating misunderstanding among members
    (c) Creating awareness among the members
    (d) Any other
23. Whether these organisations attached to any political parties?
    (a) Yes (b) No

(a) If Yes, state the reasons

(a) To get the support of the politicians

(b) To enter into politics

(c) To get power (may bring changes)

(d) Any other

(b) If No, state the reasons

(a) It is social organisation

(b) It is caste organisation

(c) It is independent organisation

(d) Any other

24. At present according to you, which factors are responsible for increasing the caste and sub-caste organisations?

(a) Divide and Rule policy of upper castes

(b) Selfish interest of leaders

(c) To expose they strength

(d) Any other

25. Do you think that, caste and subcaste organisations are giving proper direction to their members?

(a) Yes (b) No

(a) If Yes, mention the reasons

(a) Bring we feeling

(b) Knowing each others

(c) Discuss their problems

(d) Any other

(b) If No, mention the reasons

(a) Creating superior and inferior feeling

(b) Conflict for power

(c) Abuse each others

(d) Any other

26. State the reasons for formation of sub-caste organisations
    (a) Increasing subcaste feeling
    (b) Increasing feeling for getting powers in the organisations
    (c) Increasing feeling of neglecting the interests of sub-castes
    (d) Any other
27. At present which caste and sub-caste organisations are working effectively?
    (a) KSDSS
    (b) DSS (M&J)
    (c) DSS (M)
    (d) MRHS
    (e) Lambani
    (f) Any other
28. It is possible to merge all subcastes organisation into one major scheduled caste organisation?
    (a) Yes (b) No

(a) If Yes, state the reasons
    (a) Through committed leaders
    (b) Learn to give due respect to others
    (c) Protest the interest of all sub-caste members
    (d) Involve ageold, politicians, religious leaders officers and youth in the process of discussion

(b) If No, state the reasons
    (a) Lack of sacrifice leaders
    (b) Selfish nature is increasing
    (c) Vote bank of political leaders
    (d) Any other

Bibliography

Abbasayulu. Y.B. (1979), "The Emergence of Scheduled Caste Elite: Factors and Process" in IJSR Vol. 19, New Delhi. p. 95-100.

Abdullah, Aslam (1980), "Neo-Buddhist Youth Organisations", *A Study of Protest Management*, Journal of Youth Affairs, Vol. 2.1 March, New Delhi.

Akinchan S. (1995), *Caste, Class and Politics*, Emerging Horizons of Political Sociology, Gyan Publishing House, New Delhi, p. 247.

Anita Matto (1991), *Reform Movements and Social Transformation in India*, The Reliance Publishing House, New Delhi, p. 13.

Benjamin, Joseph (1991), "Social Mobility Among the Scheduled Castes in Bihar", A case study of Barh Block, Journal Social Action, Vol. 41, 4, Oct.-Dec., New Delhi, pp. 442-453.

Bhatt, S.G. (1997), *Encyclopaedia of District Gazetteers of India*, South Zone, Vol. 1, Gyan Publishing House, New Delhi, p. 454.

Bottomore, T.B. (1956), *Elite and Society*, Middle Sex, Penguin.

Buckle, H.T. (1964), Development of Social Thought.

Chandra Kanchan (2000), Elite Incorporation in Multithnic Societies, Asian Survey, Sept.-Oct., New Delhi.

David, L. Sills (1968), International Encyclopaedia of the Social Sciences, Vol. 2, The Macmillan Company and the Free Press, USA, pp. 297-98.

Dronberger IISC (1971), *The Political thought of Max Weber*, Meredith Corporation, New York, p. 55.

Dwarakanath Gupta. C. (1999), *Socio-Cultural History of An Indian Caste*, Mittal Publications, New Delhi, p. 40.

Edward Harper and others (1959), Political Organisations and Leadership in a Karnataka village, in Park and R.L. Tinker, I, (Eds.) *Leadership and Political Institutions in India*, Princeton University Press, N.J., p. 389.

Gaetano Mosca (1939), *The Ruling Class*, McGraw Hill, New York, p. 49.

Gail Omvedt (1990), "Ambedkar and Dalit Labor Radicalism", Maharashtra, 1936-42, *Journal of South Asia Bulletin*, Vol. 10, 1, New Delhi, pp. 12-22.

Gail Omvedt (1982), *Land Caste and Politics in India Stats*, (ed.) Guild Publication, Delhi, pp. 32, 106.

Galanter Garc (1972), *The Abolition of Disabilities Untouchability and the Law*, In J. Micheal Mahar, (ed.); *The Untouchability in Contemporary India*, University of Arizona Press, Tucson, p. 38.

Gokhale (1990), Janakala Mela A Souvenir Published by DSS Bangalore, pp. 51-52.

Harold. R. Issacs (1965), *Indian Ex-Untouchables*, Asian Publishing House, Bombay, p. 36.

Jacob Aikar (1980), *Scheduled Castes and Higher Education*, A Study of College Students in Bombay, Daṣtane Ramachandra and Co., Poona, p. Forword.

Jogdand P.G. (1991), *Dalit Movement in Maharashtra*, Kanak Publications, New Delhi, pp. 92-95.

Joseph Mathew (1988), "Ideology Protest and Social Mobility" *A Case Study of Mahars and Pulayas*, Inter-India Publications, New Delhi, p. 110.

Joseph Mathew (1986), *Ideology Protest and Social Mobility*, Inter India Publications, New Delhi, pp. 109-113.

Joshi, Barbara, P. (1987), "Recent Developments in Inter-Regional Mobilization of Dalit Protest in India", Journal, *South Asia Bulletin*, Vol. 7, 1-2, New Delhi, pp. 86-96.

Juergensmeyer M. (1988), "Religious Rebels in the Punjab", *The Social Vision of Untouchables*, Ajanta Publication, New Delhi, pp. 45-56.

Karanth G.K. and Charesely Simon (ed.) (1998), Challenging Untouchability, *Dalit Initiative and Experience in Karnataka*, Sage Publication, New Delhi, p. 41.

Kharata (1990), "Dr. Babasaheb Ambedkaranchi Patre", Idrayni Sahitya, Shaniwar Pet, Pune, pp. 6-14.

Kosare (1984), Vidarbhatil Dalit Chalwalich Itihas, Gyan Deep Prakashan Nagpur, pp. 115-122.

Kothari, Rajni (1994), "Caste, Communalism and the Democratic Process", Journal, South Asian Bulletin, Vol. 14, 1, p. 7-13.

Krishna. P.S. (1993), "Untouchability and Atrocities", *Journal of Sociology*, Vol. 43, 4, Oct.-Dec., pp. 412-426.

Kshirasagar (1994), *Dalit Movement in India an its Leaders*, M.D. Publications Pvt. Ltd, New Delhi, pp. 73-74.

Lata Chandrasekharan (1992), "Social Mobility Amount the Madiga of Karnataka", Sociological Bulltein, 41 (I & II), March, Sept. p, 123.

Lata Murugkar (1991), *Dalit Panther Movement in Maharashtra*, Popular Prakashan, Bombay, pp. 237-239.

Laxmidevi H. (1993), A Sociological study of the Korchas of Karnataka in an Urban setting: A case study of Korchas of Raichur, Ph.D. thesis, Gulbarga University, Gulbarga.

Mamtaź Ali Khan (1980), *Scheduled Castes and their Status in India*, Uppal Publishing House, New Delhi, pp. 2-3.

Mark Juergensmeyer (1982), *Religion as a Social Vision*, University of California Press, Brkeley, pp. 62-63.

Murthy. B.S. (1971), *Depressed and Oppressed*, Asian Publishing House, Bombay, p. 45.

Natarajan. S.A. (1959), *Century of Social Reform in India*, Asia Publishing House, Bombay, p. 8.

Oommen, T.K. (1984), "Sources of Deprivation and Styles of Protest", The Case of the Dalits in India, *Journal of Contributions to Indian Sociology—New Series*, Vol. 18, 1. Jan.-June, New Delhi, p. 4561.

Parvathamma C. (1984), Role of Protest Movements in Social Transformation" Guru Nanak, Journal of Sociology, Vol. 7, 1 Apr, pp. 1-22.

Pundir J.K. "A Comparative study of Education Social Mobility and Quality of Life in a Scheduled Caste" paper submitted in The XXXXII Indian Sociological Conference, Mangalore, Dec. 29-31.

Reobert Hardgrave and Other (1969), "The Nadar of Tamil Nadu" The Political Culture of a Community in Change California Press, Berelery University, p. 114.

Sabine G.H. (1961), *History of Political Theory*, Oxford publishing company, Calcutta, p. 21.

Sachchidananda (1977), *The Harijan Elite*, Thomas Press India Ltd., New Delhi, pp. 162-165.

Sachchidanand (1974), "Research on Scheduled Castes with Special Reference to Change" in ICSSR A survey of Research in Sociology and Social Anthropology, Vol. I, Popular Prakashan, Bombay, pp. 276-310.

Saraswathi, (1974), "Minorities in Madras State, Impex India", Delhi, pp. 14, 72-74.

Shyam Sunder. B. (1987), "They Burn, Dalit Sahitya Academy", Bangalore, pp. 16-18.

Singh, K.S. (1986), *Scheduled Castes studies in India*, ed. by G.S. Hallen, *Survey of Sociological Research in India*, M/s. Asha Printers, New Delhi, p. 77.

Syam Lal (2002), *Untouchable Movements in India*, Sublime Publication, Jaipur, pp. 147-149.

Upadhyay A.K. (1992), "Scheduled Caste Leader in Rural Setting in Eastern UP", P. Mhil Project in Sociology Meerut Univeristy, Meerut.

Venkateshwarlu (1990), "Harijan-Uppar Class Conflicts", Cited in p. 14, Dr. K. Rathnah (1991), *Social Change Among Malas*, Discovery Publishing House, New Delhi.

Venkateswamy P.R. (1955), *Ours Struggle for Emancipation*, Vol. I & II, Hyderabad, pp. 18-21.

Vilfredo Pareto (1963), *The Mind and Society, The Theory of General Society*, Rower Publishers, New York, pp. 516-519.

Vishwantham and K. Narashima Reddy (1985), *Scheduled Caste a Study in Educational Achievement*, Nutun Art Printers, Hyderabad.

Yogendra Singh (1958), "The Changing Power Structure of Village Community", *A Case Study of Six Villages in Eastern, U.P.*, in Desai Ar, *Rural Sociology in India*, (Ed.), Popular Prakashan, Bombay, p. 72.

Index

C

D